The New York Times
Southern Heritage Cookbook

The New York Times Southern Heritage Cookbook

Jean Hewitt

G. P. PUTNAM'S SONS
New York

Copyright © 1972 and 1976 by The New York Times Company
Introduction copyright © 1976 by Jean Hewitt

All rights reserved. This book, or parts thereof,
must not be reproduced in any form without permission.
Published simultaneously in Canada by Longman Canada
Limited, Toronto.

Drawings by Ray Skibinski

SBN: 399-11768-7

Library of Congress Cataloging in Publication Data

Hewitt, Jean.
　The New York times southern heritage cookbook.

　Includes index.
　1. Cookery, American—Southern States.　I. New York
times.　II. Title.　III. Title: Southern heritage
cookbook.
TX715.H5745　　1976　　641.5′975　　76-13363

Printed in the United States of America

Acknowledgments

The publication of this book would not have been possible without the cooperation of many people throughout the South who made their recipes available to *The New York Times*. Some contributed their recipes anonymously, and others received a credit line when their recipes appeared in *The New York Times*. I wish to thank them all for their generosity. The credited names are listed below in the order in which their recipes appear in these pages.

Enrique Ucan, *Conch Seviche;* Annie Rooney, *Shrimp Paste;* Alex Hawkes, *Conch Chowder;* Mrs. Wiley Hill, *She-Crab and Lobster Soup;* Paul E. Welsh, *Maryland Clam Chowder;* Mrs. Van Exem, *Tomato Soup;* Mrs. Lionel Legge, *Cream of Spinach Soup.*

Delton Harrison, *Crab Stew;* Ina Mae Heathman, *Deviled Oysters;* E. Lysle Aschaffenburg, *Pontchartrain Creole Gumbo*

John Shinn, *Southern Fried Chicken III* and *Chicken Cream Gravy;* Mrs. Yohe, *Chicken Olivette;* Mary Randolph, *Chicken Pudding;* Ruby Craven, *Barbecued Chicken;* Mrs. Robert Murphy, *Seven Hearths Chicken;* Maida Heatter, *Poulet Floride;* Mrs. Van Exem, *Pressed Chicken;* Kathleen Claiborne, *Chicken Spaghetti;* Ruby Craven, *Chicken Bog;* Mrs. Robert Murphy, *Brunswick Stew;* J. Tunkie Saunders, *Pressed Duck;* Mrs. E. V. Lewis, *Fresh Quail with Grits and Gravy;* Mrs. Wiley Hill, *Baked Christmas Mushroom Omelet;* Mrs. John DeReamer, *Cheese Grits Casserole.*

Mrs. Jackson Porter Dick, Jr., *Green Beans, Southern Style;* Mrs. Robert Murphy, *Cabbage Casserole;* Celia Marks, *Celery with Egg and Lemon Sauce;* Bessie Bogan, *Stuffed Eggplant;* Mrs. Howell Newton, *Fried*

Hominy Grits; Sarah Walker, *Sarah's Oando;* Miss Francille Killion, *Baked Hominy and Tomatoes* and *Southern-Style Turnip Greens;* James Sparks, *Steamboat Rice;* Mrs. John DeReamer, *Cauliflower Slaw.*

Miss Mae Creswell, *Spoon Bread;* Mrs. Morris Whitehurst, *Batter Bread;* Mrs. Jackson Porter Dick, Jr., *Crackling Bread Cakes* and *Lacy Hoe Cakes;* Mrs. Mescal Johnston, *Corn Meal Muffins;* Mrs. Van Exem, *Light Rolls.*

Mrs. Mescal Johnston, *Sweet Potato Pie;* Richard Hougen, *Chocolate-Butterscotch Pie* and *Kentucky Lemon Pie;* Mrs. Simon Waring, *Lemon Chiffon Pie;* Mrs. Mescal Johnston, *Peach Cobbler;* Hazel Detwiler, *Rum and Rhubarb Chess Pie;* Mae Butler, *Orange Cake;* Miriam Smith, *Butter Cake;* Mrs. Van Exem, *Poundcake I;* Mrs. Thomas Milford, *Poundcake II;* Celia Marks, *Sugar Plum Cake;* Mrs. Philip Licalzi, *Applesauce Fruitcake;* Mrs. Mescal Johnston, *Rice Custard with Lemon Sauce* and *Banana Pudding;* Maida Heatter, *Flan;* Mrs. Mescal Johnston, *Cooked Custard Ice Cream* and *Sugar Cookies.*

Mrs. Mescal Johnston, *Fig Preserves;* Martha Adams, *Louisiana Sauce Remoulade;* Pat DeReamer, *Pendennis Club Barbecue Sauce;* John Scott, *John's Eggnog;* Mrs. Robert Murphy, *Edenton Punch;* Augusta Claiborne Barnwell, *Chocolate Candy* and *Caramels.*

Contents

Introduction	11
Appetizers and Soups	17
Fish and Shellfish	49
Meat, Poultry, Game and Other Main Dishes	89
Vegetables, Main Dish Accompaniments and Salads	141
Breads	175
Pies, Cakes, Desserts and Cookies	193
Miscellaneous	
Pickles, Relishes and Preserves	239
Sauces	257
Beverages	268
Candies	273
Index	279

Introduction

America is a land where cultures merge from one generation to the next, but in Southern kitchens there are men and women who continue to take pride in preserving the traditions of the past. Southern cooking is eclectic and has been influenced by the heritage of its people, who came from Spain, France, Mexico, Britain, Africa and Germany, and by the bountiful harvests from its farms, shores and woodlands. There are many theories on where the South begins and ends, but for the purposes of this book it includes Maryland, Virginia, West Virginia, the Carolinas, Georgia, Florida, Mississippi, Alabama, Louisiana, Arkansas, Tennessee and Kentucky.

Regional food differences within the South are enormous so that a collection of favorite Southern recipes could run the gamut from Sally Lunn and Smithfield ham to chitterlings and grits, gumbo and beignets. But if any ingredients are common to all sections, they must include pork, white corn meal and hominy, sweet potatoes and chicken. Every part of the pig, from the snout to the tail, is used, and every Southern cook knows that "fat" means pork fat or lard. There's the elegant greens-stuffed Maryland ham, the famous North Carolina barbecue, souse and neck bone stew of soul cookery and hundreds of recipes for pork cuts in between.

Almost every repast served in the South is accompanied by a myriad variety of hot breads that include tender buttermilk biscuits, lacy corn and crackling breads. And calorie counting is forgotten when such luscious Southern-style desserts as lane cake, Lady Baltimore cake, chess tarts and Key lime pie are set forth.

Bountiful feasts and gracious hospitality are hallmarks of Southern living and can be enjoyed at an alfresco, family fish fry under the trees, an elaborate hunt breakfast, a New Orleans Mardi Gras buffet or an old fashioned Acadian hog-butchering picnic. A pot of collard greens with fatback simmering on the back of the stove is as fragrant and inviting to the hungry as breakfast at Brennan's with bourbon milk punch, eggs Sardou and bananas flamed with rum—and the welcome will be warm and friendly at both places.

Now let's look more closely at some of the local delicacies included under the umbrella of Southern cooking. Mention of fried chicken, for instance, brings a smile to a Southerner's face, but no two people will agree on the way it should be prepared. Some season and dip; others soak and dip, brown and bake, batter and fry, covered or uncovered. The variations are endless, but the results delectable whether eaten hot with cream gravy, Maryland style, or cold and crunchy at a picnic with homemade potato salad.

Maryland is also famous for its blue crabs, sautéed and eaten in entirety after their shells are shedded or dusted with spices and steamed for a crab boil. Then the bright-red creatures are spread on newspaper-covered tables, and there's plenty of beer to wash down the tasty morsels extracted from the shells. And one can begin dreaming of crab cakes, deviled crab, crab Imperial and sautéed crab meat, with a dash of sherry, made from meat picked from the leftover crabs.

The Eastern Shore of Maryland is the place to buy, and enjoy, fish and shellfish of all kinds—the finest, sweetest oysters, the best rock fish (called striped bass in the North) and the tenderest of clams.

Moving south into Virginia, one can recognize its English heritage in such Colonial dishes as Sally Lunn, trifle, fruitcake and syllabub. However, most travelers associate the state with ham, and most especially Smithfield ham. Cut from peanut-fed hogs, the hams are dry cured, slow smoked and aged to produce a salty, smoky, spicy and chewy meat that is very rich. It is served, thinly sliced, on a buffet with hot biscuits and relishes. The country ham is a second cousin to the Smithfield and can be bought from roadside smokehouses throughout much of the South; it is infinitely superior to and is less salty and more tender, has a milder flavor than any supermarket product.

Smithfield and country hams have to be scrubbed, soaked if overly salty, simmered in water to cover until tender and then glazed and baked for a dish fit for a king with homemade pickled peaches and watermelon rind. A slice of country ham, fried and served with red eye gravy and grits, is breakfast Southern style. And you can be sure that where there is country ham there will be beaten biscuits. Crunchy from banging with a hammer or mallet, yet the perfect partner for slivers of ham.

The ham bone goes into black bean soup, a mess of greens or a Brunswick stew which is that glorious mélange of chicken, onion, tomatoes, lima beans and corn that both Virginians and Georgians claim to have originated. Peach-fed hams, fried peach turnovers and fresh peach pie are other delicacies that visitors to Georgia have come to expect. The state also provides great hunting for the sportsman with the bonus of wild duck, quail and doves for the table. And there's game aplenty too in the backhill country of the Carolinas to eat along with pokeweed cooked with fatback. Barbecue is another dish synonymous with North Carolina, and this means whole hogs turning over smoldering coals for hours on end until the meat almost drops from the carcass. Then it is chopped, never ground, along with spices and hot red peppers for a fabulous feast.

Yams or sweet potatoes are an important crop in North Carolina, and they are cooked into savory dishes with apples, sausage and nuts and go into biscuits, breads, pies and cakes. The first blueberries of the season come from North Carolina to Northern markets, but back home they are baked into mouth-watering pies, cobblers, shortcakes and muffins. Sesame-seed-topped breads and benne (sesame) wafers show the influence of African slaves who brought the seeds to the New World.

No glance at the culinary heritage of the Carolinas would be complete without mention of the seafood delights associated with their long shoreline. Oysters, clams and crabs, striped bass, mullet, porgy and scup are but a sampling from the sea off the Outer Banks that are served up with freshly fried hush puppies and lacy corn bread in every seaside café.

Hopping John, which is a mixture of black-eyed peas and rice, is another dish found in the Carolinas, and throughout a good part of the South for that matter, including Kentucky where it is often on the menu with Burgoo. This odd-sounding concoction is a rich, hearty stew originally made in huge iron caldrons over an open fire with rabbit, squirrel and other wild creatures. A more modern version calls for beef, pork, veal, lamb and chicken cooked up with a mess of fresh vegetables, including okra, and hot red pepper pods. Okra is also said to have come from Africa hundreds of years ago.

The Kentucky hills used to be dotted with spirals of smoke rising from the hollows marking the location of the nearest moonshine still, and the commercial production of bourbon is still centered in the state. The fragrant liquor perfumes eggnog, candies, cookies and cakes and is the principal ingredient in the famous mint juleps that are as much a part of Derby Day as horses and elaborate buffets.

Another kind of Southern buffet, equally bounteous and satisfying, might feature smothered pork chops, chitterlings (fried hog intestines), fried chicken, barbecued ribs, pig's feet, catfish, collard greens with "pot likker," crackling bread and sweet potato pie. This is the food of the poor, black and white, in the deep South and within the last decade or so has been labeled soul food. It originated in the slave quarters of the opulent plantations, where nothing was wasted and everyone ate well.

Similar dishes, plus hog jowl, possum 'n' taters and homemade pork sausage, are favorites in backwoods kitchens of Tennessee. Grits and corn bread come with every meal.

Florida and Louisiana are the two Southern states that have unique cuisines, while preserving many of the standard Southern treats. Subtropical Florida's agricultural bounty of citrus, avocados, vegetables, coconuts and hearts of palm is reflected in a long list of menu specialties. They include the famous Key lime pie, coconut cake, ambrosia and hearts of palm salad. From Florida waters there are conch, mullet, mackerel, grouper, stone crabs, red snapper and pompano to delight the seafood lover and to provide first-rate ingredients for many dishes.

Crawfish from the bayous of Louisiana are the cornerstone of the Creole and Acadian or Cajun cuisines that show the influence of Indian, African, German and Spanish settlers and warrant a book to themselves. Meat from the spiny creatures goes into bisques, jambalayas and gumbos, and there is no substitute. The grand cuisine of wealthy Creoles with its oysters Rockefeller and pompano en papillot and the country-style Acadian cooking with its spicy étouffés, and pungent gumbos have tended to merge over the years. A carefully made brown roux from cooking fat and flour until it is nut brown is an important basic ingredient in both cuisines.

Rice is also a popular ingredient in Creole and Acadian kitchens. Three of the more unusual rice-based dishes are Dirty Rice made with chicken giblets, rice and red beans, and calas, or hot rice cakes, served with cane syrup for breakfast. Gumbos are served over, or with, rice, and jambalayas have the grain mixed into the shrimp and/or ham mixtures. And the question whether to thicken a gumbo with okra, an African import, or file powder, an Indian legacy, used to vary with the seasons. When there was no fresh okra, file powder, which is the crushed leaves of the sassafras plant, was used. Few Creole or Acadian main dishes are without the pungent hot pepper flavor imparted by the famous Tabasco sauce made on Avery Island. Grillades, thin slices of beef or veal, are also served over rice or grits, with oceans of deep rich brown gravy.

Then there are poor boys (po'boys), Louisiana's answer to the hero and submarine, and the oyster loaf, that heavenly combination of fried oysters in a hollowed-out loaf of French bread. Frugal Acadians hoard stale French bread to make pain perdu. Slices of the day-old bread are soaked in a brandy-flavored egg dip and fried in fat to be served with cane syrup for an original version of French toast. It could be a dessert, too, with its sprinkle of confectioners' sugar, if you want to pass up pecan pie, pralines and bananas baked with rum. Whichever dessert you choose, it will be well complemented by the orange and spice flavored café brûlot which is dramatically flamed with brandy, tableside, in the finest homes and restaurants.

America's Southern states offer a kaleidoscope of dining experiences, and sampling from the recipes that follow will be a fine preliminary to a trip from Maryland to Arkansas and back north to Tennessee and Kentucky.

Appetizers and Soups

Conch* Vinaigrette
FLORIDA

- 4 large conchs
- ½ cup olive oil
- 2 tablespoons wine vinegar or juice of one lime
- Salt and freshly ground black pepper to taste
- 1 clove garlic, finely minced
- 2 tablespoons finely chopped parsley
- 1 tablespoon finely chopped chives (optional)
- ¼ teaspoon oregano.

1. Scrub the conchs with a brush and drop them into boiling water. Cover and simmer thirty minutes to one hour, depending on the size of each conch and until part of the body protrudes from the shell. Drain and cover immediately with cold water. Remove the meat and cut off the hard outer cover with a paring knife.

2. Cut the meat into one-half-inch slices and add the remaining ingredients. Toss well and serve at room temperature.

Yield: Six servings.

*For a description of conch, see page 52.

Conch Seviche
FLORIDA

- 5 to eight conchs
- 1 small red onion, peeled and finely chopped
- ½ cup freshly squeezed lime juice or lemon juice
- 2 small tomatoes, peeled, cored and chopped
- 1 small hot green pepper, seeded and finely chopped
- Salt and freshly ground black pepper to taste
- 3 tablespoons peanut oil, approximately
- 1 tablespoon finely chopped cilantro (Chinese parsley, see note), optional.

1. If conchs in the shell are bought, rinse them thoroughly and crack the base of two shells together. If they cannot be cracked in this manner, use a large hammer to crack the shell. Using a knife and the fingers, press or pull out the flesh from the interior. Pare or scrape away the soft matter and carefully trim away the horny claw-like structure attached. Slit the outer covering of the flesh. Pull or pare away this covering.

2. Split the firm white conch flesh down the center, but do not cut in half. Using a heavy mallet, pound the flesh lightly but firmly. Slice the pounded meat into thin slivers and place in a bowl. Add the remaining ingredients. Add more peanut oil if desired. Toss and chill.

Yield: Four or more servings.

Note: Cilantro is available in Spanish and Chinese markets.

Deviled Crab Meat I
MARYLAND

- 1 pound lump crab meat, picked over to remove bits of shell and cartilage
- ¼ cup dry sherry
- Dash of Worcestershire sauce
- 2 tablespoons butter
- 1½ tablespoons flour
- ½ teaspoon dry mustard
- 1 cup milk
- Salt and freshly ground black pepper to taste
- 2 egg yolks, lightly beaten
- 1 hard-cooked egg, finely chopped
- Lemon juice to taste
- ½ teaspoon grated horseradish
- Cayenne pepper to taste (optional)
- ½ cup buttered soft bread crumbs
- Lemon wedges.

1. Preheat the oven to 375 degrees.

2. Put the crab meat in a mixing bowl and pour the sherry over the crab. Add the Worcestershire and set aside.

3. Melt the butter in a saucepan and stir in the flour and mustard with a wire whisk. Add the milk, stirring rapidly with the whisk. When the mixture is thickened and smooth, simmer two to three minutes.

4. Add the salt and pepper. Remove the sauce from the heat. When sauce cools slightly, stir in the egg yolks, beating rapidly with the whisk.

5. Add the crab meat, hard-cooked egg, lemon juice and horseradish. If desired, season with a bit of cayenne. Mix well, but do not break up the crab lumps.

6. Fill crab shells or individual ramekins with the mixture and sprinkle with the bread crumbs. Bake ten minutes, or until golden brown. Serve with lemon wedges.

Yield: Four servings.

Deviled Crab Meat II
MARYLAND

- 4 tablespoons butter
- ½ cup finely chopped onion
- ½ cup plus four teaspoons soft bread crumbs
- 1 cup heavy cream
- ½ teaspoon dry mustard
- ¼ teaspoon cayenne pepper, or to taste
- Tabasco sauce to taste
- 2 egg yolks, beaten
- Salt to taste
- 1 pound lump crab meat, picked over to remove bits of shell and cartilage
- Parsley for garnish.

1. Preheat the oven to 375 degrees.

2. Melt two tablespoons of the butter in a skillet and cook the onion in it until wilted. Add one-half cup of the bread crumbs, the cream, mustard, cayenne, Tabasco, egg yolks and salt. Gently mix with the crab meat.

3. Spoon the mixture into four individual ramekins, dot with the remaining butter and sprinkle with the remaining bread crumbs. Bake until golden brown. Serve garnished with parsley.

Yield: Four servings.

Crab Sauté
MARYLAND

4	tablespoons butter	4	to six slices thin toast
1	pound lump crab meat, picked over to remove bits of shell and cartilage		Chopped herbs (see note) Black peppermill Lemon wedges.
	Salt to taste		

1. Melt the butter in a skillet. When butter starts to sizzle, add the crab meat. Cook, stirring as gently as possible, until crab is piping hot. The crab lumps should remain as whole and firm as possible. Season with salt.

2. Spoon the crab onto the toast and sprinkle with chopped herbs if desired. Serve with a peppermill and lemon wedges.

Yield: Four to six servings.

Note: Chopped fresh herbs that go well with crab include parsley, tarragon, chives and chervil. Or use a mixture of all four.

Hot Crab Meat Puffs
VIRGINIA

2	egg whites, stiffly beaten	Tabasco sauce to taste
1	cup mayonnaise	Toast rounds
1	cup flaked and picked-over crab meat	Paprika.
1	teaspoon Worcestershire sauce	

Fold together the egg whites, mayonnaise and crab meat. Stir in the lemon juice, Worcestershire and Tabasco. Spoon onto toast rounds, sprinkle with paprika and broil until bubbly.

Yield: Three dozen to four dozen.

Oyster Appetizer
MARYLAND

12	shucked oysters	Lemon juice
6	thin slices bacon, cut in half	Worcestershire sauce.
	Finely ground black pepper	

1. Place an oyster at one end of a piece of bacon. Season with pepper, lemon juice and Worcestershire. Roll bacon up to enclose oyster.

2. Place on broiler pan and repeat with remaining ingredients. Broil in a preheated broiler, turning frequently until the bacon is crisp.

Yield: Four servings.

Oysters with Cocktail Sauce
LOUISIANA

1 cup catchup	3 dashes Tabasco sauce
Juice of one lemon	½ cup finely chopped hearts of celery
2 tablespoons horseradish, or to taste	24 freshly shucked oysters or oysters on the half shell.
2 teaspoons Worcestershire sauce	

Combine all ingredients except the oysters. Chill. Serve sauce separately with oysters.

Yield: Four servings.

Cucumber and Shad Roe
MARYLAND

3 tablespoons butter	1 teaspoon onion juice or one tablespoon finely chopped chives
1 pair shad roe	
3 medium-size cucumbers	Worcestershire sauce to taste
Salt and freshly ground black pepper to taste	Hollandaise sauce (see page 258).

1. Melt the butter in a skillet and gently add the shad roe. Cover and cook over low heat, turning once, just until the roe are cooked through, five to twelve minutes, depending on size. Let cool slightly. Discard the connecting membrane of the roe.

2. Preheat the oven to 375 degrees.

3. Peel the cucumbers. Hollow out the whole cucumbers using an apple corer or the small scoop of a melon ball cutter.

4. Gently mash the shad roe and season with salt, pepper, onion juice or chives and Worcestershire. Stuff the cucumbers with the roe mixture.

5. Butter three squares of aluminum foil and place one stuffed cucumber in the center of each. Wrap in foil and seal envelope fashion. Place on a baking sheet and bake twenty to forty minutes, or until cucumbers are tender. Remove foil, place cucumbers on hot dish and serve with hollandaise sauce.

Yield: Six servings as a first course.

Note: Cucumbers may also be stuffed with a mixture of crab meat, lemon juice and tarragon to taste.

Shrimp with Lamaze Sauce
LOUISIANA

1	cup mayonnaise, preferably homemade	½	pimento, chopped
1	cup chili sauce	1	tablespoon chopped celery
¼	cup India relish	1½	teaspoons prepared mustard
1	to two hard-cooked eggs, chopped		Salt and freshly ground black pepper to taste
½	teaspoon chopped stuffed olive	1½	teaspoons steak sauce
¼	green pepper, seeded and chopped		Dash of paprika
		36	shrimp, cooked, shelled and deveined
			Water cress for garnish.

Combine all the ingredients except the water cress and chill. Serve garnished with water cress.

Yield: Six servings.

Shrimp Cocktail with Celery-Tomato Sauce
MISSISSIPPI

¾	cup catchup		Tabasco sauce to taste
½	cup finely chopped heart of celery	1	tablespoon horseradish, preferably freshly grated
2	tablespoons finely chopped green pepper		Salt to taste (optional)
		6	or more lettuce leaves
1	teaspoon Worcestershire sauce, or to taste	36	shrimp, cooked, shelled and deveined
	Juice of one lemon		

1. Combine all the ingredients except the lettuce and shrimp and chill.
2. Arrange the lettuce leaves in six ramekins, shells or cocktail dishes and cover with equal portions of shrimp.
3. Spoon equal portions of cocktail sauce over each serving.

Yield: Six servings.

Shrimp with Hot Sauce
ALABAMA

¼ pound butter	pepper to taste
Juice of two lemons	Tabasco sauce to taste
6 tablespoons Worcestershire sauce	2 pounds shrimp, cooked, shelled, and deveined.
Salt and freshly ground black	

Combine all the ingredients except the shrimp in a chafing dish. Serve the shrimp separately on a bed of ice. Skewer the shrimp with toothpicks and let guests serve themselves by dipping shrimp into the hot sauce.

Yield: Eight or more servings.

Pickled Shrimp
ALABAMA

3 cups oil	4 teaspoons Worcestershire sauce
3 teaspoons dry mustard	
4 teaspoons sugar	3 pounds shrimp, cooked, shelled, and deveined
⅔ cup cider vinegar	
⅔ cup catchup	3 medium-size sweet onions, sliced wafer-thin
Freshly ground black pepper to taste	6 bay leaves.
4 to six cloves garlic	

1. This dish should be made two days in advance, and it must be made in two operations.
2. Combine the oil, mustard, sugar, vinegar, catchup, pepper, garlic and Worcestershire and blend half the mixture in an electric blender.
3. Arrange half the shrimp in a layer in a deep serving dish. Arrange over them half the onion slices and bay leaves. Pour the blended oil mixture over all.

4. Blend the remaining half of oil mixture. Repeat layers of remaining shrimp, onion slices and bay leaves and pour the oil mixture over all. Cover and refrigerate two days before using.

Yield: Eight or more servings.

Shrimp Remoulade
LOUISIANA

2 pounds shrimp	Freshly ground black pepper to taste
1 bay leaf	
1 rib celery with leaves	½ teaspoon chopped fresh tarragon or one-quarter teaspoon dried tarragon
2 sprigs parsley	
12 peppercorns	
Salt to taste	1 clove garlic, finely minced
3 tablespoons tarragon vinegar	1 tablespoon chopped parsley
¼ cup Creole mustard (if unavailable use Düsseldorf mustard and add Tabasco to taste)	1 scallion, including green part, chopped
	3 tablespoons horseradish, preferably fresh
5 anchovies, finely chopped	Tabasco sauce to taste
¾ cup oil (may be a mixture of olive oil and vegetable oil)	Chopped lettuce.

1. Day before, peel each shrimp and make a small incision along the curved back. Reserve the shrimp shells. Rinse the shrimp under cold running water to remove the sandy vein along the back.

2. Place the shrimp, shells, bay leaf, celery, parsley sprigs, peppercorns and salt in a saucepan and add water to cover. Bring to a boil and simmer about five minutes. Drain the shrimp and let cool.

3. Place the shrimp in a mixing bowl. Chill. Combine the remaining ingredients except chopped lettuce and pour over the shrimp. Let stand overnight in the refrigerator. Next day, bring to room temperature before serving. Serve on chopped lettuce.

Yield: Four to six servings.

Chilled Gulf Coast Shrimp Creole
LOUISIANA

- 2 cups mayonnaise
- ½ small onion, grated
- 1 clove garlic, finely minced
- ½ cup Creole mustard or Düsseldorf mustard with Tabasco added to taste
- 1 tablespoon grated horseradish, or to taste
- ½ cup finely chopped parsley
- Juice of one lemon
- 3 pounds shrimp, cooked, shelled and deveined.

1. Blend the mayonnaise with the onion, garlic, mustard, horseradish, parsley and lemon juice.
2. Stir in the shrimp and refrigerate at least two hours before serving.

Yield: Eight or more servings.

Shrimps Wilder
ALABAMA

- 2 pounds shrimp
- 2 cloves garlic, finely chopped
- ½ cup peanut oil or olive oil
- ¼ cup soy sauce
- ½ cup lime or lemon juice
- 3 tablespoons finely chopped parsley
- 2 tablespoons finely minced scallions, including green part
- Salt and freshly ground black pepper to taste
- Lime or lemon wedges.

1. Shell and devein the shrimp, but leave on the last tail segment. Dry and place in a shallow dish.
2. Combine the remaining ingredients and pour over shrimp. Let stand three to four hours.
3. Thread the shrimp on skewers and place them on a grill over hot coals. The coals should be approximately three inches from the shrimp. Cook quickly, about three minutes on one side, basting with the marinade. Turn and cook three to five minutes longer, basting occasionally. Serve with lime or lemon wedges.

Yield: Four to six servings.

Shrimp Paste
ALABAMA

2 pounds shrimp, cooked, shelled and deveined	Juice of one lemon
6 tablespoons butter	Salt to taste
¾ cup catchup	Tabasco sauce to taste
1 teaspoon onion juice	Lettuce
1½ tablespoons Worcestershire sauce	Mayonnaise.

1. Put shrimp through a meat grinder twice, using the finest blade.
2. Cream the butter; add shrimp and the remaining ingredients except lettuce and mayonnaise. Blend with a wooden spoon until mixture is the consistency of mayonnaise. Mold with hands into a loaf and press into a six-cup loaf pan. Refrigerate six hours. Unmold and slice in one-quarter-inch slices. Serve on lettuce with mayonnaise.

Yield: Six to eight servings.

Sea Food and Southern Cocktail Sauce
ALABAMA

2 cups mayonnaise	Salt to taste
1 hard-cooked egg, sieved	Coarsely ground black pepper to taste
1 cup catchup	Chopped parsley
2 teaspoons Worcestershire sauce	4 cups cooked, cleaned shrimp, oysters, clams, lobster pieces, crawfish.
Juice of one lemon	
2 teaspoons anchovy paste	
Tabasco sauce to taste	

1. Place the mayonnaise in a mixing bowl and stir in the egg. Gradually stir in the catchup; then add the Worcestershire, lemon juice, anchovy paste, Tabasco, salt and pepper.
2. Sprinkle with parsley before serving as a dip for the sea food.

Yield: About ten servings.

Chilled Red Snapper Appetizer
LOUISIANA

2 pounds red snapper fillets	¾ cup finely chopped scallions, including green part
4 cups court bouillon (see below)	⅓ cup drained capers
4 hard-cooked eggs	2 teaspoons Creole mustard, or to taste (if unavailable, use Düsseldorf mustard and add Tabasco sauce to taste)
1 tablespoon dry mustard	
⅓ cup lemon juice	
¼ teaspoon salt	
½ cup mayonnaise	Boston lettuce leaves.

1. Simmer the snapper in the court bouillon until fish flakes, about fifteen minutes. Cool the fish; bone and skin. Chill.

2. Mash the yolks of three of the eggs and add the dry mustard, lemon juice and salt.

3. Add the mayonnaise, scallions, capers and Creole mustard. Chop or sieve the whites of three of the eggs and stir in.

4. Arrange the chilled fish on the lettuce leaves and spoon the sauce over. Garnish with remaining egg cut into slices.

Yield: Four servings.

Court Bouillon
LOUISIANA

1 cup white wine	½ small onion
4 cups water	½ rib celery
Bones and head of snapper and/or other white fish	¼ teaspoon thyme
	½ bay leaf
6 peppercorns, bruised	2 sprigs parsley.
½ teaspoon salt	

1. Place the wine, water, fish bones and head, peppercorns, salt and onion in a saucepan. Sprinkle the inside of the celery with the thyme, cover with the bay leaf and parsley sprigs and tie into a bundle. Add bundle to the pan.

2. Bring to a boil and simmer twenty-five minutes. Strain through a double thickness of cheesecloth.

Yield: About one quart.

Escabeche of Red Snapper
FLORIDA

- 4 red snapper fillets, each about one-inch thick and each weighing about one-half pound
- Flour
- Salt and freshly ground black pepper
- ½ cup peanut oil
- 2 cloves garlic, peeled and cut in half
- ½ cup olive oil (see note)
- 2 tablespoons cider vinegar
- Juice of one sour orange or lime (see note)
- Tabasco sauce to taste.

1. Day before, dredge the fish fillets in a mixture of flour, salt and pepper. Cook the fish in hot peanut oil with the garlic six to eight minutes to a side. Transfer the fish to a flat baking dish.

2. Heat the olive oil and let it cool. Stir in the vinegar, orange or lime juice, Tabasco and salt and pepper to taste. Beat vigorously and pour the mixture over the fish. Cover and refrigerate overnight. Next day, serve cold.

Yield: Four to six servings.

Note: Some recipes call for using the oil in which the fish cooked rather than using the olive oil recommended in this recipe.

Sour Seville oranges are available in February and March.

Ham and Egg Canapés
VIRGINIA

- 4 slices white bread
- Melted butter
- 1 cup ground baked Virginia or country ham
- 2 hard-cooked eggs
- Paprika.

1. Preheat the oven to 400 degrees.

2. Using a small biscuit cutter, cut each slice of bread into four rounds. Brush generously with melted butter and place on a baking sheet. Bake, turning once, until golden brown.

3. Spoon one tablespoon of ham onto each round of toast and return to the oven just to heat through.

4. Meanwhile, split the eggs in half. Press the whites through a sieve

or ricer. Press the yolks through another. Sprinkle the canapés first with white of egg, then with yolk. Dust with paprika and serve hot.
Yield: Sixteen.

Ham Biscuits
KENTUCKY

1 cup flour	3 tablespoons shortening
2 teaspoons baking powder	1 cup ground cooked country-style ham
⅛ teaspoon salt	
¼ teaspoon dry mustard	½ cup milk, approximately.

1. Combine the flour, baking powder, salt and mustard in a bowl. With the finger tips or a pastry blender, mix in the shortening.
2. Preheat the oven to 450 degrees.
3. Add the ham and mix to a soft dough with the milk. Knead thirty seconds on a lightly floured board. Roll out to three-eighths-inch thickness. Cut into tiny rounds and place on a lightly greased baking sheet.
4. Bake ten minutes, or until done. Serve hot with or without butter.
Yield: Eighteen to two dozen.

Eggs Sardou
LOUISIANA

1 cup hot creamed spinach	2 poached eggs
2 artichoke bottoms, canned and reheated or freshly cooked	Easy hollandaise sauce (see page 30).

1. Spoon the spinach onto two hot plates. Top with the artichoke bottoms.
2. Place one egg on each artichoke bottom. Cover with hollandaise sauce.
Yield: Two servings.

Easy Hollandaise Sauce
LOUISIANA

3 egg yolks	⅛ teaspoon cayenne pepper (optional)
2 tablespoons lemon juice	½ cup butter, melted and hot
¼ teaspoon salt	

1. Place the yolks, lemon juice, salt and cayenne if desired in an electric blender and blend on low speed.
2. Maintaining the blender at low speed, gradually pour in the butter and continue blending until sauce is thick and smooth.

Yield: About three-quarters cup.

Stuffed Cherry Tomatoes
FLORIDA

48 cherry tomatoes	2 tablespoons chopped chives
2 tablespoons wine vinegar	2 teaspoons chopped onion
6 tablespoons olive oil	2 anchovies, finely chopped
Salt and freshly ground black pepper to taste	2 teaspoons chopped parsley
	Tabasco sauce to taste
2 three and one-half-ounce cans tuna	4 drops Worcestershire sauce
4 tablespoons chopped capers	2 tablespoons mayonnaise, or more to taste
2 hard-cooked eggs, finely chopped	1 teaspoon lemon juice

1. With a sharp paring knife, trim off a tiny portion from the base of each tomato. This will give a slight base to help them stand upright. Cut a small slice from the top of each tomato. Run the tip of the knife around the inside of each tomato and scoop out the inside to leave the shell.
2. Place the hollowed-out tomatoes in a mixing bowl and add the vinegar, oil, salt and pepper. Refrigerate one hour or longer, tossing occasionally.
3. Combine the remaining ingredients in a mixing bowl. Mash and whip to blend well. Drain the tomatoes and fill them with the stuffing.

Yield: Four dozen.

Tomato Freeze
with Avocado Topping
FLORIDA

1	three-ounce package cream cheese	2	cups tomato juice
¼	cup Roquefort cheese		Salt and freshly ground black pepper to taste
½	teaspoon grated onion	2	egg whites, beaten stiff but not dry
½	teaspoon Worcestershire sauce	1	ripe avocado
3	tablespoons lemon juice	⅛	teaspoon Tabasco sauce.

1. Cream the cream cheese and Roquefort together. Stir in the onion, Worcestershire and two tablespoons of the lemon juice. Slowly stir in the tomato juice. Season with salt and pepper.

2. Pour into a freezer tray and freeze until frozen around the edges but still mushy in the middle. Beat mixture until smooth but not completely melted. Fold in the egg whites and refreeze.

3. Peel and pit the avocado. Mash or puree the avocado and mix in the remaining lemon juice and Tabasco. Serve tomato freeze topped with avocado.

Yield: Six servings.

Cheese Balls
MISSISSIPPI

1½	cups finely grated Swiss cheese or Cheddar cheese		Dry bread crumbs
3	egg whites, beaten stiff but not dry	2	egg yolks, lightly beaten
			Fat or oil for deep-frying.

1. Place the cheese in a bowl and fold in the egg whites. Shape mixture into one-inch balls and roll in bread crumbs.

2. Dip in the egg yolks and again in crumbs. Fry until golden, a few at a time, in a fry basket in fat or oil heated to 365 degrees. Drain on paper towels.

Yield: About two dozen.

Herb Dip for Raw Vegetables
ALABAMA

- 1 cup cottage cheese
- ½ cup sour cream
- 1 cup homemade mayonnaise
- 2 tablespoons chopped chives
- 1 tablespoon chopped parsley
- 2 cloves garlic, finely minced
- 2 tablespoons grated onion
- ½ teaspoon Worcestershire sauce
- ¼ teaspoon Tabasco sauce
- Salt and freshly ground black pepper to taste.

Place the cottage cheese in a mixing bowl and add the sour cream. Beat with a fork or wire whisk until smooth, or blend in a blender. Stir in the remaining ingredients and serve chilled as a dip for raw vegetables such as cauliflower, celery and carrots.
Yield: About three cups.

Pat's Favorite Dip
KENTUCKY

- 1 egg
- 3 tablespoons cider vinegar
- 3 tablespoons sugar
- 1 eight-ounce package cream cheese, softened
- 3 tablespoons finely chopped onions
- 3 tablespoons chopped pimento
- 3 tablespoons chopped green pepper
- Salt and freshly ground black pepper to taste.

1. Put the egg, vinegar and sugar in the top of a double boiler and cook over hot water, stirring until thick.
2. Stir in the remaining ingredients and cool. Chill and serve with fresh raw vegetables.
Yield: About two cups.

Benne Seed Wafers
SOUTH CAROLINA

- ⅔ cup sesame seeds
- 2 cups flour
- Salt to taste
- Cayenne pepper to taste
- ½ cup butter
- ¼ cup shortening
- ¼ cup ice water, approximately.

1. Preheat the oven to 300 degrees.

2. Place the sesame seeds on a baking sheet and bake, stirring occasionally, until lightly browned, about twenty minutes.

3. Combine the flour, salt and cayenne in a mixing bowl. Add the butter and shortening and cut in with two knives or a pastry blender until mixture has the texture of coarse corn meal. Add the water, a little at a time, using a two-pronged fork to toss the mixture. Add just enough water so that the dough will hold together. Knead in the seeds.

4. Roll the dough on a lightly floured board and cut into small round wafers with a biscuit cutter. Place on a baking sheet and bake fifteen to twenty minutes. Remove from the oven and sprinkle, while hot, with a little salt.

Yield: Two dozen to three dozen wafers, depending on size.

Cheese Straws
ALABAMA

1¼	pounds sharp Cheddar cheese, grated	1¾	cups flour
8	tablespoons butter	¼	teaspoon cayenne pepper
		⅓	teaspoon salt.

1. Preheat the oven to 350 degrees.

2. Using an electric mixer, cream together the cheese and butter. Gradually add the flour and remaining ingredients. Work into a dough with the fingers.

3. Press the dough through a cookie press onto a baking sheet. Bake twenty to thirty minutes, or until crisp and lightly browned.

Yield: Six dozen to eight dozen, depending on size.

Deep-Fried Grits Balls
SOUTH CAROLINA

2	cups water		Freshly ground black pepper to taste
½	teaspoon salt		
½	cup quick cooking grits	2	eggs
1	cup grated sharp Cheddar cheese or Gruyère cheese	1½	teaspoons peanut oil
		1½	cups soft bread crumbs
¼	teaspoon cayenne pepper		Fat for deep-frying.
¼	teaspoon grated nutmeg		

1. Bring the water to a boil and add salt. When water is boiling vigorously, add the grits slowly. Return to a boil and cook over direct heat, stirring occasionally, two and one-half to five minutes. Chill the grits.

2. Mash grits with a fork and stir in the cheese, cayenne, nutmeg and pepper. With hands, shape into approximately forty balls. Beat the eggs and oil together. Dip balls in mixture; then roll in the bread crumbs.

3. Fry in hot fat (375 degrees) about two minutes, or until golden brown.

Yield: Forty appetizers.

Salted Pecans
GEORGIA

2 cups oil	1 pound shelled pecans (about 2½ pounds in shell).
Salt	

1. Heat the oil in a small saucepan over medium heat until the temperature reaches 360 degrees as registered on a candy thermometer.

2. Drop in one-half cup of the pecans and stir to prevent them from browning on the bottom of the pan. Cook until golden brown. Remove a few on a slotted spoon to check color. Do not overcook or burn.

3. Remove the nuts with a slotted spoon. Drain on a paper towel. Transfer to a clean paper towel and salt to taste. Repeat with the remaining pecans.

Yield: One pound salted pecans.

Conch Chowder
FLORIDA

4 raw conchs	1 one-pound can Italian-plum tomatoes
¼ pound salt pork, cut into small cubes	4 large potatoes, peeled and cut into cubes
2 tablespoons butter	8 cups water
2 cups finely chopped onions	Salt and freshly ground black pepper to taste.
1 large green pepper, peeled, seeded and cored	

1. Wash and scrub the conchs. Remove the meat from the shell. Skin the flesh and remove the intestinal vein. Clean well. Grind the meat.

2. Cook the salt pork in the butter until almost crisp. Add the onions and green pepper and cook, stirring, until onions are wilted. Add the tomatoes, ground conch, potatoes and water. Season with salt and pepper. Simmer until potatoes are mushy, about one hour. This chowder is better if it is removed from the heat, cooled, then reheated.

Yield: Four servings.

One of the genuine delicacies of the Louisiana scene is the abundant crawfish or crayfish which come primarily from the Cajun country in the southern part of the state. The finest sources are said to be the Atchafalaya River basin and the region around the Belle River. The town of Breaux Bridge is said to be the crawfish capital of the world.

Because crawfish come from swamps and other shallow freshwater sources, their flavor is a trifle earthy. They have a texture that more closely resembles lobster than shrimp, although a cooked crawfish tail is about the size of a small shrimp.

An appreciation of crawfish is by no means limited to Louisiana. Each August the Swedes have a crawfish festival and the French, who call them écrevisse, use crawfish in countless dishes.

The commonest uses for crawfish in Louisiana are in a bisque and in étouffée. The bisque is a thickened soup garnished with stuffed crawfish heads. The étouffée is a form of stew.

Crawfish Bisque

LOUISIANA

12 to fifteen pounds live crawfish	¼ cup lemon juice
Boiling salted water	3 tablespoons plus one-half cup chopped parsley
3 tablespoons butter	1 teaspoon thyme
4 onions, finely chopped	1 cup finely chopped scallions, including green part
5 ribs celery, finely chopped	
2 green peppers, seeded and finely chopped	3 slices stale white bread
	¾ cup flour
6 cloves garlic, finely chopped	¾ cup oil
Salt and freshly ground black pepper to taste	3 quarts hot water
	1 lemon, thinly sliced
3 tablespoons Worcestershire sauce	1 bay leaf
	Cooked rice.

1. Preheat the oven to 350 degrees.
2. Wash the crawfish and boil in the salted water for ten minutes. Remove meat from the tail and clean. Remove fat from heads and reserve. Clean the heads, rinse in cold water and drain.
3. Melt the butter and sauté two of the onions, three of the celery ribs, one of the green peppers and three of the garlic cloves in it until tender.
4. Grind two-thirds of the crawfish tails and add. Cook five minutes. Add salt and pepper to taste, two tablespoons of the Worcestershire, the lemon juice, three tablespoons of the parsley, the thyme, one-half cup of the scallions and one-half of the reserved crawfish fat.
5. Soak the bread briefly in water, squeeze and add. Simmer mixture ten minutes, stirring constantly. Use mixture to stuff heads. Pack tightly. Bake fifteen minutes and set aside while preparing bisque.
6. Combine the flour and oil in a saucepan and heat, stirring, until mixture forms a brown roux. Add the remaining onions, celery, green pepper and garlic and cook until tender.
7. Add the hot water all at once and blend well. Season with the remaining Worcestershire and salt and pepper and add the lemon slices. Add remaining crawfish fat and the bay leaf and cook for one hour.
8. Remove bay leaf. Add remaining crawfish tails. Cover pot and cook ten minutes longer. Add stuffed heads, remaining scallions and remaining parsley. Cook five minutes. Serve over rice.

Yield: Eight to ten servings.

Shrimp Bisque
LOUISIANA

½	cup diced salt pork	2	sprigs parsley
⅓	cup finely chopped shallots	½	teaspoon thyme
⅓	cup finely chopped celery	1½	pounds shrimp, shelled and deveined
1	cup one-half-inch cubes potato	1½	cups heavy cream
4	cups fish stock or bottled clam juice and water	¼	cup dry white wine or one teaspoon lemon juice
1	bay leaf		Cooked rice.

1. In a heavy kettle, render the salt pork until it gives up its fat and is crisp. Drain the bits and reserve.
2. Sauté the shallots and celery in the pork fat until tender. Add the po-

tato cubes, fish stock or clam juice and water and the bay leaf, parsley and thyme tied in a muslin bag. Bring to a boil and simmer fifteen minutes, or until potato pieces are barely tender.

3. Add the shrimp and cook about eight minutes, or until shrimp turn pink. Remove the muslin bag. Add the cream, reserved salt pork and wine or lemon juice and reheat. Check the seasoning. Serve in deep soup plates over rice.

Yield: Four servings.

She-Crab and Lobster Soup
ALABAMA

4 cups Italian plum tomatoes	Cayenne pepper to taste
1 cup shelled green peas	¼ teaspoon ground ginger
Salted water	1 tablespoon Worcestershire sauce
1 cup milk	
2 cups heavy cream	½ cup plus six tablespoons dry sherry
1 pound lump crab meat, picked over to remove bits of shell and cartilage	6 tablespoons whipped cream
	Paprika
1 one and one-half-pound lobster, cooked	Finely chopped parsley.
Salt and freshly ground black pepper to taste	

1. Cook the tomatoes over moderate heat about thirty minutes, or until reduced to a paste. The tomatoes must be stirred frequently to prevent sticking and burning.

2. Cook the peas in salted water to cover until tender. Put them through a sieve or food mill and add to the tomatoes.

3. Add the milk, cream and crab meat. Remove all the meat from the lobster shell and cut lobster meat into bite-size pieces. Add to the stew. Add the salt, pepper, cayenne, ginger and Worcestershire. Cook over low heat, stirring frequently, for one hour. Add one-half of the sherry.

4. When ready to serve, add one tablespoon sherry to each of six heated soup bowls. Ladle the soup over and garnish each serving with one tablespoon whipped cream sprinkled with paprika and parsley.

Yield: Six servings.

She-Crab Soup
MARYLAND

4 tablespoons butter	¼ cup cracker crumbs
¼ cup onion, finely minced	Nutmeg to taste
2 cups milk	Cayenne pepper to taste
½ teaspoon grated lemon rind	Salt and freshly ground black pepper to taste
1 pound lump crab meat, picked over to remove bits of shell and cartilage	1 tablespoon dry sherry
	¼ to one-half cup crab roe, if available.
2 cups heavy cream	

1. Heat one tablespoon of the butter in the top of a double boiler. Add the onion and cook, stirring, until onion is wilted. Add the milk and lemon rind and simmer five minutes.

2. Add the crab meat to the onion and milk. Add remaining butter and the cream and simmer over boiling water fifteen minutes, stirring occasionally. Stir in the crumbs, nutmeg, cayenne, salt and pepper. Let stand until ready to serve. Before serving, stir in the sherry and roe. Heat thoroughly.

Yield: Six servings.

South River Club Crab Soup
MARYLAND

2 tablespoons butter	1 pound back fin crab meat, picked over to remove bits of shell and cartilage
1½ tablespoons flour	
2½ cups milk	
1 teaspoon salt	1 cup heavy cream
¼ teaspoon freshly ground black pepper	2 hard-cooked eggs, pressed through a sieve
⅛ teaspoon cayenne pepper	¼ cup dry sherry, or to taste.

1. Melt the butter in a saucepan. Blend in the flour and cook, stirring, one minute. Remove from heat and gradually stir in the milk. Add the salt, pepper and cayenne.

2. Bring to a boil, stirring constantly until sauce thickens. Cook two minutes. Add the crab meat and cream and reheat. Add the eggs and then the sherry. Serve at once.

Yield: Six servings.

Maryland Clam Chowder

3	quarts chicken broth or broth and water mixed	¼	teaspoon white pepper
1	whole chicken breast	1	cup sliced carrots
1	teaspoon salt	1	cup diced potatoes
2	ribs celery with leaves	1	ten-ounce package frozen corn
1½	cups Chesapeake Bay soft-shelled clams (about 36)	1	ten-ounce package frozen peas
1	tablespoon chopped chives	1	pimento, finely chopped
2	tablespoons minced onion	1	cup clam juice
½	teaspoon celery salt	1	teaspoon finely chopped parsley.
¼	teaspoon thyme leaves		

1. Combine the broth, chicken breast, salt and celery. Bring to a boil, cover and simmer thirty minutes.

2. Discard celery. While chicken broth simmers, separate the bodies of the clams from tough outer ring; refrigerate bodies and mince the outer rings.

3. Remove chicken and chop meat finely. Add the remaining ingredients except clam juice, parsley, chicken and clam bodies, to broth. Simmer twenty minutes.

4. Add chicken, clam juice and parsley. Continue cooking five minutes. Add clam bodies just before serving.

Yield: Four quarts; about sixteen servings.

Black-Eyed Pea Soup
LOUISIANA

2	cups dried black-eyed peas		Salt to taste
	Cold water	4	peppercorns
1	small ham hock	4	thin slices lemon
4	cups boiling water		Paprika
1	bay leaf	1	teaspoon finely chopped parsley.
2	ribs celery, coarsely chopped		
1	onion, studded with two whole cloves		

1. Soak the black-eyed peas overnight in cold water to cover. Next day, drain and place in a two-quart kettle. Add the ham hock, boiling water,

bay leaf, celery, onion, salt and peppercorns and bring to a boil. Cook until peas are tender, two and one-half to three hours. As the soup cooks, skim the surface as necessary.

2. Remove the ham hock and bay leaf and puree the soup either through a sieve or in an electric blender. Spoon into four hot soup plates and top each with a slice of lemon. Dot the center of each lemon slice with a little paprika and one-quarter teaspoon chopped parsley.

Yield: Four servings.

**Potage d'Haricots Rouges
(Louisiana Red Bean Soup)**

4	cups dried Louisiana red beans or kidney beans	1	teaspoon sage
½	pound lean slab bacon, without rind, cut into cubes		Salt and freshly ground black pepper to taste
			Tabasco sauce to taste
2	large onions, finely chopped		Chopped parsley
2	cloves garlic, finely minced		Chopped hard-cooked egg
1	teaspoon celery seeds		Garlic croutons (optional).

1. Soak the beans overnight in water that extends one inch above their level.

2. Next day, drain the beans and put them in a heavy kettle. Add three quarts of water and bring to a boil.

3. Cook the bacon in a skillet until most of the fat is rendered. Add the onions and garlic and cook until onions are translucent. Add the celery seeds and sage. Season with salt, pepper and Tabasco and pour the mixture into the beans. Simmer the beans until they are very tender, two to two and one-half hours.

4. Let the beans cool and put them through a food mill or sieve or puree them, a little at a time, in an electric blender. If necessary, they may be thinned with a little broth or water. This soup will keep well in the refrigerator.

5. Heat the soup thoroughly and serve sprinkled with chopped parsley and hard-cooked egg and, if desired, garlic croutons.

Yield: Three and one-half quarts; about one dozen servings.

Black Bean Soup
SOUTH CAROLINA

1½	cups dried black beans	⅛	teaspoon mace
	Cold water	1	teaspoon salt
8	cups water		Pinch of cayenne pepper
¼	pound salt pork, diced	2	tablespoons flour
1	onion, chopped	1	tablespoon butter
1	carrot, quartered	¾	cup dry sherry
2	ribs celery, diced	2	hard-cooked eggs, chopped
2	whole cloves	1	lemon, thinly sliced.

    1. Day before, wash and pick over the beans. Cover with cold water and let soak overnight. Next morning, drain beans and place in a large kettle.
    2. Add the eight cups water. Cook the salt pork until the fat has been rendered. Add the onion and sauté until tender.
    3. Add the onion to the kettle along with the carrot, celery, cloves, mace, salt and cayenne. Bring to a boil, cover and simmer about three hours, or until beans are very tender. Stir occasionally and add more water if necessary.
    4. Press mixture through a sieve or a food mill. Mix the flour with a little water. Stir in a little of the hot soup and return to the pan. Bring to a boil, stirring. Cook three minutes. Check the seasoning.
    5. Add the butter and sherry. Serve in soup bowls. Garnish with the chopped egg and the lemon slices.
    Yield: Six servings.

Cream of Corn Soup
SOUTH CAROLINA

6	ears corn	¼	teaspoon freshly ground
3	tablespoons butter		black pepper
2	hard-cooked egg yolks	1	cup heavy cream
1½	tablespoons flour	1	egg yolk.
1	teaspoon salt		

    1. Cut the kernels from the corn cobs and grind in a meat grinder. Place the cobs in a saucepan, barely cover with water and boil fifteen minutes. Remove and discard the cobs. Reserve liquid.

2. Mix together the butter, hard-cooked egg yolks and flour in a saucepan. Gradually stir in the corn cob liquid. Add the corn and bring to a boil, stirring. Cook five minutes. Press through a sieve or puree in an electric blender.

3. Season with salt and pepper. Mix the cream with the egg yolk, add a little hot soup and return all to the pan. Cook only to just below boiling.

Yield: Six servings.

Pumpkin Soup
VIRGINIA

4 cups diced peeled pumpkin pulp (about one medium-size pumpkin)	6 cups chicken broth
	1 cup heavy cream
	Salt and freshly ground black pepper to taste
3 carrots, diced	
3 ribs celery, diced	½ teaspoon nutmeg
1 small onion, finely chopped	1 tablespoon sugar
1 bay leaf	Boiling milk.

1. Place the pumpkin, carrots, celery and onion in a large kettle. Add the bay leaf and broth. Bring to a boil. Cover and simmer about one hour, or until pumpkin is tender.

2. Pass mixture through a strainer, food mill or electric blender and return to the kettle. Stir in the remaining ingredients except the milk. Adjust the consistency with the milk.

Yield: Six servings.

Tomato Soup
SOUTH CAROLINA

4 cups finely chopped, peeled tomatoes	Salt and freshly ground black pepper to taste
¾ teaspoon baking soda	
2 cups light cream or milk	2 tablespoons butter
2 large soda crackers, made into fine crumbs	¼ cup finely grated Cheddar cheese.

1. Cook the tomatoes for about fifteen minutes, stirring to prevent sticking. Add the baking soda and stir until it stops effervescing.

2. Stir in the cream or milk and the cracker crumbs. Reheat. Season with salt and pepper. Whirl in the butter.

3. Serve in hot bowls and sprinkle one tablespoon of the cheese over each serving.

Yield: Four servings.

Cream of Spinach Soup
SOUTH CAROLINA

1½ pounds fresh spinach or one package frozen spinach	4 cups milk or half milk and half heavy cream
2 tablespoons butter	Cayenne pepper to taste
½ cup finely minced onion	Whipped cream for garnish.
2 tablespoons flour	
Salt and freshly ground black pepper to taste	

1. If fresh spinach is used, pick it over well and wash in several changes of cold water. Tear off and discard any tough stems. Cook the spinach in a covered kettle in the water that clings to the leaves. If frozen spinach is used, cook according to package directions. Drain spinach well and set aside.

2. Heat the butter in a saucepan and add the onion. Cook until onion is wilted. Sprinkle with the flour, salt and pepper. Add the milk, stirring rapidly with a wire whisk.

3. Put the spinach through a food mill or sieve or add to the sauce and blend in an electric blender. Add cayenne, bring just to a boil and serve hot or cold with a garnish of whipped cream.

Yield: Six to eight servings.

Celery Chowder
FLORIDA

¼ pound salt pork, diced	3 cups celery, diagonally sliced into small pieces
3 onions, thinly sliced	
4 cups milk	2 tablespoons flour
3 large potatoes, peeled and diced	Salt and freshly ground black pepper to taste.

1. Cook the salt pork in a heavy kettle or pan until crisp and brown. Remove the pork pieces and reserve.
2. Sauté the onions in the pork fat remaining in the pan or kettle until tender but not browned.
3. Heat all but one-quarter cup of the milk to boiling and add to the pan with the potatoes and celery. Bring to a boil, cover and simmer about twenty minutes, or until potatoes are tender.
4. Blend the flour with the remaining milk, add a little of the hot soup and mix. Return to the pan and cook, stirring, until soup thickens. Season with salt and pepper and sprinkle with reserved salt pork.

Yield: About two quarts; eight to ten servings.

Field or Cow Pea Soup
SOUTH CAROLINA

2 cups dried field or cow peas	½ cup chopped celery
Water	2 teaspoons salt
1 ham bone	Freshly ground black pepper to taste
8 cups water	
1 onion, chopped	6 slices lemon.

1. Cover the peas with water and let soak overnight.
2. Next day, drain peas and put in a kettle with the ham bone, two quarts water, onion, celery and salt and cook until peas are soft. Remove bone and puree soup in an electric blender or push through a sieve.
3. Reheat soup and add pepper. Serve in hot soup plates and garnish each serving with a slice of lemon.

Yield: Six servings.

Okra Ham Soup
SOUTH CAROLINA

2 pounds okra, finely sliced (frozen okra can be used)	Salt and freshly ground black pepper to taste
1 tablespoon bacon drippings	Water or chicken broth, if necessary
1 tablespoon cider vinegar	
1 ham bone	1½ cups corn kernels, cut from cob
6 tomatoes, peeled and chopped, or four cups canned	3 cups hot cooked rice.
1 cup fresh butter or lima beans	
1 small sprig thyme or one-half teaspoon dried thyme	

    1. Cook the okra quickly in a skillet with the bacon drippings and vinegar until okra loses its slimy consistency, stirring constantly.
    2. Transfer to a kettle and add the ham bone, tomatoes, beans and thyme. Season with salt and pepper. Bring to a boil and simmer until meat on bone is very tender. Remove bone. Chop ham and return to kettle. Check consistency and, if too thick, add water or chicken broth.
    3. Add corn kernels to soup. Cook three minutes. Serve over the rice.
Yield: Six servings.

Okra Soup
LOUISIANA

2 pounds beef shin	2 pounds young fresh okra, cut into one-quarter-inch thick slices
2 large onions, coarsely chopped	
1 carrot, quartered	1 tablespoon chopped fresh basil or one teaspoon dried
1 bay leaf	
6 sprigs parsley	1 tablespoon butter
10 roughly crushed black peppercorns	1 tablespoon flour
	Salt and freshly ground black pepper.
2 teaspoons salt	
3 quarts water, approximately	
3 pounds ripe tomatoes, peeled and chopped	

1. Place the beef, onions, carrot, bay leaf, parsley, peppercorns, salt and enough water to cover in a large kettle. Bring to a boil and skim. Cover and simmer three to four hours.
2. Strain the broth into a clean kettle. Cut the meat from bones, dice and add to the broth. Add the tomatoes and cook twenty minutes.
3. Add the okra and basil. Cook until the okra is tender, but do not overcook.
4. Blend the butter and flour together and whisk into the soup bit by bit to thicken. Season to taste with salt and pepper.

Yield: Ten servings.

Chilled Peach Soup
GEORGIA

2	tablespoons butter	1/8	teaspoon oregano
1	tablespoon finely chopped scallion, including green part	1/4	teaspoon cinnamon
		1/4	teaspoon freshly ground black pepper
1	tablespoon grated carrot		
1	tablespoon finely chopped celery with leaves	2	cups light cream
		2	to four tablespoons dark rum or cognac (optional)
1	tablespoon finely chopped parsley	1/2	cup heavy cream, whipped
1	tablespoon flour	2	tablespoons toasted almond slivers.
2	cups chicken broth		
4	cups peeled, thinly sliced ripe peaches		

1. Heat the butter in a heavy saucepan. Sauté the scallion, carrot, celery and parsley in it until golden. Sprinkle with the flour and cook, stirring, one minute longer.
2. Add the broth, peaches, oregano, cinnamon and pepper. Bring to a boil and simmer gently about thirty minutes.
3. Force the mixture through a food mill. Chill well.
4. Before serving, stir in the light cream and rum or cognac if desired. Pour soup into individual bowls and top with the whipped cream and almonds.

Yield: Six servings.

Strawberry Cooler
FLORIDA

4 cups strawberries	1 tablespoon lemon juice
1 cup orange juice	1 cup buttermilk
1½ tablespoons cornstarch	Sesame wafers.
½ cup sugar	

1. Reserve several berries for garnish; place remainder in an electric blender with the orange juice.
2. Blend until smooth and strain into a saucepan. Mix the cornstarch with a little of the strained mixture and add to remaining mixture in the pan. Heat, stirring, until mixture comes to a boil; then cook one minute.
3. Remove from heat and add the sugar, lemon juice and buttermilk. Chill thoroughly. Serve in chilled bowls, garnished with reserved strawberries and wafers.

Yield: Four to six servings.

Cream of Peanut Soup
VIRGINIA

⅓ cup butter	4 cups chicken broth
2 tablespoons finely chopped onion	1 teaspoon salt
	¼ teaspoon freshly ground black pepper
2 tablespoons finely chopped celery	1 cup heavy cream
1½ tablespoons flour	⅓ cup finely chopped unsalted peanuts.
1 cup peanut butter	

1. Melt the butter in a heavy saucepan and sauté the onion and celery in it until tender but not browned. Sprinkle with the flour and cook one minute longer.
2. Remove from the heat and stir in the peanut butter. Gradually stir in the broth, salt and pepper. Bring to a boil, stirring, and simmer, covered, twenty-five minutes.
3. Strain mixture and add the cream. Reheat, but do not boil. Serve garnished with the peanuts.

Yield: Six servings.

Almond Soup
VIRGINIA

- 1 large whole chicken breast
- 2 cups chicken broth
- 1 bay leaf
- 1 rib celery
- Salt and freshly ground black pepper to taste
- ¼ cup blanched almonds, finely grated
- 1 cup heavy cream.

1. Place the chicken breast in a skillet with the broth, bay leaf, celery, salt and pepper.
2. Bring to a boil, cover and simmer fifteen minutes. Remove chicken from the bone and mash together with the almonds with a wooden spoon or in an electric blender. Mix in two tablespoons of the cream.
3. Strain the chicken broth and add gradually, while stirring, to the chicken-almond mixture. Bring to a boil and add the remaining cream. Reheat, but do not boil.

Yield: Four servings.

Fish and Shellfish

**Clam-Stuffed Baked Rock Fish
(Striped Bass)**
MARYLAND

1 eight-pound or two four-pound rock fish, heads and tails removed	1 clove garlic, finely chopped
	2 cups shucked soft-shelled clams with liquor
Salt and freshly ground black pepper to taste	1 teaspoon plus one tablespoon lemon juice
½ cup butter	¼ teaspoon oregano
1 onion, finely chopped	2 tablespoons chopped parsley
2 tablespoons finely chopped green pepper	8 slices stale white bread, finely cubed
1 rib celery, finely chopped	8 slices bacon.

1. Preheat the oven to 350 degrees.
2. Season the fish inside and outside with salt and pepper.
3. Melt half the butter and sauté the onion, green pepper, celery and garlic in it until tender. Add the clams and liquor and cook until edges of clams just curl.
4. Add one teaspoon of the lemon juice, the oregano, parsley, bread and salt and pepper to taste.
5. Stuff the cavity of the fish with the stuffing. Sew or skewer to close. Make gashes on top of fish and fit the bacon in the gashes. Set fish in a greased baking dish.

6. Sprinkle with remaining lemon juice and dot with remaining butter.

7. Bake about one and one-quarter hours for an eight-pound fish and forty-five minutes for two four-pounders, or until fish flakes.

Yield: Eight servings.

Baked Stuffed Striped Bass
(Rock Fish)
MARYLAND

2	slices salt pork, diced	¼	cup chopped toasted almonds
2	tablespoons butter		Freshly ground black pepper
½	cup finely chopped onion	1	four-pound striped bass,
¼	cup chopped celery		dressed, with head and tail
2	tablespoons chopped green pepper		left on
			Melted butter
1	cup soft bread crumbs		Salt
1	teaspoon thyme	4	slices bacon.

1. Preheat the oven to 400 degrees.

2. Render the salt pork in a heavy pan until crisp. Add the butter, onion, celery and green pepper. Cook until the vegetables are tender but not brown. Add the crumbs, thyme, almonds and pepper to taste.

3. Use the mixture to stuff the cavity of the fish. Secure by sewing, toothpicks or skewers. Place on a sheet of aluminum foil. Brush with melted butter. Season with salt and pepper.

4. Arrange the bacon over the fish. Place on a baking sheet. Close the foil and bake twenty-five minutes. Open the foil and bake ten minutes longer, or until the fish is done.

Yield: Six servings.

Baked Catfish
MISSISSIPPI

- 2 pounds skinned catfish fillets, cut into serving pieces
- 1 teaspoon salt
- 1/8 teaspoon freshly ground black pepper
- 1/2 cup chopped scallions, including green part
- 1 lemon, thinly sliced
- 1/2 cup catchup
- 2 tablespoons melted butter
- 2 tablespoons dry white wine.

1. Preheat the oven to 350 degrees.
2. Place the fillets in a single layer in a shallow baking dish. Season with the salt and pepper.
3. Sprinkle with the scallions and top with the lemon slices. Combine the remaining ingredients and pour over fish. Bake twenty-five minutes, or until fish flakes easily.

Yield: Four servings.

Catfish Gumbo
LOUISIANA

- 1/4 cup pork fat rendered
- 1/2 cup finely chopped celery
- 1/2 cup chopped green pepper
- 1/2 cup chopped onion
- 1 clove garlic, finely chopped
- 2 cups beef broth
- 1 one-pound can tomatoes
- 1/2 pound fresh okra or one ten-ounce package frozen okra, sliced
- 2 teaspoons salt
- 1/2 teaspoon freshly ground black pepper
- 1/4 teaspoon thyme
- 1 bay leaf
- Few drops of Tabasco sauce
- 1 pound skinned catfish fillets, cut into one-inch pieces
- 1 1/2 cups hot cooked rice.

1. Heat the fat and sauté the celery, green pepper, onion and garlic in it until tender. Stir in the broth, tomatoes, okra, salt, pepper, thyme, bay leaf and Tabasco.
2. Bring to a boil and simmer thirty minutes.
3. Add the fish and simmer about ten to fifteen minutes longer, or until fish flakes easily. Remove bay leaf.

4. Place one-quarter cup of the rice in each of six hot bowls and fill with gumbo.

Yield: Six servings.

Maryland Fried Clams

- 4 cups shucked soft-shelled clams with liquor
- 2 eggs, beaten
- 2 tablespoons milk
- ½ teaspoon salt
- ⅛ teaspoon freshly ground black pepper
- 3 cups dry bread crumbs
- Fat or oil for deep-frying
- Tartar sauce (see page 259).

1. Drain the clams. Combine the eggs, milk, salt and pepper. Dip clams in egg mixture and roll in the bread crumbs.
2. Fry a few clams at a time until golden in a fry basket in fat or oil heated to 350 degrees. Drain on paper towels. Serve with tartar sauce.

Yield: Six servings.

Conchs are big sea snails, and the early settlers of the Florida Keys said that the flesh or juices of fresh conch would give those who partook of it perpetual youth. The flesh of conch may be marinated and eaten raw or it may be cooked.

Raw Conch Salad

FLORIDA

- 4 raw conchs
- Salt and freshly ground black pepper to taste
- 2 to four tablespoons lime juice
- ½ cup tomato juice
- ¾ cup finely chopped heart of celery
- ½ cup finely chopped white onion or scallions, including green part
- ¼ cup finely chopped green pepper
- Tabasco sauce to taste
- Lettuce (optional).

1. Wash and scrub the conchs. Remove the meat from the shell. Skin the flesh and remove the intestinal vein. Clean well.
2. Slice the conchs and pound the meat with a mallet. Cut the meat into

small cubes and combine with the remaining ingredients. Refrigerate several hours.

3. Serve chilled, with lettuce if desired.

Yield: Six to eight servings.

Crab Cakes I
MARYLAND

2 cups back fin crab meat, picked over to remove bits of shell and cartilage	½ cup soft bread crumbs
	2 eggs, well beaten
	1 teaspoon Worcestershire sauce
¼ cup milk	4 tablespoons butter
2 tablespoons finely chopped parsley	Lemon wedges
Salt to taste	Tartar sauce (recipe below).

Blend the crab meat with the milk, parsley, salt, bread crumbs, eggs and Worcestershire. Shape into four to six cakes and cook in the butter on all sides until golden brown. Serve with lemon wedges and tartar sauce.

Yield: Four to six servings.

Tartar Sauce
MARYLAND

1 cup mayonnaise	1 teaspoon finely chopped onion (optional)
2 tablespoons finely chopped parsley	1 tablespoon finely chopped capers
1 tablespoon finely chopped chives	1 small sour pickle, finely chopped
1 tablespoon finely chopped tarragon	Finely minced garlic (optional).
1 tablespoon finely chopped chervil (optional)	

Combine all ingredients except the garlic and blend well. If desired, add a little finely minced garlic.

Yield: About one and one-quarter cups.

Crab Cakes II
MARYLAND

¼ cup chopped parsley	⅛ teaspoon freshly ground black pepper
3 tablespoons chopped scallions including green part	1 teaspoon dry mustard
1 pound crab meat, picked over to remove bits of shell and cartilage	1 egg
	½ cup fine dry bread crumbs
½ teaspoon salt	8 tablespoons butter.

Combine the parsley, scallions, crab meat, salt, pepper, mustard and egg and mix well. Shape into small cakes, roll in the bread crumbs and cook in butter until golden brown on all sides.
Yield: Eight to ten cakes.

Crab Stew
LOUISIANA

2 tablespoons butter	2 tablespoons finely chopped parsley
2 tablespoons finely chopped shallots or scallions, including green part	2 tablespoons finely chopped chives
4 white mushrooms, thinly sliced	1¼ cups heavy cream
Juice of half a lemon	Tabasco sauce to taste
2 ripe tomatoes, peeled, seeded and cubed	Salt and freshly ground black pepper to taste
1 pound lump crab meat, picked over to remove bits of shell and cartilage	2 tablespoons warm cognac
	Cooked rice.

1. Heat the butter in a skillet or chafing dish and add the shallots or scallions. Cook about three minutes and add the mushrooms. Sprinkle with the lemon juice and cook briefly, stirring. Add the tomatoes and simmer five minutes.

2. Add the crab meat, but treat it gently so as not to break up the lumps. Add the parsley and chives and simmer five minutes. Stir in the cream, Tabasco, salt and pepper. Add the cognac and ignite it. Serve immediately with rice.
Yield: Four to six servings.

Deep-Fried Soft-Shelled Crabs
MARYLAND

6 soft-shelled crabs	2 eggs, lightly beaten
Milk	2 cups soft bread crumbs
Salt and freshly ground black pepper to taste	Fat for deep-frying
	Tartar sauce (page 259).

1. Wash the crabs well to remove all sand. Place them "face" down and, with a sharp knife, cut out the face. Remove the spongy gills under the side points and sand bags from under either side of the shell. Remove the small pointed lower portion known as the apron. Soak the crabs in milk seasoned with salt and pepper.

2. Dip each crab in the egg, then in the bread crumbs, in egg again and then again in crumbs. Heat the fat to about 375 degrees and cook the crabs, turning once, until golden brown. Drain on paper towels. Serve with tartar sauce.

Yield: Six servings.

Crab Gumbo
LOUISIANA

12 live hard-shelled crabs	3 sprigs fresh parsley
Boiling water	4 cups tender okra
Salt and freshly ground black pepper to taste	2 tablespoons bacon drippings
¼ cup butter	1 bay leaf
8 large tomatoes, cored and peeled	½ pod seeded red pepper
2 large onions, chopped	Cayenne pepper to taste
3 sprigs fresh thyme or one teaspoon dried thyme	Boiled rice.

1. Place the crabs in a kettle and add boiling water to cover. Let stand briefly; then drain. Pull away the front "apron" on the underside of the crabs. Take away and discard the "dead man's fingers," a spongy, lunglike substance inside the crabs. Crack the crab claws and cut the body of the crab into quarters. Season with salt and pepper. Wipe the kettle with a clean cloth.

2. Heat half the butter in the kettle and add the crab pieces. Cover closely and cook over low heat about five minutes. Chop the tomatoes and

drain, but reserve both the pulp and juice. Add pulp to the kettle. Add the onions, thyme and parsley and stir to prevent scorching. Cook about five minutes. Brown the okra separately in bacon drippings. Add to the crab. Cook, stirring, until most of the moisture in the kettle has evaporated.

3. Add the bay leaf and reserved tomato juice. Add eight cups boiling water and the pepper pod and simmer, stirring frequently, for one hour. Season with cayenne. Serve hot with boiled rice.

Yield: Six or more servings.

One of the greatest delights of Florida's costal regions is stone crabs or Morro crabs, with their hard shell and meat-filled claws which have a delicate flavor and admirable texture. Stone crabs are not plentiful and, when available, they are expensive. There are a few sea food shops in coastal areas, especially in the Keys, where these crabs may be bought alive.

One of these shops is Sid and Roxie's in Islamorada. The whole crabs may be purchased, but the claws alone may be ordered. The body of the stone crab has a delicious flavor, but there is not much meat to be had.

Steamed Stone Crab
FLORIDA

24	whole stone crabs (see above)	3	ribs celery with leaves
	Water	½	teaspoon thyme
1	cup dry white wine	2	carrots, quartered
	Salt to taste	2	bay leaves
20	peppercorns	3	tablespoons cider vinegar.
1	large onion, coarsely chopped		

1. Take special care when dealing with the crabs because they have powerful claws and their grip is dangerous.

2. In a large kettle place enough water to cover the crabs to the depth of one inch and add the wine, salt, peppercorns, onion, celery, thyme, carrots and bay leaves. Simmer fifteen minutes and add the vinegar. Immediately add the crabs, cover and bring to a boil. Simmer ten to fifteen minutes. Crack the claws and cut the bodies into quarters. To serve, see note.

Yield: Four to six servings.

Note: Stone crabs may be served hot with melted butter and lemon or lime juice or cold with mustard, mayonnaise or vinaigrette sauce.

Crab Meat Imperial
MARYLAND

1	large green pepper, diced
2	pimentos, diced
½	teaspoon salt
½	teaspoon freshly ground white pepper
1	tablespoon dry mustard
	Mayonnaise
2	eggs, lightly beaten
3	tablespoons dry sherry
2	pounds lump crab meat, picked over to remove bits of shell and cartilage
	Paprika.

1. Preheat the oven to 350 degrees.
2. Mix the diced pepper and pimentos. Add the salt, pepper, mustard, three tablespoons mayonnaise, the eggs and two tablespoons of the sherry. Mix well.
3. Carefully fold the crab meat into the pepper mixture so as not to break up the pieces of crab. Add the remaining sherry and place the mixture in a buttered casserole.
4. Coat the top of the casserole with a thin layer of mayonnaise and sprinkle with paprika. Bake fifteen minutes.

Yield: Six servings.

Steamed Hard-Shelled Crabs
MARYLAND

12	hard-shelled crabs	1	cup stale beer
1	teaspoon crushed red pepper flakes		Lemon wedges
	Salt to taste		Melted butter.
2	tablespoons crab boil (see note) or pickling spices		

1. Place the crabs on a rack in a steamer and sprinkle with the pepper flakes, salt, crab boil and beer.
2. Cover closely and bring to a boil on top of the stove. Steam the crabs twenty to thirty minutes, or until the aprons begin to lift. Serve with lemon wedges and melted butter.

Yield: Four to six servings.

Note: Crab boil is available in packages in many grocery stores.

Broiled Soft-Shelled Crabs
FLORIDA

- 6 soft-shelled crabs
- 6 tablespoons melted butter
- Juice of half a lemon
- Salt and freshly ground black pepper to taste
- Few drops of Tabasco sauce
- Toast (optional).

1. Wash the crabs to remove all sand. Place them "face" down and, with a sharp knife, cut out the face. Remove the spongy gills (sometimes called "dead man's fingers") from under the side points and sand bags from under either side of the shell. Remove the small pointed lower portion known as the apron.

2. Combine the remaining ingredients. Dip the crabs in the mixture and broil or grill the crabs five to ten minutes. Pour over the remaining melted butter mixture. Serve on toast if desired.

Yield: Three servings.

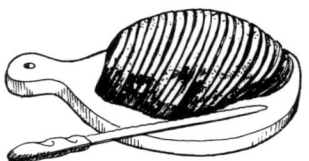

Crawfish à la Nage
LOUISIANA

- 1 carrot, cut into rounds
- 1 large onion, sliced
- 2 shallots or scallions, including green part, coarsely chopped
- 2 cups water
- 2 cups dry white wine
- Salt to taste
- 12 peppercorns
- 2 sprigs parsley
- 1 bay leaf
- Pinch of thyme
- 48 to sixty crawfish
- Parsley for garnish.

1. Combine the carrot, onion, shallots or scallions, water, wine, salt, peppercorns, two sprigs parsley, bay leaf and thyme in a kettle and bring to a boil. Simmer fifteen minutes.

2. Wash the crawfish well and drop them into the court bouillon. Return to a boil and remove from the heat. Let the crawfish cool in the liquid. Drain and arrange in a pile with the parsley for garnish. Eat with the fingers.

Yield: Four to six servings.

Crawfish Étouffée
LOUISIANA

3 tablespoons vegetable oil or olive oil
¾ cup chopped onion
1 clove garlic, finely chopped
2 cups tomatoes, preferably Italian plum style
Salt and freshly ground black pepper
2 tablespoons butter
1 cup chopped scallions, including green part
¼ cup crawfish stock (see note)
5 pounds crawfish tails
⅔ cup crawfish fat (see note)
Cayenne pepper to taste
¼ teaspoon each ground rosemary, marjoram, thyme, oregano, sage and basil
Cooked rice.

1. Heat two tablespoons of the oil and add the onion and garlic. Cook, stirring, until onion is translucent. Add the tomatoes and sprinkle with salt and pepper. Cook, stirring occasionally, approximately one hour, or until sauce is thickened. There should be about one cup of sauce.

2. Melt the butter in a large Dutch oven or kettle and add the remaining oil. Add half the scallions and cook briefly. Add sauce, crawfish stock and crawfish tails and season lightly with salt and pepper. Stir briefly and bring to a boil.

3. Add the crawfish fat and seasonings. Cook, stirring occasionally, thirty to forty minutes. Before serving, sprinkle with remaining scallions. Serve piping hot with rice.

Yield: Eight to ten servings.

Note: Crawfish stock is made by boiling shells and other discarded portions of the crawfish in water barely to cover. If the shells are not available, substitute chicken broth. When shelled crawfish are purchased, there is always a certain amount of crawfish fat clinging to the meat.

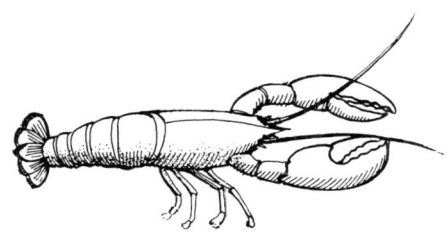

Dolphin Fillets Norsaga

FLORIDA

- 2 dolphin fillets, each weighing approximately one-half pound
- Milk
- Oil
- ½ cup melted butter
- Salt and freshly ground black pepper
- Juice of half a lemon or lime
- 3 tablespoons finely chopped parsley or equal parts finely chopped parsley, tarragon and dill
- Lemon wedges.

1. Place the dolphin fillets in a pan and cover with milk. Let stand one hour.
2. Fifteen minutes before cooking, preheat the broiler to high.
3. Drain the dolphin fillets and wipe with paper towels. Rub the broiler rack lightly with oil. Place the fillets on the rack and brush with half the butter. Sprinkle with salt and pepper. Broil five minutes and brush again. When the fillets are browned, remove them to plates or a hot serving platter. Pour the remaining butter over them and sprinkle with the lemon or lime juice and parsley. Serve immediately with lemon wedges.

Yield: Four servings.

Out Island Grouper

FLORIDA

- 1 two-and-one-half-pound grouper
- ½ cup lime juice
- Salt and freshly ground black pepper to taste
- 1 egg
- ⅓ cup cold water
- ¼ cup flour
- Oil for deep-frying
- Lemon wedges
- Tartar sauce (page 259).

1. Cut the grouper into finger-size pieces and place in a mixing bowl. Add the lime juice, salt and pepper and cover. Let stand one hour or so in the refrigerator.
2. Place the egg and water in a bowl and beat in the flour. Add salt and pepper.
3. Drain the fish and dry with paper towels. Dip a few fish pieces at a

time in the batter and deep-fry in oil heated to 370 degrees. As the fish is cooked, drain on paper towels. Serve with lemon wedges and tartar sauce.
Yield: Four to six servings.

There is a giant crustacean in Florida waters that goes by the name of lobster and crawfish. Actually, it more nearly resembles the langosta or langouste of European waters. Most of the meat in a Florida lobster is in the tail and it is delicious hot or cold.

Steamed Florida Lobster

4 Florida lobsters or crawfish	3 ribs celery with leaves
2 cups dry white wine	½ teaspoon thyme
Salt to taste	2 carrots, quartered
20 peppercorns	2 bay leaves
1 large onion, coarsely chopped	3 tablespoons cider vinegar.

1. The lobsters should be alive when cooked. They should be cooked in a kettle large enough to hold them.
2. Add enough water to the kettle to immerse the lobsters completely. Add the wine, salt, peppercorns, onion, celery, thyme, carrots and bay leaves. Bring to a boil and simmer ten minutes. Add the vinegar. When the water is boiling violently, add the lobsters. Cover the kettle and simmer exactly fifteen minutes. Drain the lobsters; to serve, see note.
Yield: Four servings.
Note: The lobsters may be served hot with melted butter or cold with mayonnaise and lemon wedges.

How to Salt Mackerel
FLORIDA

6 mackerel, each weighing one and one-half to two pounds	salt, preferably coarse salt (do not use iodized salt).
2 cups, approximately, pure	

1. If possible, procure a small wooden bucket (approximately four-quart capacity) with lid. Wash the bucket inside and outside and rinse well to

remove all trace of soap or detergent. Soak the bucket in pure clean water. This will act as a "seal." Test the bucket by filling it with water to ensure that it does not leak. If it leaks, seal it on the outside wherever necessary with sealing wax. A stone crock or enamel utensil may be substituted for the bucket.

2. Have the fish filleted. Add a layer of salt to the bucket. Arrange two fillets on the salt. Continue adding layers of salt and of mackerel, ending with a layer of salt. Cover and refrigerate two weeks or longer. The fish will produce its own brine.

Yield: Six salt mackerel fillets.

How to Cook Salt Mackerel
FLORIDA

Remove as many pieces of salt mackerel as desired from the brine. Rinse well under cold water. Place the fish in a dish and cover with cold water. Let stand twelve hours or longer in a cool place. Change the water occasionally. When ready to cook, drain the fish and add equal parts milk and cold water to cover. Bring to a boil and simmer five to twelve minutes. Serve with melted butter and lemon wedges.

Deviled Oysters
MISSISSIPPI

4 cups shucked and drained oysters	Salt and freshly ground black pepper to taste
8 tablespoons butter	12 to sixteen soda crackers, approximately.
2 cups finely chopped celery	
1 cup finely chopped onions	
2 teaspoons Worcestershire sauce	

1. Preheat the oven to 325 degrees.

2. If the oysters are large, cut them in half. Melt two tablespoons of the butter in a large skillet and add the oysters. Cook just until the edges curl.

3. Cook the celery and onions in two tablespoons of the remaining butter, but do not brown. When the onions are wilted and transparent, add the oysters, Worcestershire, salt and pepper. Crumble the crackers and add about half of them to the oysters. Continue adding just enough crackers until all liq-

uid is absorbed. Spoon the mixture into a two-quart baking dish. Sprinkle with the remaining crackers, dot with the remaining butter and bake twenty-five to thirty minutes.

Yield: About eight servings.

Oysters Johnny Reb
MISSISSIPPI

- 4 cups shucked and drained oysters
- 6 tablespoons finely chopped parsley
- 6 tablespoons finely chopped scallions, including green part
- Salt and freshly ground black pepper to taste
- Tabasco sauce to taste
- 2 teaspoons Worcestershire sauce
- 1 tablespoon lemon juice
- 4 tablespoons butter
- 1 cup cracker crumbs
- 1 teaspoon paprika
- ⅓ cup heavy cream.

1. Preheat the oven to 375 degrees.
2. Place half the oysters in a generously buttered one-quart baking dish. Sprinkle with half the parsley, half the scallions, salt, pepper, Tabasco, half the Worcestershire, half the lemon juice, half the butter and half the crumbs. Make a layer with the remaining oysters and top with the remaining parsley, scallions, salt, pepper, Tabasco, Worcestershire, lemon juice, butter and crumbs.
3. Sprinkle with paprika and, using a knife, make six or so "holes" in the top of the casserole to pour in the cream. Bake thirty minutes or until firm.

Yield: One dozen to fifteen servings.

Oysters Bienville

LOUISIANA

½	pound mushrooms, finely chopped
2	tablespoons finely chopped shallots or scallions, including green part
5	tablespoons butter
6	tablespoons flour
¼	cup dry white wine
1½	cups fish stock or clam juice
¾	cup milk
¾	cup heavy cream
2	egg yolks
	Salt and freshly ground black pepper to taste
12	cooked shrimp, shelled, deveined and finely chopped
1	ounce anise liqueur such as Pernod, Ricard, anisette, etc. (optional)
48	oysters on the half shell
	Rock salt
½	cup freshly grated Parmesan cheese.

1. Cook the mushrooms and shallots or scallions in butter until mushrooms give up their liquid. Sprinkle with flour.

2. Meanwhile, combine the wine and stock or clam juice and bring to a boil. Simmer five minutes and add to the mushroom mixture, stirring vigorously with a wire whisk. Add the milk, stirring. Combine the cream and egg yolks; add a little of the hot mixture; then stir this into the sauce. Bring just to a boil and add salt, pepper and shrimp. Add the anise liqueur, if desired.

3. Preheat the oven to 450 degrees.

4. Loosen the oysters on their half shells. Make a reasonably thick layer of rock salt in four pie tins. Arrange one dozen oysters on the half shell in each tin. Place in the oven and bake briefly until edges of oysters start to curl. Carefully pour off the water from each shell and replace shells on the rock salt. Spoon a generous amount of sauce over each and sprinkle lightly with Parmesan cheese. Return to the oven and bake until lightly browned. Serve immediately.

Yield: Four servings.

Hot Oysters à la Louisiane
LOUISIANA

1 cup catchup	1 cup minced celery
1 cup chili sauce	½ cup finely chopped parsley
3 tablespoons Worcestershire sauce	Tabasco sauce to taste
4 tablespoons butter	48 oysters, shucked and drained
Grated rind of one lemon	Buttered toast or crackers (optional).
Juice of half a lemon	

1. Combine the catchup, chili sauce, Worcestershire, butter and lemon rind. Bring just to a boil and stir until butter is melted and blended. Remove the sauce from the heat and add the lemon juice, celery, parsley and Tabasco. The sauce may be refrigerated at this point.

2. When ready to serve, heat the sauce again to the simmering point. Add the oysters and cook just until the edges of the oysters curl. Do not overcook or the oysters will toughen. Serve with buttered toast or crackers if desired.

Yield: Four to eight servings.

Oysters Casino
LOUISIANA

48 oysters on the half shell	⅓ cup finely chopped heart of celery
Rock salt	
1 cup sweet butter	½ cup finely chopped parsley
⅓ cup finely chopped shallots or scallions, including green part	Juice of one lemon
	48 small squares bacon
¼ cup finely chopped chives	48 strips pimento.

1. Preheat the oven to 450 degrees.

2. Loosen the oysters in their half shells. Make a reasonably thick layer of rock salt in four pie tins. Arrange one dozen oysters on the half shell in each tin. Place in the oven and bake briefly until edges of oysters start to curl. Carefully pour off the water from each shell and replace shells on the rock salt.

3. Cream together the butter, shallots or scallions, chives, celery, parsley and lemon juice. Spoon a little of the creamed mixture atop each oyster.

4. Place the bacon briefly under the broiler to cook partly. Top each oyster with a strip of pimento and a square of bacon. Return the oysters to the oven and bake until bacon is browned, five to eight minutes.

Yield: Four servings.

Fried Oysters
MARYLAND

12	large plump oysters	Salt and freshly ground black pepper to taste
1	egg	Fat for deep-frying
2	tablespoons water	Lemon wedges.
	Yellow corn meal	

1. Drain the oysters and dry on paper towels.

2. Beat the egg with water. Dip the oysters one at a time in the egg, then in corn meal seasoned with salt and pepper. Dip them in egg again, then again in corn meal. Let stand thirty minutes.

3. Preheat the fat to 375 degrees. Fry the oysters in it until corn meal is golden brown. Drain on paper towels. Serve with lemon wedges.

Yield: Two to four servings.

Oysters en Brochette
VIRGINIA

48	small oysters, shucked and drained		Lemon juice to taste
	Salt and freshly ground black pepper		Tabasco sauce to taste (optional)
8	slices bacon	4	slices white or wholewheat toast.
6	tablespoons butter		
2	tablespoons chopped fresh parsley		

1. Sprinkle the oysters with salt and pepper.

2. Cut each slice of bacon into six cubes. Arrange the oysters alternately with cubes of bacon on four skewers. Melt the butter. Dip the skewered

food into it. Place the skewers on a grill over hot charcoal or place under the broiler. Grill or broil until bacon browns and oysters curl.

3. Add the parsley, lemon juice and Tabasco to the remaining butter. Pour the butter over the skewered food and serve immediately with or on toast.

Yield: Four servings.

Oysters Rockefeller
LOUISIANA

- 1 pound spinach
- 8 scallions, including green part trimmed and chopped
- ½ cup coarsely chopped heart of celery
- 1 cup firmly packed, coarsely chopped parsley
- ½ pound butter, melted
- ¼ cup finely chopped chives (optional)
- ½ teaspoon crushed anise seeds or fennel seeds
- 1½ cups soft bread crumbs
- 1 tablespoon anchovy paste
- 2 tablespoons Worcestershire sauce
- Salt and freshly ground black pepper to taste
- 1½ ounces anise liqueur such as Pernod, Ricard, anisette, etc.
- 48 oysters on the half shell
- Rock salt
- ¾ cup freshly grated Parmesan cheese.

1. Rinse the spinach in several changes of cold water. Drain. Place spinach in a large pot, cover and cook in the water that clings to the leaves. Do not add salt. Drain the spinach well, pressing to remove most of the moisture.

2. Place the spinach, scallions, celery and parsley in an electric blender. Pour in the melted butter and blend well. It may be necessary to blend this in two batches.

3. Spoon the mixture into a mixing bowl and add the chives, anise seeds, bread crumbs, anchovy paste, Worcestershire, a little salt (the anchovy paste is salty), pepper and anise liqueur.

4. Preheat the oven to 450 degrees.

5. Loosen the oysters on their half shells. Make a reasonably thick layer of rock salt in four pie tins. Arrange twelve of the oysters on the half shell in each tin. Place in the oven and bake briefly until edges of oysters start to curl. Carefully pour off the water from each shell and replace shells on the rock salt. Spoon a generous amount of sauce over each and sprinkle lightly

with the cheese. Return to the oven and bake until lightly browned. Serve immediately.

Yield: Eight servings.

Creamed Oysters
ALABAMA

- 4 cups shucked oysters with liquor
- Light cream, if necessary
- 4 tablespoons butter
- ½ cup flour
- 1 small clove garlic, finely minced
- 1 teaspoon chopped fresh basil or one-half teaspoon dried basil
- 2 teaspoons finely chopped parsley
- 1 tablespoon lemon juice
- Tabasco sauce to taste
- 1 tablespoon Worcestershire sauce
- 1 tablespoon catchup
- Salt and freshly ground black pepper to taste
- ½ teaspoon paprika
- 1 tablespoon dry sherry or cognac
- Toast
- Additional chopped parsley (optional).

1. Drain the oysters and reserve the liquor.
2. Place the oysters in a skillet or saucepan and cook just until they curl. Drain oysters again and combine hot liquid with reserved liquor. If necessary, add enough cream to make three cups of liquid.
3. Melt the butter over gentle heat in a heavy iron skillet. Add flour and stir constantly for about thirty minutes until flour is almost caramel-colored.
4. Add oyster liquid a little at a time while stirring rapidly with a wire whisk. Stir in the remaining ingredients. Finally, add the oysters. Serve on toast, sprinkled, if desired, with additional chopped parsley.

Yield: Six to eight servings.

Southern Scalloped Oysters
MISSISSIPPI

4 tablespoons butter	1 teaspoon celery salt
1½ cups dry bread crumbs	1 teaspoon paprika
2 cups shucked oysters with liquor	¼ teaspoon nutmeg
1 cup heavy cream	1 teaspoon Worcestershire sauce
1 tablespoon finely chopped chives	Tabasco sauce to taste
1 tablespoon finely chopped parsley	½ cup freshly grated Parmesan cheese.
Salt and freshly ground black pepper to taste	

1. Preheat the oven to 400 degrees.
2. Heat the butter in a small skillet and add the bread crumbs. Stir until crumbs are coated with butter. Spoon half the crumbs over the bottom of a nine-inch baking dish.
3. Drain the oysters and empty them into a mixing bowl. Add the remaining ingredients except the cheese and remaining crumbs. Spoon mixture over the crumb-lined pan.
4. Blend remaining crumbs with cheese and spread this over the oysters. Bake ten minutes, or until thoroughly hot and lightly browned.

Yield: Four to six servings.

Oyster Roast for 24
SOUTH CAROLINA

48 dozen oysters	Juice of four lemons
3 pounds butter	Tabasco sauce to taste.
6 tablespoons Worcestershire sauce, or to taste	

1. Place a large cast iron slab on supports, leaving enough space beneath for a giant fire. Prepare a fire beneath the slab and keep it going for two hours or longer.
2. Rinse the oysters well and add them to the slab. Dip enough burlap bags in cold water to cover the oysters. Soak them thoroughly. Cover the

oysters with the burlap bags and douse with water. Roast the oysters until they are easily opened, about fifteen minutes or longer, depending on heat of the fire.

3. Meanwhile, melt the butter to bubbling and add the remaining ingredients. Equip each guest with thick gloves and oyster knives and serve the oysters with the butter sauce.

Yield: Two dozen servings.

Oyster Pie
VIRGINIA

- 3 tablespoons butter
- 3 tablespoons flour
- ¾ cup oyster liquor
- ¾ cup light cream
- Salt and freshly ground black pepper to taste
- ⅛ teaspoon mace
- 2 cups drained oysters
- ½ cup finely chopped celery
- Unbaked pastry for a one-crust pie.

1. Preheat the oven to 400 degrees.
2. Melt the butter, blend in the flour and then gradually stir in the oyster liquor and cream. Bring mixture to a boil, stirring. Season with salt, pepper and mace. Simmer five minutes.
3. Stir in the oysters and celery and turn into a one-and-one-half-quart deep baking dish. Top with the pastry. Make a steam hole and bake twenty to twenty-five minutes, or until pastry is browned and cooked.

Yield: Four servings.

Pompano Baked en Papillote
FLORIDA

- 4 pompano fillets (see note)
- ¼ cup butter
- 5 tablespoons flour
- 1 cup clam juice or milk, preferably clam juice
- 1 egg yolk
- ¼ cup heavy cream
- Salt and freshly ground black pepper to taste
- 1 tablespoon finely chopped shallots or scallions, including green part
- ¼ cup dry white wine
- 1 tablespoon cognac (optional)
- 1 cup crab meat, picked over to remove bits of shell and cartilage
- 16 to twenty-four raw or cooked shrimp, shelled and deveined.

1. Preheat the oven to 400 degrees.
2. Split the fillets lengthwise and trim away the tiny bone unit down the center of each. Cut or tear off sheets of heavy parchment paper or heavy-duty aluminum foil, each large enough to enclose one fillet envelope style. Rub the center of each sheet lightly with the butter, reserving three tablespoons for a sauce, and put one fillet on each sheet.
3. Melt the three tablespoons butter in a saucepan and blend in the flour, using a wire whisk. Add the clam juice, and milk all at once, stirring vigorously with the whisk. Continue stirring until the sauce is thickened and smooth. Continue to cook, stirring frequently, for five minutes. The sauce will be very thick.
4. Blend the egg yolk with the cream. Add a little of the hot sauce to the egg yolk mixture and stir until blended. Add the egg mixture to the hot sauce, stirring rapidly. Heat until mixture starts to bubble, but do not boil. Season with salt and pepper.
5. Meanwhile, combine the shallots, or scallions and wine in a saucepan and cook until reduced by half. Strain the wine into the hot sauce. Blend. Stir in the cognac if desired.
6. Sprinkle each fish fillet with an equal portion of crab meat and divide the sauce among the portions. Arrange four to six shrimp over the sauce on each portion. Bring the edges of the paper or foil up and enclose the fish envelope style. Press down on edges to seal fish tightly. Bake for eighteen to twenty minutes, or until fish flakes easily when tested with a fork. Serve directly from the package.

Yield: Four servings.

Note: Small sole fillets may be substituted for the pompano.

Pompano Meunière
LOUISIANA

4 pompano fillets	¼ cup peanut oil, approximately
Milk	
Flour	½ cup butter
Salt and freshly ground black pepper to taste	¼ cup finely chopped parsley.

1. Place the fillets in a dish and add milk barely to cover. Let stand one hour.
2. Drain the fish, wipe lightly and dredge in flour seasoned with salt and pepper.

3. Cook the fish until golden brown on all sides in hot oil, turning once. Remove the fish to a warm platter.

4. Quickly wipe out the skillet and add the butter. When the butter is hot and foamy, pour it over the fish. Sprinkle with parsley.

Yield: Four servings.

Pompano Grenoble Style
LOUISIANA

Follow the above recipe for "Pompano Meunière." When the butter is added to the skillet, add two tablespoons small whole or chopped capers. Sprinkle with small bits of chopped lemon as well as parsley.

Sea Food with Eggs
MARYLAND

½ pound shrimp, cooked, shelled and deveined	Salt and freshly ground black pepper to taste
½ pound crab meat, picked over to remove bits of shell and cartilage	12 eggs
	6 slices white toast, crusts removed
3 tablespoons dry sherry	1 tablespoon chopped chives
6 tablespoons butter	1 tablespoon chopped parsley
2 tablespoons flour	1 teaspoon chopped tarragon (optional).
¾ cup heavy cream	

1. Combine the shrimp, crab meat and sherry in a mixing bowl and set aside.

2. Heat two tablespoons of the butter in a saucepan and stir in the flour, using a wire whisk. When blended, add the cream, stirring rapidly with the whisk. When thickened and smooth, add salt and pepper. Add shrimp and crab and keep hot.

3. Heat remaining butter in a large skillet. Beat the eggs lightly and add to the skillet. Cook, stirring over low heat, until eggs are partially cooked. Do not let them scramble in the usual fashion. Add salt and pepper to taste and, while eggs are still soft, stir in the sea food mixture. Heat thoroughly and serve equal portions on the toast. Serve sprinkled with a mixture of chives and parsley and, if desired, tarragon.

Yield: Six servings.

Artichoke and Sea Food Casserole
MARYLAND

4 tablespoons butter	1 tablespoon freshly snipped dill weed
2 tablespoons chopped shallots	
1 clove garlic, finely chopped	1 pound shrimp, cooked, shelled and deveined
½ pound mushrooms, sliced	
¼ cup flour	1 pound lump crab meat, picked over to remove bits of shell and cartilage
1 cup milk	
⅔ cup dry white wine, fish stock or clam juice	
1½ cups grated Swiss cheese or Gruyère cheese	1 package frozen artichoke hearts, cooked and drained
Salt and freshly ground black pepper to taste	3 tablespoons buttered soft bread crumbs.

1. Preheat the oven to 375 degrees.
2. Melt the butter in a skillet and sauté the shallots and garlic in it until tender. Add the mushrooms and cook two minutes longer.
3. Sprinkle with the flour, stir and cook one minute.
4. Gradually stir in the milk and wine, stock or clam juices. Bring to a boil, stirring until thick. Remove from the heat and stir in one cup of the cheese until it melts. Season with salt and pepper and add the dill.
5. Stir in the shrimp, crab meat and artichoke hearts and pour into a buttered casserole. Sprinkle with the remaining cheese and the bread crumbs. Bake twenty-five minutes, or until bubbly, and glaze under the broiler if desired.

Yield: Six servings.

Shad Stuffed with Mousse and Roe
SOUTH CAROLINA

¾ pound boneless scrod or cod	2 boneless fillets of fresh shad
3 shallots, finely chopped	1 pair shad roe
4 tablespoons finely chopped parsley	3 hard-cooked eggs
	5 tablespoons butter
1⅔ cups heavy cream	1½ cups thinly sliced mushrooms
⅔ cup soft bread crumbs	1 cup dry white wine
Salt and freshly ground black pepper to taste	1 tablespoon flour
	1 teaspoon lemon juice
Cayenne pepper to taste	Boiled potatoes.

1. Preheat the oven to 400 degrees.

2. Cut the scrod or cod into small cubes and add to the container of an electric blender. Blend, stirring down with a rubber spatula, until well blended. Do not let the spatula touch the blender blades. It may be necessary to stop the machine at times to "stir down." When blended, add one tablespoon of the chopped shallots and one tablespoon of the parsley. Gradually add two-thirds cup of the cream. When the cream has been added, carefully scoop the mousse from the blender into a mixing bowl. Stir in the bread crumbs. Season with salt, pepper and cayenne.

3. Lay one of the shad fillets, skin side down, in a buttered baking dish. There are two "flaps" on either side of the fillet where the bones were removed. Open these "flaps" and spread half the scrod mixture up and down the center of the fillet. Split the pair of shad roe in two and place the two parts tip to tip down the center of the mousse.

4. Quarter the eggs. Arrange six quarters along one side of the roe. Arrange the other six down the other side. Spread the remaining mousse mixture over the roe and eggs.

5. Open the "flaps" on the other shad fillet and place this fillet, skin side up, over the stuffed fillet. This will in effect form a "box" with the mousse and roe enclosed. Tie the "box" crosswise in about four places with string.

6. Sprinkle the fish with salt and pepper and spread fish generously on top with four tablespoons of the butter. Sprinkle fish with the remaining shallots and parsley and scatter the mushrooms all around. Pour the wine around and cover with aluminum foil. Bake forty to fifty minutes, lifting the foil occasionally and basting with the wine.

7. Remove the fish to a warm platter. Remove string and keep fish warm.

8. Pour the sauce into a saucepan and reduce sauce over high heat to about two-thirds of its original volume. Add the remaining cream and cook about ten minutes. Blend together the remaining tablespoon butter and the flour and stir, bit by bit, into the sauce. When thickened, add the lemon juice.

9. Peel the skin from the top of the shad and pour a little of the sauce over and around the fish. Serve the remaining sauce separately. Serve with boiled potatoes.

Yield: About six servings.

Shrimp Gumbo
LOUISIANA

- ¼ cup flour
- 8 small white onions, peeled
- 7 tablespoons butter
- 2 eight-ounce bottles clam juice
- 1 large can Italian plum tomatoes, drained
- 1 bay leaf
- 1 teaspoon Worcestershire sauce
- Salt, if necessary
- ¼ teaspoon thyme
- Freshly ground black pepper to taste
- Red pepper flakes to taste
- ½ teaspoon sugar
- 2 pounds shrimp, cooked, shelled and deveined
- 1 package frozen okra
- 1 green pepper, seeded and cut into strips
- 2 ribs celery, trimmed and cut into one-half-inch pieces
- ½ teaspoon filé powder (optional)
- Chopped parsley.

1. Preheat the oven to 350 degrees.
2. Place the flour on aluminum foil and bake, stirring occasionally, until hazelnut brown, about ten minutes.
3. Combine the onions and four tablespoons of the butter in a saucepan. Toss briefly. Cover and cook until onions start to become translucent, about five minutes.
4. Sprinkle the onions with the browned flour. Stir in the clam juice with a wire whisk. Continue stirring until mixture is thickened and smooth. Add the tomatoes, bay leaf, Worcestershire, seasonings and sugar. Add the

shrimp and cook ten minutes. Add the okra and cook, stirring, until pieces of okra separate.

5. Cook the green pepper and celery in the remaining butter about three minutes, stirring. The vegetables must remain crisp.

6. Add the vegetables to the onion mixture and cook ten to fifteen minutes longer, or until celery is tender but still somewhat crisp. Stir in the filé powder, sprinkle with chopped parsley and serve.

Yield: Four to six servings.

Shrimp à la Turque
FLORIDA

2 pounds shrimp in the shell	1 teaspoon thyme
1 cup oil	Salt and freshly ground black pepper to taste
1½ teaspoons chili powder	
1 tablespoon cider vinegar	2 tablespoons finely minced shallots
1 teaspoon plus one tablespoon chopped fresh mint	4 lemon wedges.

1. Split the shrimp down the back with a sharp knife or with scissors. Rinse the shrimp under cold water to remove the small intestinal vein down the back. Pat dry.

2. Pour the oil into a mixing bowl. Combine the chili powder, vinegar and one teaspoon of the mint to make a paste. Add to the oil along with the thyme, salt, pepper, shallots and remaining mint. Stir well to mix and add the shrimp. Mix well and let stand four hours or overnight.

3. Preheat the broiler.

4. Pour the shrimp and the marinade into a broiler pan.

5. Broil the shrimp five or six inches from the flame. Broil six to ten minutes, depending on size, turning once. Serve, if desired, with a little of the marinade poured over. Garnish with lemon wedges.

Yield: Four servings.

Steamed Live Shrimp
FLORIDA

36	live shrimp (the kind that are sold for bait)	1	small onion, sliced
8	cups water	1	carrot, quartered
1	cup dry white wine (optional)	1	bay leaf
2	tablespoons salt	2	sprigs parsley
12	peppercorns	¼	teaspoon thyme
1	rib celery with leaves, halved	2	tablespoons cider vinegar.

1. Place the shrimp in cold running water until ready to use.
2. Place the two quarts water and the wine if desired in a large saucepan and add the salt, peppercorns, celery, onion and carrot. Tie the bay leaf, parsley and thyme in cheesecloth and add. Bring to a boil and simmer ten minutes. Add the vinegar and shrimp. Return to a boil and remove from the heat. To serve, see note.

Yield: Three to six servings.

Note: Serve hot with melted butter or lukewarm or cold with cocktail sauce, mustard mayonnaise or with lukewarm French dressing.

Shrimp in Sour Cream
LOUISIANA

6	tablespoons butter	¼	teaspoon freshly ground black pepper
3	shallots, finely chopped		
1½	pounds shrimp, shelled and deveined	¼	teaspoon thyme
		2	cups sour cream
½	pound mushrooms, sliced	3	to four tablespoons dry sherry.
2	tablespoons flour		
1	teaspoon salt		

1. Melt the butter and sauté the shallots in it until tender but not browned.
2. Add the shrimp and cook over high heat, stirring occasionally, five minutes, or until shrimp just turn pink.
3. Add the mushrooms and cook three minutes longer. Sprinkle with the flour, salt and pepper and cook, stirring, two minutes.
4. Sprinkle with the thyme and gradually stir in the sour cream over

low heat. Bring the mixture just to a boil, but do not allow to boil or it will curdle. Stir in the sherry.

Yield: Six servings.

Shrimp Creole
LOUISIANA

- 3 tablespoons butter or bacon drippings
- 2 cups coarsely chopped onions
- 2 cloves garlic, finely minced
- 3 ribs celery, coarsely chopped
- 1 green pepper, cored, seeded and chopped
- 3 ripe tomatoes, cored and peeled
- 1 bay leaf
- 2 sprigs fresh thyme or one-half teaspoon dried thyme
- Salt to taste
- ½ teaspoon freshly ground black pepper
- ¼ teaspoon cayenne pepper
- 2 pounds shrimp, shelled and deveined
- 1 teaspoon Worcestershire sauce (optional)
- Hot fluffy rice.

1. Melt the butter or bacon drippings in a large saucepan and cook the onions, garlic, celery and green pepper in it until tender and without browning. Add the tomatoes, bay leaf, thyme, salt, pepper and cayenne. Simmer ten minutes, stirring occasionally.

2. Add the shrimp and cover. Simmer ten minutes. If desired, season with Worcestershire. Serve with hot fluffy rice.

Yield: Four to six servings.

Charleston Breakfast Shrimp
SOUTH CAROLINA

- 3 tablespoons bacon drippings
- 1 tablespoon chopped green pepper
- 2 tablespoons chopped onion
- 1½ cups small shrimp, shelled and deveined
- 1 cup water
- Salt and freshly ground black pepper to taste
- 1 teaspoon Worcestershire sauce
- 1 tablespoon catchup
- 1½ tablespoons flour
- Grits.

1. Heat the bacon drippings and add the green pepper and onion. Cook until onion is wilted and add the shrimp. Cook, stirring, until shrimp turn pink. Add the water, salt and pepper and simmer three minutes.
2. Combine the Worcestershire, catchup and flour. Blend well and stir into the simmering mixture. When thickened, remove from the heat and serve. Serve with grits.
Yield: Four servings.

Broiled Red Snapper
FLORIDA

2 red snapper fillets, each weighing about one pound, or four large fillet pieces, each weighing about one-half pound
Melted butter
Salt and freshly ground black pepper
Chopped parsley
Lemon butter
Lemon wedges.

1. Preheat the broiler.
2. Place the fillets on a baking dish and brush generously with melted butter. Sprinkle with salt and pepper and broil about two inches from broiler heat. If fish starts to brown too quickly, reduce heat. Cook five to ten minutes, depending on size and thickness of fish. Brush the fish with additional butter during cooking. Serve fish sprinkled with parsley and lemon butter. Garnish with lemon wedges.
Yield: Two to four servings.

Red Snapper Grenobloise
FLORIDA

1 lemon
1 one-and-one-half-pound red snapper
Salt and freshly ground black pepper
½ cup butter
2 tablespoons capers
Lemon slices (optional).

1. Preheat the oven to 425 degrees.
2. Peel the lemon, removing all the white pulp. Cut the lemon into thin

slices and remove the seeds. Cut each slice into small cubes, discarding the membranes between sections. Reserve lemon cubes.

3. Thoroughly clean and scale the fish, but leave the head and tail intact. Rinse the fish under cold water and pat dry with paper towels. Sprinkle the fish inside and outside with salt and pepper.

4. Melt the butter in a skillet with ovenproof handle large enough to hold the fish. When skillet is hot, put in the fish and cook only on one side for about five minutes. Tilt the pan occasionally and spoon the butter over the fish.

5. Place the fish in the oven and bake, basting occasionally, for about twenty-five minutes, or until fish flakes easily when tested with a fork.

6. Remove the fish from the oven and transfer to a serving platter. Sprinkle with the capers, reserved lemon cubes and butter from the skillet. Garnish with lemon slices if desired.

Yield: About three servings.

Note: Bluefish, porgies, striped bass and other small fish may be cooked in the same way.

Florida Keys Red Snapper
FLORIDA

1	three-pound to four-pound red snapper	2	cups toasted soft bread crumbs
	Peanut oil or vegetable oil	¼	cup finely chopped parsley
	Salt and freshly ground black pepper	¼	cup coarsely chopped toasted almonds
¼	cup butter	6	thin tomato slices
½	cup finely chopped onion	6	thin onion slices
¼	cup finely chopped celery	6	thin orange slices
¼	cup finely chopped green pepper	6	thin lime slices
2	scallions, including green part, chopped		Juice of half a lime.

1. Preheat the oven to 350 degrees.

2. Rub the fish lightly with oil and sprinkle inside and outside with salt and pepper.

3. Melt the butter and cook the chopped onion, celery, green pepper and scallions in it until onion is wilted. Stir in the bread crumbs, parsley and

almonds. Season to taste with salt and pepper. Stuff the fish with the mixture and tie with string.

4. Place the fish on a length of aluminum foil and add alternating, slightly overlapping slices of tomato, onion, orange and lime. Sprinkle with salt, pepper and lime juice. Bring up the edges of the foil and secure it envelope style. Bake thirty minutes, or until fish flakes easily when tested with a fork.

Yield: Four to six servings.

Red Snapper Creole
LOUISIANA

1 three-pound red snapper, cleaned and scaled	1 tablespoon finely chopped parsley
½ cup flour	1 tablespoon tomato paste
Salt and freshly ground black pepper to taste	Juice of half a lemon
	½ teaspoon grated lemon rind
6 tablespoons butter	1 bay leaf
¾ cup finely chopped onion	1 teaspoon thyme
1 cup finely chopped celery	Cayenne pepper to taste
½ cup chopped green pepper	1 teaspoon Worcestershire sauce
1 clove garlic, finely minced	
3 cups fresh peeled or canned tomatoes	Lemon slices for garnish
	Parsley for garnish.

1. Preheat the oven to 350 degrees.

2. Rub the fish inside and outside with a light coating of flour. Sprinkle inside and outside with salt and pepper. Arrange fish in a baking dish.

3. Heat the butter in a saucepan, add the onion, celery and green pepper and cook until vegetables are wilted. Stir in the garlic.

4. Press the tomatoes through a sieve or food mill and season with all the remaining ingredients except the lemon slices and parsley for garnish. Bring to a boil and add this to the onion mixture. Pour the sauce around the fish and bake, basting often with the sauce, about thirty minutes, or until fish flakes easily.

5. To serve, garnish with lemon slices and parsley.

Yield: Four to six servings.

Baked Red Snapper
ALABAMA

8	tablespoons butter	1½	teaspoons chili powder
2	cups finely chopped onions		Juice of half a lemon
2	cups finely chopped celery		Salt and freshly ground black pepper to taste
1	clove garlic, finely minced		
½	cup finely chopped green pepper		Cayenne pepper or Tabasco sauce to taste
¼	cup finely chopped parsley	1	three-pound red snapper
4	cups canned Italian plum tomatoes		Flour for dredging
		3	sprigs parsley.
1	bay leaf		
1½	tablespoons Worcestershire sauce		

1. In a saucepan melt the butter and cook the onions, celery, garlic and green pepper until onions are wilted. Add the chopped parsley, tomatoes, bay leaf, Worcestershire, chili powder, lemon juice, salt, pepper and cayenne or Tabasco. Bring to a boil and simmer, stirring frequently, forty-five minutes.
2. Meanwhile, preheat the oven to 350 degrees.
3. Sprinkle the fish inside and outside with salt and pepper. Dredge fish lightly with flour. Place the parsley sprigs in the fish cavity. Place fish in a baking dish and pour the sauce over fish. Bake one-half hour or longer, basting frequently, or until fish flakes easily when tested with a fork.

Yield: Four to six servings.

Fish Stew
LOUISIANA

1	pound boned, skinned haddock or striped bass, cut into serving pieces	2	teaspoons salt
		⅛	teaspoon freshly ground black pepper
1	cup fish stock	⅛	teaspoon nutmeg
2	tablespoons butter	¼	teaspoon thyme
½	cup finely chopped shallots	3	drops Tabasco sauce
1	clove garlic, finely chopped	2½	cups milk
1	tomato, peeled and chopped	2	tablespoons Pernod
1	tablespoon finely chopped parsley	1	teaspoon grated lemon rind.

1. Simmer the fish in the stock, covered, until fish flakes easily, about eight minutes. Reserve stock and fish separately.
2. Melt the butter in a small skillet. Add the shallots and garlic and sauté until golden.
3. Add mixture to reserved stock. Add the tomato, parsley, salt, pepper, nutmeg, thyme and Tabasco. Simmer, covered, twenty-five minutes.
4. Add the milk, Pernod and lemon rind to stock. Add fish pieces. Heat before serving, but do not boil.

Yield: Four servings.

The following dish is often used in the Pee Dee section of South Carolina for large family or community meals. The name of the stew stems from the custom of cooking it in a black pot over a pine bark fire (or because it was served on pine bark).

Pine Bark Stew
SOUTH CAROLINA

- 3 quarts ripe tomatoes
- 2 tablespoons salt
- 4 tablespoons sugar
- 1 teaspoon chili powder
- 1½ teaspoons freshly ground black pepper, or to taste
- ⅛ teaspoon cayenne pepper
- ¼ pound bacon slices
- 2 green peppers, cored, seeded and chopped
- 1½ cups chopped onions
- 5 pounds white fish (rock fish, bass, bream, mullet or grouper), cut into serving pieces
- 4 cups hot water
- 2 tablespoons Worcestershire sauce
- Hot cooked rice.

1. Peel the tomatoes and chop finely. Place in a saucepan with the salt, sugar, chili powder, pepper and cayenne. Cook, uncovered, until sauce measures three cups.
2. Cook the bacon in a skillet until crisp; remove and reserve. Sauté the green peppers and onions in the bacon drippings until lightly browned.
3. Place the fish, hot water, the sautéed vegetables, reserved bacon and the three cups sauce in a kettle. Add the Worcestershire and cook for about twenty minutes, or until the fish flakes easily. Serve over rice.

Yield: Twenty-five to thirty servings.

Chesapeake Bay Fish Stew
MARYLAND

Court bouillon:

Fish	trimmings, including heads, bones, skin, crab claws and crab fat, from all fish listed below	1	leek, chopped
		2	to three sprigs fresh thyme or one-half teaspoon dried thyme
1	onion	2	sprigs parsley
1	rib celery with leaves, chopped	1	four-inch strip orange peel
		10	peppercorns
1	bay leaf	1	teaspoon salt
1	carrot, cubed	8	cups water.

Fish:

12	steamer clams	¼	pound Norfolk spot fillets, cut into two-inch pieces
12	cherrystone clams		
¼	cup water	¾	pound catfish, skinned, filleted and cut into two-inch pieces
6	hard-shelled blue crabs, claws and fat removed and back cut in half		
		½	pound sea trout fillets, cut into two-inch pieces
½	pound sea bass fillets, cut into two-inch pieces		
		⅛	teaspoon whole saffron
2	two-pound rock fish (striped bass), filleted and cut into two-inch pieces		Salt and freshly ground black pepper to taste
			Buttered, baked thin French bread slices.
1	small butterfish, filleted and cut into two-inch pieces		

    1. Place all ingredients for the court bouillon in a large kettle. Bring to a boil and simmer, uncovered, twenty minutes. Strain through a double layer of cheesecloth into a large heavy pot.

    2. Place the clams and water in a heavy pan or casserole. Cover and heat until clams open, about eight minutes. Discard those that do not open.

    3. Add the liquid from the clams to the court bouillon and, when the clams are cool enough, cut the snouts off the steamers and discard. Except for six cherrystones to be used for garnish, remove clams from shells and set aside.

    4. Add the crabs to the large pot of court bouillon and simmer fifteen minutes.

5. Add the sea bass and rock and cook three minutes. Add the butterfish and spot and cook three minutes longer. Add the catfish, sea trout and saffron and cook five minutes longer, or until all fish are cooked.

6. Return the clams, those in and those out of the shells, to the pot and reheat. Serve stew immediately in deep bowls either over the crisp bread slices or with the bread passed separately.

Yield: Six servings.

There is no dish in American cooking that speaks more vividly of a region than the various gumbos of the South. They may be made with shrimp or oysters or crab or ham or a combination of these things. But the essential ingredient is okra, whence the dish derives its name. The word is of African origin derived years ago from the Bantu language of Central Angola. The following recipe is an authentic creation of E. Lysle Aschaffenburg of the Pontchartrain Hotel in New Orleans. The gumbo is somewhat tedious to make, but it is well worth the effort.

Pontchartrain Creole Gumbo
LOUISIANA

2 pounds shrimp	2 tablespoons oil
12 live hard-shelled crabs	1 large ham bone, split in half or quartered
Boiling water	
3 slices bacon	½ pound chicken wings
4 large onions, finely chopped (about two quarts when chopped)	1 pound boneless stewing veal, cut into one-inch cubes
	⅓ cup finely chopped parsley
4 cloves garlic, finely minced	1 one-pound-three-ounce can tomatoes or four ripe tomatoes, peeled and cored
2 bay leaves	
2 tablespoons finely minced green pepper	½ teaspoon Tabasco sauce, or to taste
1 teaspoon finely chopped fresh thyme or one-half teaspoon dried thyme	
	¼ cup Worcestershire sauce
	Juice of half a lemon
1½ teaspoons sugar	2 cups shucked oysters with liquor
Salt and freshly ground black pepper to taste	
2 pounds fresh okra or two packages frozen okra	1 teaspoon filé powder (optional)
	Freshly cooked rice.

1. Using a pair of kitchen scissors, split the raw shrimp down the back. Pull off the shells and put them in a saucepan. Rinse the shrimp under cold running water and rinse or pull away the dark vein down the back. Set the shrimp aside. Cover the shrimp shells with water and bring to a boil. Simmer five minutes and set aside.

2. Drop the live crabs into boiling water. Cook exactly five minutes and drain. Break off the top shell, but save the juices and scrape away any "fat" inside the shell. Discard the shell.

3. With the fingers, pull away and discard the spongy "dead fingers" inside. Pull away and discard the small, tough sac between the eyes. Pull off and discard the "apron" on the underside of the crab. Save the crab claws and split the crabs in half and reserve.

4. Cut the bacon slices in half and put the bacon in a kettle. Cook the bacon, stirring, until it is rendered of its fat. Remove the cooked bacon and drain it on paper towels. Reserve the bacon.

5. Add the onions to the bacon drippings in the kettle. Cook, stirring, until the onions are golden brown. Add the garlic, bay leaves, green pepper, thyme, sugar, salt and pepper. Cook slowly, stirring, until green pepper is wilted.

6. Cut the fresh or frozen okra crosswise into one-half-inch lengths and add to the kettle. Continue cooking, stirring occasionally, about five minutes.

7. In another large skillet heat the oil, add the ham bone, chicken wings and veal. Cook over relatively high heat, shaking the skillet occasionally and turning the pieces so that they brown well on all sides. Pour off any excess fat from the skillet and add the browned meat and bones to the kettle. Add a cup or so of water to the skillet and stir with a wooden spoon to dissolve the brown particles that cling to the bottom and sides. Pour this liquid into the kettle.

8. Add to the kettle the parsley, tomatoes, Tabasco, Worcestershire and lemon juice. Add the pieces of crab, the reserved peeled shrimp, the oysters and cooked bacon. Strain the liquid from the shrimp shells into the kettle. Add enough water to cover all the ingredients. The water level should be about one inch over the ingredients. Add salt and pepper to taste and bring to a boil. Care should be taken that this gumbo does not burn. It may be wise to pour the gumbo at this point into a clean kettle. Bring the gumbo to a boil and cook thirty minutes, skimming the surface frequently to remove scum, foam and excess fat. Stir occasionally as the gumbo cooks. When it is ready to serve, bring the gumbo to a boil and turn off the heat. Stir in the filé powder if desired. Do not boil again.

9. To serve, spoon a quarter of a cup of cooked rice into a measuring

cup. Level off the top; then unmold the rice into the center of a hot soup plate. Do this for each serving. Ladle the gumbo around the rice and serve immediately. If desired, pass a bottle of Tabasco sauce with the gumbo for those who require more heat.

Yield: One dozen servings.

Jambalaya
MISSISSIPPI

6	tablespoons butter	¼	teaspoon ground cloves
1	cup finely chopped onions		Tabasco sauce to taste
2	cloves garlic, finely minced	4	cups canned Italian plum tomatoes
1	green pepper, cored, seeded and chopped		Salt and freshly ground black pepper to taste
1	rib celery, chopped		
1	cup diced cooked ham preferably country ham	1	teaspoon Worcestershire sauce
1½	cups chicken broth	2	cups oysters with their liquor
1	teaspoon chopped fresh thyme or one-half teaspoon dried thyme	1½	pounds shrimp, shelled and deveined
¼	cup chopped parsley	1	cup rice, cooked according to package directions.
¼	teaspoon nutmeg		

1. Melt the butter in a large saucepan and add the onions, garlic, green pepper, celery and ham. Cook, stirring, until onions are translucent. Add the broth, thyme, parsley, nutmeg, cloves, Tabasco and tomatoes. Add salt, pepper and the Worcestershire. Simmer fifteen minutes.

2. Add the oysters, shrimp and rice and simmer ten minutes longer.

Yield: Six to eight servings.

Chartres Street Trout
LOUISIANA

6	trout, filleted		Juice of one lemon
	Salt and freshly ground black pepper	¼	cup capers
		¼	cup freshly chopped parsley
½	cup butter, approximately		Buttered toast.

1. Preheat the oven to 350 degrees.
2. Cover a baking sheet with aluminum foil and butter it well. Arrange the fish fillets on the foil and sprinkle with salt and pepper. Dot fillets liberally with the butter and cover with another sheet of aluminum foil. Bake eight to ten minutes, or just until the fish flakes easily when tested with a fork.
3. Transfer the fish to hot dinner plates and sprinkle with lemon juice, capers and parsley. Serve with buttered toast.

Yield: Six main course servings or one dozen servings as a first course.

Trout Meunière
LOUISIANA

6 trout fillets	⅓ cup vegetable oil or peanut oil
1 cup milk	
½ cup flour	¼ cup butter
Salt and freshly ground black pepper to taste	Chopped parsley
	Lemon wedges.

1. Dip the fillets in the milk and let stand until ready to cook.
2. Blend the flour with salt and pepper. Drain the fillets, but do not dry. Dip them in seasoned flour.
3. Heat the oil in a large skillet and cook the fillets until golden brown, turning once. Transfer to a warm serving platter. Wipe out the skillet.
4. Add the butter to the skillet and cook until butter just begins to brown. Pour the butter over the fish, sprinkle with parsley and garnish with lemon wedges.

Yield: Three to six servings.

Trout Amandine
LOUISIANA

Follow the recipe above for "Trout Meunière," but cook one-half cup slivered blanched almonds in the butter before pouring it over the fish.

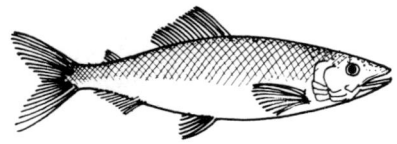

Meat, Poultry, Game and Other Main Dishes

Piccadillo
FLORIDA

¼ cup peanut oil	¼ teaspoon oregano
1 clove garlic, finely minced	Salt and freshly ground black pepper to taste
2 large onions, chopped	
1 large green pepper, cored, seeded and chopped	1 tablespoon capers
	¼ cup chopped stuffed olives
1 pound ground round steak	½ cup raisins, chopped
1 one-pound can tomatoes, preferably Italian plum style	1 tablespoon cider vinegar
	Cooked rice and black beans.

1. Heat the oil in a large skillet and cook the garlic, onions and green pepper in it until onions are wilted.

2. Add the meat and cook, stirring and chopping, until meat is thoroughly crumbled and loses its red color. Add the tomatoes with their liquid and break up tomatoes with a fork.

3. Add the oregano, salt and pepper. Add the capers, olives, raisins and vinegar. Cover and simmer over low heat about one hour. Stir occasionally to prevent the piccadillo from sticking or scorching. Serve with rice and black beans.

Yield: Four to six servings.

Tamale Pie
MISSISSIPPI

- 1 cup finely chopped onions
- ½ cup finely chopped green pepper
- 2 cloves garlic, finely minced
- 2 tablespoons olive oil or bacon drippings
- 2 cups shredded boiled chicken or braised beef
- 1 tablespoon chili powder, or more to taste
- 1 cup finely chopped and drained canned or fresh tomatoes
- ½ cup chicken broth or braised beef gravy
- Salt to taste
- ½ teaspoon ground or crushed cumin seeds
- 2 cups white or yellow corn meal
- 5 cups boiling water
- 2 tablespoons butter or lard.

1. Preheat the oven to 350 degrees.
2. Cook the onions, green pepper and garlic in the oil or drippings until onions are wilted.
3. Grind the chicken or beef and add to the onion mixture. Add the chili powder, tomatoes, broth or gravy, salt and cumin seeds. Beat well with a wooden spoon.
4. Gradually add the corn meal to the boiling water, stirring vigorously with a wire whisk. When the mixture is boiling and smooth, add the butter or lard.
5. Butter a two-and-one-half-quart casserole and add about three-quarters of the mush. Using a spoon, push the mush against the bottom and sides of the casserole to make a well in the center. Spoon in the meat mixture and add the remaining mush to cover. Bake about one hour.

Yield: Four to six servings.

Tamale Pie with Hominy Grits
ALABAMA

- 3 cloves garlic
- ¼ cup olive oil
- ¾ pound ground round steak
- 2 green peppers, cored, seeded and chopped
- 2 cups finely chopped onions, preferably the red Italian variety
- 2 teaspoons chili powder, or to taste
- Salt to taste
- 1 pepperone (Italian hot sausage), cut into small pieces
- 4 ripe tomatoes, peeled, seeded and chopped
- 2 cups homemade or canned tomato sauce
- 3 leaves fresh basil, finely chopped, or dried basil to taste
- 1½ cups hominy grits
- Boiling salted water.

1. Cook the garlic in the oil until garlic starts to brown. Remove the garlic and discard.

2. Add the ground meat, stirring to break up lumps, and cook until it loses its red color. Add the green peppers and onions and cook until onions are wilted, stirring frequently. Add the chili powder, salt and pepperone. Stir. Add the tomatoes, tomato sauce and basil and simmer thirty minutes.

3. Preheat the oven to 300 degrees.

4. Meanwhile, cook the hominy in boiling salted water according to package directions. When hominy is thickened and done, spread it on a two-inch-deep oval or round platter or deep pie plate and smooth out the center to make a "shell" resembling a pie shell with a thick rim. Fill the hollow with the meat mixture and bake, uncovered, about thirty minutes.

Yield: Six to eight servings.

Cuban Round Roast

FLORIDA

3	pounds eye of beef round	1	tablespoon chopped green chilies (optional)
¼	pound smoked ham, preferably country style		Salt and freshly ground black pepper to taste
¼	pound bacon	¼	cup lard or bacon drippings
1	cup finely chopped onions	1	cup beef broth or water
2	tablespoons finely chopped capers	½	cup homemade or canned tomato sauce
1	clove garlic, finely minced	1	tablespoon cider vinegar.
¼	cup chopped green olives		

1. Preheat the oven to 350 degrees.
2. Run a long, sharp, thin-bladed knife through the center of the roast. The incision should be about one and one-half to two inches deep, depending on the thickness of the roast.
3. Chop or grind the ham and bacon and mix well. Blend the ham mixture with the onions, capers, garlic, olives and chilies. Stuff the roast with the mixture. Season the roast with salt and pepper.
4. Heat the lard or bacon drippings in a Dutch oven or heavy casserole and brown the roast in it thoroughly on all sides. Do not let the fat burn.
5. Add the broth, tomato sauce and vinegar and bake, uncovered, basting occasionally, until the meat is very tender, two to two and one-half hours. Add water, if necessary, during cooking.

Yield: Eight to ten servings.

The town of Natchitoches on the western side of Louisiana is famous for its "Hot-ta-Meat Pies," which are shaped like a half-moon with delicately fluted edges and a spiced meat filling. The name of the town is pronounced, incidentally, NACK-i-tosh. The pies date from before the Civil War.

Hot-ta-Meat Pies
LOUISIANA

Filling:
- 2 tablespoons flour
- 1 tablespoon bacon drippings
- 1½ cups finely chopped onions
- 1 clove garlic, finely minced (optional)
- ½ pound ground beef
- 1½ pounds ground pork
- 6 scallions, including green part, trimmed and finely chopped
- 3 tablespoons finely chopped parsley
- 1 tablespoon finely chopped hot green pepper or a dash of cayenne pepper to taste.
- Salt and freshly ground black pepper to taste.

Pastry:
- ½ cup shortening
- 4 cups flour
- 2 teaspoons baking powder
- Salt to taste
- 2 eggs
- ¼ cup milk, approximately
- 4 cups oil or shortening.

1. The filling should be prepared and cooled before the pastries are made.

2. Blend the flour with the bacon drippings in a skillet and cook, stirring, until flour is golden. Add the onions and garlic and cook until onions are lightly browned. Add the meat and cook, breaking up the meat with the side of a spoon and stirring, until meat loses its color. Add the remaining ingredients and remove the mixture from the heat. Cool thoroughly.

3. To prepare pastry, melt the shortening and let it cool slightly.

4. Sift together the flour, baking powder and salt into a mixing bowl. Make a well in the center and add the eggs. Stir with a wooden spoon and add the shortening. When blended, mix with the fingers, adding a little milk at a time. Continue kneading, adding just enough milk to make a stiff, manageable dough. Chill the dough if desired.

5. Divide the dough into quarters and roll it out one-eighth-inch thick or less. Using a saucer six inches in diameter, cut out circles of dough. If desired, these circles may be rolled slightly to make them larger or the pastry thinner. Spoon a little of the filling into the center of each circle. Brush the edges of each circle with cold water; then fold dough over. The water helps

seal the dough. Crimp the edges with a fork. Using a sharp knife, make two small incisions in the top of each turnover to permit the escape of steam.

    6. Heat the oil or shortening in a deep-fryer to 370 degrees. Drop in the turnovers, a few at a time, and, when thoroughly brown on one side, turn them to brown on the other. Drain on paper towels and serve hot.

    Yield: One dozen or more pies.

    One of the best dishes in Louisiana—and one that is particularly recommended for breakfast—is known as grillades. It is a braised meat dish generally made with veal, but it may be made with round steak. The usual accompaniment for breakfast grillades is grits.

Grillades
LOUISIANA

2 pounds veal or round steak, cut into six thin slices, each slice measuring about four by six inches	¼ teaspoon thyme
	¼ teaspoon cayenne pepper
	1 bay leaf
	Salt and freshly ground black pepper to taste
6 tablespoons bacon drippings	
¼ cup flour	2 cups beef broth
2 cups finely chopped onions	Worcestershire sauce to taste (optional)
3 tablespoons tomato paste	
1 clove garlic, finely minced	Chopped parsley
½ cup finely chopped scallions, including green part	Chopped scallions for garnish.

    1. Pound the meat, if desired.

    2. Heat two tablespoons of the bacon drippings in a skillet and brown the meat in it on both sides.

    3. Heat the remaining drippings in a two-quart saucepan and add the flour. Cook over moderate heat, stirring with a wooden spoon, until flour is lightly browned. Add the onions and continue cooking and stirring until onions are golden brown. Add the tomato paste and cook, scraping the bottom of the saucepan until tomato paste browns slightly. Add the garlic, scallions, thyme, cayenne, bay leaf, salt and pepper and stir well. Pour in the broth, stirring rapidly.

4. Return the meat to the sauce and simmer one to one and one-half hours, stirring occasionally from the bottom. Add Worcestershire if desired.
5. Serve sprinkled with parsley and scallions.
Yield: Six servings.

Tripe Creole
LOUISIANA

3 pounds honeycomb tripe, cut into one-and-one-half-inch cubes	2 cloves garlic, minced
	2 sprigs thyme, finely chopped, or one-half teaspoon dried thyme
Salt to taste	
4 small onions, thinly sliced (about two cups)	1 bay leaf (see note)
	2 cups chicken broth, approximately
½ pound mushrooms, sliced	
2 cups peeled, chopped, ripe tomatoes or an equal amount canned Italian plum tomatoes	Freshly ground black pepper to taste
	Tabasco sauce to taste
2 green peppers, cored, seeded and sliced	Boiled potatoes.

1. Preheat the oven to 375 degrees.
2. Place the tripe in a kettle and add water to cover. Bring to a boil and cook five minutes. Drain.
3. Return the tripe to the kettle and add the remaining ingredients. Bring to a boil, cover closely and bake four hours, stirring occasionally. If the tripe seems to cook too fast, reduce the oven heat and continue cooking. If it is deemed necessary, add a little more chicken broth as tripe cooks. Serve with boiled potatoes on the side.

Yield: Four to six servings.

Note: The bay leaf may be added whole, but it is better finely chopped. To chop it, break the leaf into quarters and combine it with the chopped garlic and thyme. Chop until finely minced.

Some recipes for tripe creole also call for a last-minute addition of cognac, but it is not generally considered an ingredient in the traditional sense.

Roast Marinated Pork Loin
VIRGINIA

1	three- to five-pound pork loin	1	teaspoon peppercorns
1½	cups dry white wine	1	teaspoon thyme
3	cloves garlic, crushed	1	large bay leaf
½	cup sliced carrot	1	teaspoon juniper berries.
½	cup sliced onion		

1. Place the pork in a dish large enough to hold it. Add the remaining ingredients and cover. Refrigerate. Let the pork stand in the refrigerator, turning occasionally in the marinade, three or four days. If this is not feasible, let pork stand overnight and the following day.
2. Preheat the oven to 325 degrees.
3. Drain the pork and reserve the marinade. Wipe the pork with paper towels and place it on a rack in a baking pan. Roast forty minutes to the pound, basting occasionally with the marinade. When cooked, the roast should be quite brown. When cooked, turn off the oven and let the pork stay there ten minutes longer. This roast when served should be neither hot nor cold.

Yield: Four to six servings.

Pork Chops Bermudiana
FLORIDA

4	pork chops, each one and one-half inches thick	4	thick slices Bermuda onion
	Salt and freshly ground black pepper	1	cup fresh or canned chicken or beef broth
1	tablespoon butter	1	tablespoon finely chopped parsley
4	tablespoons uncooked rice	1	tablespoon finely chopped chives
4	slices peeled tomato		
4	slices green pepper	½	bay leaf.

1. Preheat the oven to 350 degrees.
2. Sprinkle the chops with salt and pepper. Brown the chops on both sides in butter and transfer to a baking dish. Spoon one tablespoon uncooked rice atop each chop. Top each with a slice of tomato, green pepper and onion

and sprinkle with salt and pepper. Pour the broth around the chops and sprinkle with parsley and chives. Add the bay leaf half and cover. Bake one hour.

 Yield: Four servings.

Smothered Pork Chops
MISSISSIPPI

6 loin pork chops, each one-inch thick	Shortening or lard
3 tablespoons flour	3 onions, sliced
1 teaspoon salt	⅓ cup water or broth.
¼ teaspoon freshly ground black pepper	

1. Coat the chops with the flour mixed with the salt and pepper.
2. Preheat the oven to 325 degrees.
3. Heat the shortening to a depth of ¼-inch in a heavy iron skillet. Brown the chops quickly in hot shortening, turning once. Drain and place in a heavy casserole.
4. Pour off all but three tablespoons fat from the skillet. Add the onions and cook until golden. Scatter the onions over the chops. Stir the water or broth into the skillet and stir while cooking to loosen browned-on bits. Pour over the chops. Cover and bake forty-five minutes.

 Yield: Six servings.

Boiled Spareribs
ALABAMA

2 sides baby spareribs	1 onion, studded with two whole cloves
Boiling water	
Salt and freshly ground black pepper to taste	Sauerkraut, cooked rice or mashed potatoes.

1. Cut the sides of spareribs in half or quarters and place in a kettle large enough to hold them. Pour boiling water to cover over them and add salt, pepper and the onion.
2. Bring to a boil and simmer one to two hours, depending on size of

spareribs, until thoroughly tender. Serve with sauerkraut, rice or mashed potatoes, or deep-fry the spareribs (recipe below). The cooking liquid may be used to cook rice.

Yield: Four to six servings.

Deep-Fried Spareribs

GEORGIA

- 2 sides baby spareribs, boiled (recipe above)
- 1 cup self-rising flour
- Freshly ground black pepper to taste
- 3 eggs
- ¼ cup milk
- Oil for deep-frying
- Cooked rice
- Tomato sauce (optional).

1. When the spareribs are cooked and cool enough to handle, cut them into individual ribs or, if they are not very meaty, cut them into two-rib sections.
2. Dredge the ribs in flour seasoned with pepper.
3. Beat the eggs and add the milk. Dip the ribs in the mixture and deep-fry in hot oil just until they are crisp and golden brown. Serve hot with rice. The ribs may also be served with tomato sauce.

Yield: Four to six servings.

Barbecue

NORTH CAROLINA

- 1 pork shoulder, eight to ten pounds, or four pounds spareribs
- 2 teaspoons salt
- 1 cup vinegar
- 1 cup water
- 2 hot red pepper pods, chopped
- ¼ cup butter
- 1 medium onion, finely chopped
- 1 clove garlic, finely chopped
- Rind of one lemon, slivered
- 1 tablespoon lemon juice
- ½ cup vinegar
- ¼ cup water
- 1 cup catchup
- 2 tablespoons Worcestershire sauce
- 2 tablespoons brown sugar
- ½ teaspoon dry mustard.

1. Spit barbecue the shoulder or ribs over charcoal very slowly. The shoulder will take five and a half hours and the ribs two hours. While they are cooking, brush with a mixture made by combining the salt, one cup vinegar, one cup water and red pepper pods.

2. Meanwhile, heat the butter in a saucepan. Add the onion and garlic and cook until tender but not browned. Add the remaining ingredients. Bring to a boil and simmer ten minutes. Use this sauce to baste the pork shoulder, or ribs, during the last thirty minutes of cooking, being careful not to burn the meat.

3. When the pork shoulder is very well done, remove from the spit. Remove the meat from the bone and shred or chop very finely; do not grind. Moisten with additional vinegar and hot pepper basting liquid and cool. If necessary make more vinegar basting liquid. The ribs are ready to cut up and serve as is once they are well done.

Yield: Ten to twelve servings pork shoulder barbecue or four servings ribs.

Pork-Stuffed Peppers
GEORGIA

4	pork chops or two pounds lean shoulder of pork	Freshly ground black pepper to taste
	Boiling water	¾ cup finely chopped onion
	Salt to taste	1 tablespoon butter
1	cup leftover grits (page 153)	8 large green peppers, halved, membranes and seeds scooped out to give shells for stuffing
1	cup crumbled baking powder biscuits (page 188)	
2	eggs, lightly beaten	

1. Cover the meat with boiling water and add salt. Bring to a boil and simmer until meat is fork-tender. Drain, reserving a little of the cooking liquid. Shred or grind the meat.

2. Preheat the oven to 350 degrees.

3. In a mixing bowl combine the meat with the grits, biscuits, eggs and black pepper. Cook the onion in the butter until onion is translucent and add to the stuffing. Mix well. Add just enough cooking liquid to moisten.

4. Meanwhile, drop the green pepper in boiling water to cover and simmer three minutes. Drain immediately.

5. Fill the peppers with the pork mixture and place them, stuffed side

up, in a buttered baking dish. Bake ten to fifteen minutes, or until thoroughly heated.

Yield: Eight servings.

Sausage with Cream Gravy and Biscuits
TENNESSEE

1½	pounds sausage meat		Salt and freshly ground black pepper to taste
⅓	cup flour		
1	cup water	6	hot biscuits, split.
2	cups evaporated milk or heavy cream		

1. Shape the sausage meat into twelve patties and fry in a heavy skillet until brown and thoroughly cooked. Remove patties and keep warm.
2. Remove all but one-third cup fat from the skillet. Sprinkle the flour over fat in skillet and mix. Gradually add the water, stirring constantly.
3. Stir in the milk or cream. Season with salt and pepper. Bring to a boil, stirring. Return patties to skillet and reheat.
4. Serve on top of the biscuits.

Yield: Six servings.

Cuban Sausages
FLORIDA

3	pounds pork that is both lean and fat	3	cloves garlic, finely minced
2½	tablespoons salt	1	teaspoon ground oregano
	Freshly ground black pepper to taste	½	cup achiote coloring (see note)
		2	yards pork intestines.

1. Grind the meat twice. Add the salt, pepper, garlic, oregano and achiote and mix well.
2. Use the mixture to stuff the pork intestines, using a sausage stuffer or a large funnel. These sausages may be hung for a short time in a cool, dry place. Before hanging, prick them in several places. Twist the sausage in several places to make individual sausages.

Yield: About three pounds stuffed sausages; twelve servings.

Note: Achiote coloring is available in Spanish markets.

Head Cheese (Fromage de Tête)
LOUISIANA

- 1 pig's head
- Coarse salt
- 1 pound salt pork
- 2 large carrots
- 2 medium-size onions, each studded with two whole cloves
- 1 clove garlic, peeled
- 4 sprigs parsley
- 3 ribs celery
- 2 bay leaves
- 4 sprigs thyme or one teaspoon dried thyme
- Salt to taste
- 20 peppercorns
- 1 tablespoon cider vinegar
- Freshly ground black pepper to taste, if necessary.

1. This will require a large kettle. First, however, the pig's head must be thoroughly singed, cleaned and scraped to remove all traces of hair. Remove the tongue and brains. Discard the fat part of the throat. Keep tongue and brains separate. Have the head cut into quarters.

2. Rub the head and tongue with coarse salt and place in a large bowl with the salt pork. Let stand in a cool place at least four hours. Place the head, tongue, salt pork, carrots, onions, garlic, parsley, celery, one bay leaf and half the thyme in a large kettle. Add salt, the peppercorns and water to cover.

3. Bring to a boil and simmer one and one-half hours, skimming the surface, as necessary. Remove the tongue and reserve it. Continue cooking the head and other ingredients two and one-half hours longer. Let cool to lukewarm.

4. Meanwhile, soak the brain in cold salted water. Drain and place in a saucepan. Add water to cover, one bay leaf, the remaining thyme and the vinegar. Bring to a boil and simmer two minutes. Remove from the heat and let cool.

5. Lift the pig's head from the broth and cut off all meat from the bones. Cut the brains, meat and tongue into one-half-inch squares. Reserve the pig's ears. Season meat and tongue with salt and pepper if necessary.

6. Bring the cooking liquid to a boil and cook rapidly over high heat to reduce by one-third. Strain.

7. Cut the salt pork and pig's ears into strips. Arrange layers of salt pork, pig's ears, brains, meat and tongue in a bowl and pour in enough of the strained cooking liquid to cover. Let cool slightly. Cover with aluminum foil or wax paper and add a weight to cover. Let cool twenty-four hours. Serve unmolded or directly from the bowl as an appetizer, preferably with sour pickles, the kind the French call *cornichons*.

Yield: One dozen or more servings.

Head Cheese Vinaigrette
LOUISIANA

Cut head cheese (recipe page 101) into cubes and arrange on lettuce leaves. Serve sprinkled with cider vinegar, oil, chopped onion, salt and freshly ground black pepper.

Chitterlings
MISSISSIPPI

10 pounds chitterlings (see note)	1 onion, finely chopped
Lemon juice	1 clove garlic, crushed
Salt to taste	3 bay leaves
1 tablespoon cider vinegar	Vinegar
Seasoning salt to taste	Hot sauce.

1. Place the chitterlings in a basin and add cold water, a little lemon juice and salt. Clean chitterlings thoroughly, removing as much of the fat as possible. Change the water, adding more lemon juice and salt as necessary. Rinse chitterlings thoroughly and put them in a pot.

2. Add cold water to cover, the juice of one lemon and the remaining ingredients and bring to a boil. Cover and simmer until chitterlings are thoroughly tender, about four hours. Serve hot with vinegar and hot sauce on the side.

Yield: Eight servings.

Note: Chitterlings are the intestines of the hog and it is important to remove all excess fat and clean them thoroughly. After boiling until tender, the chitterlings may be drained, dipped in corn meal and fried, or dipped in a batter made of two cups flour, two eggs and one and one-half cups milk and deep-fried.

This recipe is as Southern as grits and red eye gravy and is always eaten on New Year's Day along with turnip greens or collards and some sort of corn bread. This is good luck for the New Year—the peas are coins, the greens are folding money, the jawl is for luck and the corn bread is to stick to your ribs.

Mrs. Jackson Porter Dick's Black-Eyed Peas and Hog Jawl (Jowl)
GEORGIA

- 1 one-pound package dried black-eyed peas
- 1 four-inch to five-inch piece of smoked hog jawl, sliced
- Salt
- 1 bird's eye pepper or other small hot red pepper (see note)
- Worcestershire sauce to taste.

1. Day before, rinse and pick over the peas. Cover with water and soak overnight.
2. Next day, sprinkle the jawl with three teaspoons salt and then fry in a skillet until browned. Transfer to a kettle. Add the soaked peas, enough water to cover by one inch, salt to taste and the pepper. Bring to a boil.
3. Cover and simmer three to four hours. Add additional water during cooking if necessary. Add Worcestershire.

Yield: Eight servings.

Note: Bird's eye peppers grow in Georgia and Bermuda.

Souse (Jellied Pork)
TENNESSEE

- 1 hog's head, split, eyes and brain removed
- 4 pig's feet
- 2 pig's ears
- Salt
- Freshly ground black pepper
- Sage
- Crushed hot red pepper.

1. Remove excess fat from head and clean thoroughly.
2. Singe hairs off feet and ears and scrub well under hot water.
3. Place head, feet and ears in a large kettle and cover with hot water. Bring to a boil, cover, and simmer several hours, or until meat is very tender.
4. Remove meat from the bones and season with one teaspoon each salt, pepper, sage and red pepper for each quart meat. Press into a bowl and chill. To serve, see note.

Yield: Two dozen servings.

Note: Serve cold with vinegar or cut into slices, dip in egg and bread crumbs and fry in hot lard. Hog's head cheese is prepared as above, but the meat is ground, seasoned as above plus three teaspoons allspice and two teaspoons ground cloves and mixed with two to three cups of the cooking broth before pressing into a bowl. Broth forms jelly.

Smithfield or Smithfield-Style Virginia Ham

1 ten-pound to twelve pound country ham (see note).

1. Soak the ham in cold water to cover overnight.
2. Preheat the oven to 500 degrees.
3. Scrub the ham to remove the pepper coating and any mold that may be present. Place the ham in a covered roaster with six cups cold water. Close all vents.
4. Bake ham twenty minutes. Turn oven off. Allow ham to remain in oven without opening door three hours.
5. Turn oven heat to 500 degrees and leave fifteen minutes. Turn off the heat and allow ham to remain in the oven for at least three hours or more, or ham can be left in overnight.
6. Remove ham from roaster and cut off the rind. Ham is ready to serve or may be glazed if desired.

Yield: About two dozen servings.

Note: Country hams are dry cured, salty and usually have a pepper coating.

Boiled and Baked Country Ham
KENTUCKY

1	country-style ham	¾	cup light brown sugar
6	onions, sliced	2	tablespoons dry mustard
2	cups cider vinegar	1	cup soft bread crumbs
2	bay leaves		Whole cloves.
½	cup unsulphured molasses		

1. Day before, scrub the ham, removing any pepper coating and mold. Place in a large kettle, cover with water and let soak overnight.
2. Next day, drain ham. Put back in the kettle and cover with fresh wa-

ter. Add the onions, vinegar, bay leaves and molasses; stir to mix. Bring to a boil and simmer gently fifteen to twenty minutes to the pound.
3. Allow ham to cool in the broth.
4. Preheat the oven to 375 degrees.
5. Remove skin from ham and score fat in diamond pattern. Combine the sugar, mustard and bread crumbs. Place cloves in centers of diamonds and pat bread crumb mixture over all. Bake twenty minutes, or until brown.

Yield: About twenty servings.

Southern Maryland Stuffed Ham

1 twelve-pound to fourteen-pound plump, thick country ham with thin layer of fat	1 whole stalk pascal celery, chopped
	1 hot red pepper, chopped
	6 tablespoons salt
3 pounds kale, shredded	2 tablespoons freshly ground black pepper
3 pounds water cress, tough stems removed, chopped roughly	2 tablespoons red pepper flakes
	2 tablespoons mustard seeds
2 pounds green cabbage, shredded	2 tablespoons celery seeds
	2 teaspoons Tabasco sauce.

1. If the ham is salty, cover with cold water and soak overnight. Place in a kettle, cover with water, bring to a boil and simmer, covered, twenty minutes. Let ham sit in the hot broth twenty minutes longer, remove the skin and cool.

2. In a large kettle, barely cover the kale, water cress, cabbage, celery and chopped pepper with boiling water and simmer one to two minutes, or until limp. Drain well.

3. Carving is easier if the ham is boned, but this is not essential.

4. Add the remaining ingredients and mix well. Starting at the butt end of the cooled ham, make several deep incisions either crosswise or lengthwise about two to three inches apart.

5. With the fingers, push the greens down into the slits to fill all the holes. Pile remaining greens over the top of the ham. If the ham has been boned, it is necessary to tie it at this point to retain the shape. Boned or unboned, tie in a muslin or fine cloth, securing with pins, to retain the stuffing in position.

6. Lower the ham back into the boiler with the broth in it and simmer, covered, fifteen minutes to the pound, or until tender. Allow to set in the "pot likker" at least two hours. Chill, still in the cloth, before removing and carving.

Yield: About two dozen servings.

Ham Steak and Red Eye Gravy
VIRGINIA

1 center slice about three-eighths-inch thick country ham	Black coffee (optional) Cooked grits Fried apples (page 239).

1. If the ham is salty, soak the slice in water for thirty minutes to an hour. Drain and pat dry.
2. Cook the slice in a heavy skillet slowly, until tender, about twenty minutes. Set aside on a warm platter.
3. Add one cup water to the skillet and cook, stirring to loosen all the browned particles and pieces of "red" meat. Boil two minutes. Add tablespoon or two of coffee to darken further if desired.
4. Serve ham with grits, gravy and fried apples.

Yield: Three servings.

Ham Hocks
GEORGIA

4	ham hocks	3	potatoes, diced
2	teaspoons salt	¼	large head cabbage, cut into four wedges.
3	carrots, quartered		
3	onions, sliced		

1. Place the hocks in a Dutch oven or casserole. Cover with water and add the salt. Bring to a boil and simmer, covered, one and one-half to two hours, or until tender.
2. Add the remaining ingredients and cook, covered, fifteen minutes longer, or until vegetables are tender.

Yield: Four servings.

Ham Croquettes with Egg Sauce
VIRGINIA

¾	plus one-third cups butter	4	eggs, lightly beaten
¾	cup flour		Dry bread crumbs
3½	cups milk or light cream		Fat or oil for deep-frying
	Salt and freshly ground black pepper to taste	½	cup finely chopped onion
		1	cup sliced mushrooms
2½	cups finely ground cooked country ham	1	green pepper, finely chopped
		½	teaspoon sage
½	teaspoon Worcestershire sauce	¼	teaspoon marjoram
			Light cream
½	teaspoon dry mustard	6	hard-cooked eggs, chopped.

    1. Melt three-quarters cup of the butter and blend in the flour. Gradually stir in the milk or cream. Season with salt and pepper and bring to a boil, stirring. Cook, stirring, three minutes.

    2. Place the ham in a bowl and add Worcestershire, mustard and one and one-half cups of the sauce mixed with two of the lightly beaten eggs. Set remaining sauce over hot water.

    3. Mix ham and sauce and set aside to cool. Chill. Shape the cooled mixture into croquettes, dip in remaining eggs and then in the bread crumbs. Repeat if necessary to get good coating.

    4. Fry a few croquettes at a time until golden, using a fry basket, in fat or oil heated to 365 degrees. Drain on paper towels.

    5. Heat remaining butter in a skillet and sauté the onion in it until tender. Add the mushrooms, green pepper, sage and marjoram and cook until vegetables are tender.

    6. Add enough light cream to reserved sauce to make pouring consistency. Stir in cooked vegetables and the chopped eggs. Season to taste with salt and pepper. Serve separately with croquettes.

Yield: Six servings.

Southern Fried Chicken I
MISSISSIPPI

2	three-and-one-half-pound frying chickens, cut into serving pieces		Salt to taste
	Milk to cover	1	or more teaspoons freshly ground black pepper
½	teaspoon Tabasco sauce	2	pounds lard or 4 cups oil and one-half pound butter.
1	cup flour		

1. Place the chicken pieces in a large mixing bowl and add milk to cover. Add the Tabasco and refrigerate for one hour or so.
2. Combine the flour, salt and pepper in a heavy paper bag or large plastic bag. Shake to blend.
3. Use two large heavy skillets. Heat one pound of lard or half the oil and one-quarter pound of the butter in each skillet.
4. Do not drain the chicken. Take one piece at a time and shake it in the bag until well coated. Place in skillets and cook until golden brown on one side. Turn and cook until brown on the other side. When done, drain on paper towels. Serve hot or cold.

Yield: Four to six servings.

Southern Fried Chicken II
TENNESSEE

1	two-and-one-half-pound to three-pound frying chicken, cut into serving pieces	¾	cup flour
			Salt and freshly ground black pepper to taste
1	egg		Shortening
	Juice of one lemon		Gravy
	Milk to cover		Hot biscuits.

1. Wash the chicken pieces under cold running water. Drain and dry with paper towels.
2. Beat the egg and add the lemon juice. Soak the chicken in milk to cover to which egg mixture has been added at least one-half hour or longer if possible.
3. Place the flour, salt and pepper in a medium-size brown paper bag. Add the chicken pieces, close top of bag and shake so all pieces are coated evenly and well.

4. Place melted shortening one inch deep in a ten-inch or eleven-inch skillet. Fry the chicken in it until tender, about thirty to forty minutes. Serve with gravy and hot biscuits.
Yield: Four to six servings.

Southern Fried Chicken III
ALABAMA

1 two-and-one-half-pound to three-pound frying chicken, cut into serving pieces, or four medium-size chicken breasts, halved Salt	1 cup flour ½ teaspoon white pepper Shortening, lard or oil Chicken cream gravy (next recipe) Hot biscuits.

1. Wash the chicken pieces under cold running water. Drain, but do not dry. Sprinkle liberally on both sides with salt.
2. Place the flour, pepper and one teaspoon salt in a medium-size brown paper bag. Add chicken, close top of bag and shake so all pieces are coated evenly and well. Remove chicken pieces and shake to remove excess flour.
3. Place melted shortening or lard or oil one-quarter-inch deep in a ten-inch skillet. Place over highest heat for a few minutes until fat is crackling hot. Carefully place chicken pieces in skillet side by side, fleshy side down. Cook rapidly a few minutes, making sure pieces have a firm but very light brown crust on the bottom. Turn each piece as it reaches this stage until all are turned. Continue cooking one minute over high heat. Reduce the heat to quite low and cover skillet. Cook forty minutes.
4. Remove cover and turn heat up once more to highest level. Turn each piece as the bottom becomes golden, but not too brown, and quite crisp. (The top surface of the chicken pieces will have a rather soft, dispirited look when the cover is removed, but a couple minutes turned over will change this to the desired golden crispness.)
5. Remove pieces to drain on paper towels. Serve with chicken cream gravy and hot biscuits.
Yield: Four to six servings.

Chicken Cream Gravy
ALABAMA

	Cooking fat from chicken	2	dashes Tabasco
3	tablespoons flour	2	cups milk.
	Freshly ground black pepper		

Pour through a sieve the fat left in the skillet after frying chicken. Return two or three tablespoons of the fat to the skillet, along with the brown particles remaining in the sieve. Turn the heat to high, add the flour and stir, picking up browned bits remaining in the skillet, until flour is medium brown; then turn heat off. Add a generous sprinkle of the pepper and the Tabasco. Pour in the milk all at once, turn heat to medium high and stir constantly until gravy thickens. The consistency should be similar to that of heavy cream.
Yield: Two cups.

Batter-Fried Chicken
WEST VIRGINIA

1	two-and-one-half-pound to three-pound frying chicken, cut into serving pieces		Chicken broth
		2	cups flour
		2	teaspoons baking powder
1	rib celery	2	eggs
1	carrot	1½	cups milk
1	bay leaf	2	tablespoons melted butter
1	small onion		Fat or oil for deep-frying.
	Salt and freshly ground black pepper		

1. Place the chicken pieces in a skillet. Add the celery, carrot, bay leaf, onion, salt and pepper to taste and enough broth to cover barely.
2. Bring to a boil and simmer gently fifteen minutes. Drain and dry pieces of chicken and let cool.
3. Combine the flour, baking powder and one-half teaspoon salt in a bowl. Beat the eggs with the milk and stir into dry ingredients along with the butter.
4. Dip the chicken pieces in the batter and, using a fry basket, drop into the fat or oil heated to 375 degrees. Fry until golden and drain on paper towels.
Yield: Four servings.

Chicken with Corn Bread Stuffing
ARKANSAS

Corn bread (next recipe)
⅔ cup coarsely chopped celery
⅔ cup coarsely chopped onion
⅔ cup coarsely chopped green pepper
10 tablespoons butter
2 slices toast, coarsely chopped
⅓ cup finely chopped parsley
2 raw eggs
3 or more cups chicken broth
2 hard-cooked eggs, coarsely chopped
Salt and freshly ground black pepper to taste
1 four-pound roasting chicken, cleaned and ready to stuff
Chicken giblets
3 tablespoons flour.

1. Preheat the oven to 400 degrees.
2. Crumble the corn bread into a mixing bowl. Cook the celery, onion and green pepper in three tablespoons of the butter just until vegetables are crisp-tender. Add to the corn bread. Add the toast, parsley, raw eggs and enough broth to make a moist dressing. Reserve remaining broth.
3. Add the chopped eggs, salt and pepper. Melt three tablespoons of the remaining butter and add to stuffing. Stir briefly. Use just enough filling to stuff the chicken. Spoon remaining filling into a generously buttered skillet and set aside.
4. Melt one tablespoon of the remaining butter in a skillet large enough to hold the chicken. Add the chicken and turn it around in the butter on top of the stove.
5. Place the chicken on one side and roast, uncovered, basting occasionally, about twenty minutes. Turn the chicken to the other side and continue roasting, basting, about twenty minutes longer. Turn the chicken on its back and roast, basting, twenty minutes longer.
6. Place the skillet with additional filling in the oven for the last half hour of roasting. Bake just until bubbling and golden.
7. Meanwhile, place the remaining broth in a saucepan and add the neck, gizzard and heart. Simmer about thirty minutes. Add the liver and continue cooking about ten minutes. To prepare giblet gravy, discard the neck and chop the liver, heart and gizzard. Blend the remaining butter with the flour and stir, bit by bit, into simmering broth. Serve gravy separately with chicken and stuffing.

Yield: Four to six servings.

Corn Bread
ARKANSAS

1 cup yellow corn meal	1 egg
1 cup flour	1 cup milk
1 teaspoon sugar	¼ cup melted lard or shortening.
½ teaspoon salt	
4 teaspoons baking powder	

1. Preheat the oven to 425 degrees.
2. Sift the corn meal, flour, sugar, salt and baking powder into a mixing bowl. Add the egg, milk and lard or shortening and stir with a wooden spoon until blended. Do not overbeat.
3. Grease an eight-inch square pan or iron skillet. Heat on top of the stove and pour in the batter. Place in the oven and bake twenty to twenty-five minutes.

Yield: Eight to ten servings.

Chicken 'n' Dumplings
ALABAMA

1 five-pound to six-pound hen or capon	12 peppercorns
2 ribs celery with leaves	Salt
1 large carrot, cut in half	2 cups self-rising flour
1 large onion, studded with two whole cloves	1½ tablespoons shortening
	1 cup milk.

1. Place the hen or capon in a kettle and add the celery, carrot and onion. Add water to cover and peppercorns. Do not salt. Bring to a boil and cook until chicken is tender, four to five hours. Remove the chicken and, when it is cool enough to handle, remove the meat from the bones.
2. Strain the cooking liquid and return it to the heat. Salt lightly. Cook the broth down until it is rich-flavored.
3. Meanwhile, place the flour in a mixing bowl and cut in the shortening, using a pastry blender or two knives. Stir in the milk, adding just enough so that the dough can be handled. Roll out the dough on a lightly floured board to one-quarter-inch thickness and with a sharp knife cut into one-inch circles.

4. Return the chicken to the kettle, return to a boil and drop in the dumplings a few at a time. Cook, covered, about ten minutes, stirring once, and serve immediately.
Yield: Ten to one dozen servings.

Chicken Olivette
ARKANSAS

1 five-pound fowl or two large broiler-fryers, cut into serving pieces	2 cups chopped clery
	1 medium-size green pepper, diced
½ cup olive oil	2 cups uncooked rice
6 cups water or chicken broth	½ cup chopped pimentos
Salt and freshly ground black pepper to taste	1 cup sliced stuffed olives
	1 pound shredded sharp Cheddar cheese.
1 onion, chopped	

1. Brown the fowl or broiler pieces in the oil in a heavy Dutch oven or casserole. Add the water or broth, salt and black pepper. Cover, bring to a boil and simmer until the meat is tender, about thirty minutes for broilers and one hour for fowl.

2. Strain the cooking broth and reserve. Take the meat off the bones and cut into large pieces. Discard the skin.

3. Place two or three tablespoons of the chicken fat from the top of the reserved broth in a skillet. Add the onion, celery and green pepper and sauté until barely tender.

4. Measure the reserved broth and make up to four and one-half to five cups with water and add to the skillet with the chicken pieces and the rice. Cover and cook until rice is tender, about twenty-five minutes.

5. Add the remaining ingredients and stir until the cheese melts. Check the seasoning.
Yield: Six servings.

Chicken Pudding
VIRGINIA

2	three-pound chickens	5	eggs
12	peppercorns	2	cups milk
3	celery tops	2	cups plus six tablespoons flour
½	onion		
3	sprigs parsley	4	tablespoons melted butter
½	teaspoon thyme	4	tablespoons cold butter
	Boiling chicken broth or cold water		Freshly ground black pepper to taste
	Salt to taste	2	tablespoons chopped parsley.

1. Place the chickens in a kettle and add the peppercorns, celery, onion, parsley sprigs and thyme. Add boiling broth or cold water to cover and bring to a boil. Add salt. (If broth is used, use salt sparingly because the liquid will be reduced.) Simmer until chickens are tender, at least forty minutes.

2. Remove the chickens from the broth and let cool slightly. When cool enough to handle, remove the best pieces of white and dark meat and set aside. Return the skin and bones to the kettle and continue simmering until broth is reduced by almost half. Strain.

3. Preheat the oven to 450 degrees.

4. Butter a ten-inch heavy iron skillet or similar utensil and add one-quarter cup of the simmering broth. Add the reserved chicken meat and cover with aluminum foil. Place in the oven and heat about ten minutes.

5. Meanwhile, beat the eggs lightly and add the milk. Gradually beat in two cups of the flour, salt to taste and the melted butter. Pour the mixture over the chicken and bake until the pudding is set and brown, forty-five minutes to one hour.

6. While the pudding cooks, prepare a sauce. Melt the cold butter and stir in the remaining flour with a wire whisk. When blended, add three cups of the strained broth, stirring vigorously with the whisk. When thickened and smooth, simmer ten minutes. Add pepper and chopped parsley. Serve the pudding with sauce.

Yield: Six to eight servings.

Mom's Arkansas Chicken Pie

- 1 five-pound to six-pound fowl or two broiler-fryers, cut into serving pieces
- 1 rib celery, diced
- 1 carrot, diced
- 1 onion, sliced
- cup flour.

Crust:
- 3 cups flour
- 1 teaspoon salt
- 4 teaspoons baking powder
- ½ teaspoon baking soda
- 1½ cups soured heavy cream, made by leaving at room temperature until it thickens, by adding one and one-half tablespoons white vinegar or by adding two tablespoons buttermilk and leaving at room temperature twenty-four hours, or until it thickens
- 2 eggs, beaten
- Light cream.

- 1 bay leaf
- Salt and freshly ground black pepper to taste
- 6 cups water or chicken broth
- ½ cup chicken fat or butter
- ½ cup flour.

1. Place the fowl or broilers in a deep Dutch oven or heavy casserole and add the celery, carrot, onion, bay leaf, salt, pepper and water or broth. Bring to a boil, cover and simmer until tender, about one hour for fowl and thirty-five minutes for chickens.

2. Remove chicken pieces and take meat off the bones. Discard the skin. Strain the cooking liquid and measure four and one-half cups, adding milk if necessary.

3. Preheat the oven to 350 degrees.

4. Melt the chicken fat or butter and blend in the flour. Gradually stir in the broth and bring to a boil, stirring. Season with salt and pepper. Add chicken pieces and pour into a shallow baking pan about twelve-by-eight-by-three inches.

5. To make crust, sift the dry ingredients together. Combine the heavy cream and eggs and stir into the dry ingredients. Spoon the mixture over the chicken in the baking dish and even out with a spatula. Brush with light cream and bake thirty-five minutes, or until done and browned.

Yield: Six to eight servings.

Stuffed Chicken Breasts
TENNESSEE

10	large whole chicken breasts, boned and halved	1½	cups boiling fresh or canned (twelve ounces) chicken broth
	Salt and freshly ground black pepper	2	tablespoons arrowroot or cornstarch
1	pound mushrooms	½	cup water
	Juice of two lemons	15	canned or bottled crab apples
8	tablespoons butter		Parsley for garnish.
¼	cup chopped fresh chives		
	Paprika		

1. Preheat the oven to 450 degrees.
2. Split each half breast partly through the center to make a pocket. Sprinkle the cavity with a little salt and pepper.
3. Slice the mushrooms and immediately sprinkle with lemon juice to prevent discoloration. Add half the butter to a small skillet and cook mushrooms in it until they are wilted. Add about one tablespoon of the mushrooms to each of the chicken cavities. If there are any remaining mushrooms, reserve them.
4. Arrange the chicken breasts, skin side up, in a large buttered baking dish and sprinkle with salt, pepper and chives. Sprinkle lightly with paprika and dot with the remaining butter. Cover closely with heavy-duty aluminum foil and bake twenty-five minutes. Uncover and add the boiling broth. Continue cooking.
5. Combine the arrowroot or cornstarch with the water and stir it into the baking dish. If there are any remaining mushrooms, add them. Baste the chicken until it is nicely glazed. Place the crab apples in the center of a large platter and arrange the chicken breasts around them. Garnish the platter with parsley and serve hot.

Yield: Ten to fifteen servings.

Chicken Crab Bake
MARYLAND

¾	cup butter	2	tablespoons chopped parsley
1	two-and-one-half-pound broiler-fryer, cut into small serving pieces	½	cup minced clams
		½	pound backfin crab meat, picked over to remove bits of shell and cartilage
	Salt and freshly ground black pepper to taste	1	dozen small clams in the shell
½	cup finely chopped onion		
1	cup uncooked rice	1	ten-ounce package frozen artichoke hearts, cooked
1½	cups chicken broth		
1	cup clam juice	1	cup fresh peas, cooked, or frozen peas, thawed.
⅛	teaspoon saffron		

1. Heat one-half cup of the butter in a large ovenproof skillet or shallow casserole. Season the chicken with salt and pepper and sauté in the butter until brown on all sides. Set chicken aside.

2. Add remaining butter to skillet and sauté the onion in it until tender. Add the rice and cook five minutes longer.

3. Stir in the broth, clam juice, saffron, parsley and chicken pieces. Cover and cook about thirty minutes, or until rice and chicken are cooked. Stir occasionally.

4. Preheat the oven to 350 degrees.

5. Fold in the minced clams and crab meat. Season to taste with salt and pepper.

6. Arrange the clams in the shell, artichoke hearts and peas over the top and bake, uncovered, for ten minutes, or until clams open.

Yield: Six to eight servings.

Barbecued Chicken
SOUTH CAROLINA

1	two-and-one-half-pound to three-pound frying chicken, cut into serving pieces	2	tablespoons Worcestershire sauce
		1	teaspoon paprika
2	onions, sliced		Salt and freshly ground black pepper to taste
¾	cup catchup		
¾	cup water	1	teaspoon chili powder.
3	tablespoons cider vinegar		

1. Preheat the oven to 350 degrees.
2. Place the chicken pieces in a casserole. Mix together the remaining ingredients and pour over chicken.
3. Bake, uncovered, one and one-half hours.

Yield: Four servings.

Seven Hearths Chicken
NORTH CAROLINA

3	whole chicken breasts, halved	2	tablespoons oil
		6	tablespoons flour
4	chicken thighs	2	cups rich chicken broth
2	chicken legs	¼	teaspoon thyme
	Salt and freshly ground black pepper to taste	½	cup heavy cream
		½	pound mushrooms
10	tablespoons butter	¼	cup Madeira wine.

1. Preheat the oven to 350 degrees.
2. Sprinkle the chicken pieces with salt and pepper. Heat two tablespoons of the butter and the oil in a large skillet and brown chicken on all sides. Transfer to a heavy two-quart casserole. Wipe out skillet and set aside for future use.
3. Heat six tablespoons of the butter in a saucepan and stir in the flour. When blended, add the broth, stirring rapidly. When mixture is thickened and smooth, add the thyme and simmer ten minutes, stirring frequently. Stir in the cream.
4. Add the remaining butter to skillet in which chicken cooked. Chop the mushrooms and add them to skillet. Cook until mushrooms give up their moisture and most of it evaporates.
5. Stir in cream sauce to dissolve brown particles that cling to bottom and sides of skillet. Add the Madeira and pour over chicken. Cover and bake thirty-five minutes, or until chicken is thoroughly tender.

Yield: Six servings.

Poulet Floride
FLORIDA

¼ cup catchup	1 teaspoon salt
¼ cup cider vinegar	1 teaspoon dry mustard
2 tablespoons Worcestershire sauce	1 teaspoon chili powder
	¼ teaspoon cayenne pepper
2 tablespoons butter	Few dashes Tabasco sauce
2 tablespoons light brown sugar	2 medium-size onions, sliced
	1 three-pound chicken, cut into serving pieces.
1 clove garlic, crushed	

    1. Mix all the ingredients except the sliced onion and chicken in a large saucepan. Bring to a boil and let cool.
    2. Preheat the oven to 375 degrees.
    3. Add the sliced onion and chicken to the sauce.
    4. Cut four pieces of heavy-duty aluminum foil fourteen by eighteen inches. Butter one side of each. Divide the chicken, onion and sauce evenly on the buttered foil. Fold foil in half and close by folding open edges triply. Place packages on a baking sheet and bake one hour. Serve in the foil.
    Yield: Four servings.

Pressed Chicken
SOUTH CAROLINA

1 envelope unflavored gelatin	2 tablespoons lemon juice
2 tablespoons cold water	1 teaspoon finely grated onion
½ cup boiling chicken broth	½ cup blanched almonds, split
2 cups cut-up or diced cooked chicken	½ cup heavy cream, whipped
	¼ cup mayonnaise
2 cups diced celery	½ green pepper, finely chopped
2 teaspoons salt	6 hard-cooked eggs, chopped or left whole
¼ teaspoon freshly ground black pepper	Salad greens.

    1. Soak the gelatin in the water. Add the broth and stir to dissolve the gelatin.
    2. In a bowl mix together the chicken, celery, salt, black pepper, lemon juice, onion and almonds. Fold in the cream, mayonnaise, green pepper and dissolved gelatin.

3. If the eggs are chopped, fold them into mixture. Pack mixture into a lightly oiled mold or loaf pan. If the eggs are left whole, pack half the mixture into mold or pan, arrange eggs lengthwise on top and pack in remaining mixture.

4. Chill several hours. Unmold on a bed of greens.

Yield: Four servings.

Chicken Loaf
ARKANSAS

1 cup soft bread crumbs	¼ teaspoon freshly ground black pepper
1½ cups warm milk	½ teaspoon celery seeds
2 eggs, lightly beaten	Tabasco sauce to taste
3 cups diced cooked chicken	Mushroom sauce.
½ cup chicken broth	
1 teaspoon salt	

1. Preheat the oven to 325 degrees.
2. Place the bread crumbs in a bowl and pour the milk over. Let stand five minutes.
3. Stir in the eggs. Combine the chicken and broth and add to crumb mixture. Season with the salt, pepper, celery seeds and Tabasco.
4. Pack into a greased loaf pan and bake forty-five to sixty minutes, or until set. Serve with mushroom sauce.

Yield: Four to six servings.

Chicken Gumbo
LOUISIANA

- 1 five-pound stewing chicken, cut into pieces
- ¼ cup lard or bacon drippings
- 4 cups boiling chicken broth or water
- Salt to taste
- 4 ears corn
- 3 ripe tomatoes or two cups canned tomatoes
- ½ pound okra, trimmed and sliced lengthwise or crosswise
- 5 cups water
- ¾ cup finely chopped onion
- ¾ cup finely chopped celery
- ½ cup finely chopped green pepper
- ¼ cup butter or chicken fat
- ½ teaspoon or more red pepper flakes or Tabasco sauce to taste
- ½ cup uncooked rice
- 1 teaspoon or more Worcestershire sauce (optional)
- 1 to two teaspoons filé powder (optional).

1. Brown the chicken pieces in the lard or bacon drippings and transfer the pieces to a casserole. Add the broth or water and salt and simmer, partly covered, until the meat is easily removed from the bones, one and one-half hours or longer. Drain and reserve the cooking liquid. Remove the meat from the bones and shred it. Add the meat to the cooking liquid and set aside.

2. Scrape the corn from the cobs into another saucepan. Add the tomatoes, okra and water and bring to a boil.

3. Meanwhile, cook the onion, celery and green pepper in the butter or chicken fat until vegetables are wilted. Add them to the tomato mixture. Add the pepper flakes or Tabasco and rice and return to a boil. Continue cooking until rice is tender.

4. Add the reserved meat and broth and return to a boil. Taste for seasoning and add more salt and red pepper if desired. Add the Worcestershire if desired. Moisten the filé powder with water if desired and add. Do not boil gumbo. Serve immediately.

Yield: Six or more servings.

Chicken Wings, Gumbo-Style
LOUISIANA

- ¼ pound salt pork
- 3 pounds chicken wings
- 2 cups finely chopped onions
- 2 large cloves garlic, finely minced
- 2 cups chopped green pepper
- 1½ cups chopped celery
- 1 pound ground pork
- 1 pound ground round steak
- 5 cups fresh peeled or canned tomatoes
- 1½ cups fresh or canned chicken broth
- Salt and freshly ground black pepper to taste
- ¾ cup fresh or frozen lima beans
- 1 cup corn kernels, scraped from the cob
- Worcestershire sauce to taste
- Tabasco sauce to taste
- Cooked rice.

1. Cut the salt pork into small cubes or thin slices. In a large casserole, cook the salt pork, stirring occasionally, about five minutes, or until golden. Remove and reserve the salt pork, but leave the fat in the casserole.

2. Add the chicken wings and cook until golden brown on all sides. Remove and reserve the chicken wings.

3. Add the onions, garlic, green pepper and celery and cook, stirring, until onions are wilted.

4. Add the ground pork and round steak and cook, stirring to break up the meat. Cook until meat loses color. Add the chicken wings and salt pork. Add the tomatoes, broth, salt and pepper. Simmer, stirring occasionally, thirty minutes.

5. Add the lima beans and continue cooking thirty minutes. Add the remaining ingredients and cook fifteen minutes longer. Serve in soup bowls with rice on the side. Sprinkle with pork bits.

Yield: Eight or more servings.

Chicken Jambalaya

LOUISIANA

- 1 four-and-one-half-pound to five-pound chicken, cut into serving pieces
- 3 tablespoons peanut oil or vegetable oil
- 1 carrot, sliced
- 1 onion, studded with one whole clove
- 1 cup diced celery
- 2 sprigs parsley
- 1 bay leaf
- 1 clove garlic
- Salt to taste
- 16 peppercorns
- 1½ cups uncooked rice.

1. Brown the chicken pieces lightly in the oil in a Dutch oven or heavy casserole. Add the carrot, onion, celery, parsley, bay leaf, garlic, salt, peppercorns and cold water to cover. Bring to a boil and simmer until chicken is fork-tender.

2. Remove the chicken from the broth and strain the broth. When the chicken is cool enough to handle, remove the skin and bones. Leave the chicken in large pieces and return it to the broth. Add the rice, bring the dish to a boil and simmer until rice is tender, twenty minutes or longer.

Yield: Six servings.

Chicken Creole

LOUISIANA

- 1 three-pound chicken, cut into serving pieces
- Salt and freshly ground black pepper to taste
- 3 tablespoons butter
- 1 onion, thinly sliced
- 1 tablespoon flour
- 1 cup chopped green pepper
- 1 clove garlic, finely minced
- 1 cup chopped fresh or canned tomatoes
- 2 sprigs fresh thyme or one-half teaspoon dried thyme
- 2 sprigs parsley
- 1 bay leaf
- 1 cup boiling chicken broth
- Cooked rice.

1. Season the chicken with salt and pepper and brown on all sides in the butter. Remove the chicken and add the onion. Cook, stirring, until golden brown. Add the flour and cook, stirring, until flour is lightly browned. Add the green pepper and garlic, cook briefly and add the tomatoes, thyme, parsley

and bay leaf. Bring to a boil. Return the chicken to the skillet. Cover closely and simmer twenty minutes longer.

2. Add the boiling broth, stir all around until blended, cover and continue cooking ten to fifteen minutes, or until chicken is tender. Serve with rice.

Yield: Four servings.

Chicken Spaghetti
MISSISSIPPI

2	three-pound chickens	2	ribs celery, finely chopped
2	whole ribs celery	½	pound mushrooms, sliced
1	carrot, cut into rounds	5	tablespoons flour
2	sprigs parsley	1	cup heavy cream
1	onion, studded with two whole cloves	2	cups tomato sauce (recipe below)
	Salt to taste	2	pounds spaghetti (see note)
12	peppercorns	2	cups freshly grated sharp Cheddar cheese
8	tablespoons butter		French bread
2	green peppers, cored, seeded and chopped		Freshly grated Parmesan cheese.
1	large onion, finely chopped		

1. Place the chickens in a heavy kettle and add the whole celery ribs, carrot, parsley and onion studded with cloves. Add water to cover, salt and peppercorns. Bring the mixture to a boil and simmer until chickens are tender, about forty-five minutes to one hour. Remove the chickens from the broth and, when they are cool enough to handle, remove the meat from the bones. Discard bones and skin and reserve the meat, keeping it covered. Meanwhile, continue cooking the chicken broth until it is reduced and has more body.

2. Melt half the butter in a skillet and cook the peppers, chopped onion and chopped celery in it until vegetables are nearly tender. Add the mushrooms and cook, stirring, until mushrooms give up their juices. Continue cooking until most of the liquid is evaporated and the vegetables are tender. Reserve until ready to use.

3. Melt the remaining butter in a saucepan and add the flour, stirring it with a wire whisk. When blended, add two cups of the hot chicken broth and cook, stirring vigorously with the whisk, until the mixture is thickened and smooth. Continue cooking, stirring occasionally, five to fifteen minutes. Add

the cream, blend well and return to a boil. Add the tomato sauce. Combine the sauce, chicken and mushroom mixture. The sauce should have a medium thickness. To thin it, add a little broth.

4. Cook the spaghetti according to package directions until it is nearly but not thoroughly done. (The spaghetti will cook slightly when it is reheated in the sauce.) Drain the spaghetti.

5. Use a roasting pan or other large cooking utensil and pour in a layer of sauce and a layer of spaghetti. Sprinkle with the Cheddar cheese. Continue making layers until all the sauce, spaghetti and Cheddar cheese are used, ending with a layer of cheese. This dish may be made in advance to this point.

6. If spaghetti is allowed to stand, it will absorb much of the sauce and it may be necessary to add more chicken broth. The spaghetti should be amply steeped in sauce, but not runny.

7. When ready to serve, preheat the oven to 350 degrees.

8. Place the pan in the oven and heat spaghetti and sauce until hot and bubbling, but do not overcook. Serve on hot plates with loaves of French bread and grated Parmesan cheese.

Yield: One dozen to fifteen servings.

Note: Spaghettini may be substituted for the spaghetti.

Leftover chicken broth can be reserved for another purpose.

Tomato Sauce
MISSISSIPPI

3	medium-size tomatoes (about one and one-half pounds)	½	clove garlic, finely chopped
3	tablespoons butter	½	teaspoon thyme
1½	cups coarsely chopped onions	1	bay leaf
			Salt and freshly ground black pepper to taste.

1. Peel the tomatoes. To facilitate peeling, pierce the stem end of the tomatoes with a two-pronged fork and dip them briefly into rapidly boiling water. Peel with a paring knife. Pare away and discard the core. Chop the tomatoes in a mixing bowl.

2. Melt the butter in a saucepan and cook the onions and garlic in it until wilted. Add the chopped tomatoes and the seasonings. Simmer fifteen minutes, stirring occasionally.

3. Pour the contents of the saucepan into a colander to drain. Reserve the tomatoes and reserve the liquid that flows from the tomatoes. When well

drained, return the liquid to the saucepan and cook over high heat until reduced by half. Add the cooked tomatoes to the reduced liquid and bring to a boil. Simmer five minutes.

Yield: About two cups.

Note: This sauce may be stored for several days in the refrigerator or may be frozen.

Cajun Jambalaya
LOUISIANA

- 1 three-pound frying chicken, cut into serving pieces
- Salt and freshly ground black pepper
- 2 tablespoons bacon drippings or shortening
- 2 tablespoons flour
- 1 pound smoked sausage or smoked country ham, diced
- 2 onions, chopped
- 1 green pepper, diced
- 3 cups peeled and diced tomatoes
- 1 clove garlic, finely chopped
- 2 cups shelled and deveined shrimp (about one and one-quarter pounds)
- 3 cups water
- ½ teaspoon thyme
- ½ teaspoon Tabasco sauce, or to taste
- 2 cups uncooked rice
- ¼ cup chopped parsley
- ⅓ cup finely chopped scallions, including green part.

1. Season the chicken with salt and pepper and brown on all sides in the drippings or shortening in a heavy skillet. Remove chicken.

2. Sprinkle the flour over fat remaining in the skillet and cook, stirring, until roux turns light brown. Do not allow to burn.

3. Add the sausage or ham, the chicken, onions, green pepper, tomatoes, garlic and shrimp and cook, stirring, about ten minutes.

4. Add the water, one and one-half teaspoons salt, the thyme, Tabasco, one-half teaspoon pepper and the rice. Bring to a boil and then cover and let simmer about thirty minutes, or until the rice is tender. Stir in the parsley and scallions. Cook five minutes longer.

Yield: Eight servings.

Chicken Bog
SOUTH CAROLINA

1 five-pound to six-pound hen, cut into small serving pieces	2 tablespoons salt
Chicken broth	2 teaspoons freshly ground black pepper
4 cups uncooked rice	½ cup butter.

1. Place the hen pieces in a deep casserole and add water to cover. Bring to a boil, cover and simmer until tender, about one hour.
2. Reserve the chicken and measure the broth in the casserole. Add enough broth to make eight cups.
3. Bring to a boil and add the rice, salt, pepper and butter. Cook, covered, very slowly until rice is tender, about forty-five to sixty minutes, stirring twice during cooking.
4. Add reserved chicken and reheat.

Yield: One dozen to fourteen servings.

Brunswick Stew
NORTH CAROLINA

- 1 three-pound chicken, cut into serving pieces
- 8 cups fresh or canned chicken broth (or use half chicken broth and half water)
- Salt and freshly ground black pepper to taste
- ¼ cup diced uncooked bacon
- 1 cup chopped onions
- 2 cups peeled ripe tomatoes or one one-pound-three-ounce can tomatoes, drained
- 2 cups peeled, diced raw potatoes
- 2 cups fresh baby lima beans or one ten-ounce package frozen
- 2 cups corn kernels, cut from the cob (about eight ears)
- 1 tablespoon Worcestershire sauce, or to taste
- 2 tablespoons butter.

1. Place the chicken in a kettle and add the broth. Bring to a boil and add salt and pepper. Simmer until chicken is tender, about one hour, skimming surface frequently to remove fat and foam. Remove chicken from kettle, but let stock continue to boil to reduce slightly.

2. When chicken pieces are cool enough to handle, remove meat from bones. Discard bones and skin.

3. Return meat to kettle and add the bacon, onions, tomatoes, potatoes and lima beans. Simmer one hour, skimming surface as necessary to remove all fat. Stir frequently so stew does not stick.

4. Add the corn and cook ten minutes longer. When done, stew should be a thickened mass. Stir in the Worcestershire and butter. Serve piping hot.

Yield: Six to eight servings.

This rich hearty stew was originally made in huge caldrons over an open fire and included rabbit, squirrel and other game.

Kentucky Burgoo
KENTUCKY

2	pounds beef shank	3	carrots, cut into one-quarter-inch slices
2	pounds pork shank		
2	pounds veal shank	6	tomatoes, peeled and chopped
2	pounds breast of lamb		
1	four-pound stewing chicken	2	cups corn kernels
1	tablespoon salt	2	cups lima or butter beans
	Freshly ground black pepper to taste	1	green pepper, seeded and diced
3	quarts water, approximately	2	hot red pepper pods, chopped
3	large onions, chopped	2	cups sliced okra
3	large potatoes, diced	½	cup chopped parsley

1. Place the beef, pork, veal, lamb, chicken, salt, pepper and enough water to cover in a large kettle. Bring to a boil and skim.

2. Partially cover the kettle and simmer over low heat forty-five minutes to an hour, or until the chicken is tender. Remove the chicken and set aside.

3. Continue to cook the remaining meats until they are tender, about one-and-one-half hours. Remove the meats and set with the chicken.

4. Add the remaining ingredients, except for the parsley, to the kettle. Cover and simmer one hour, or until the vegetables are tender. Add more water if necessary.

5. Meanwhile, remove the chicken and meats from the bones and

cube. When the vegetables are tender, return the cube meat back to the kettle and reheat. Add the parsley and salt and pepper if needed.
Yield: Eight to ten servings.

Deep-Fried Frogs' Legs
LOUISIANA

- 12 pairs large frogs' legs
- Milk to cover
- Fat for deep-frying
- Flour for dredging
- Salt and freshly ground black pepper to taste
- Lemon wedges
- Tartar sauce (page 259).

1. Soak the frogs' legs in the milk one hour or so.
2. Heat the fat for deep-frying (about 375 degrees).
3. Drain the frogs' legs, but do not dry. Dredge them in flour seasoned with salt and pepper and drop them, one pair at a time, into the hot fat. Cook until golden brown, turning once. Drain on paper towels and serve with lemon wedges and tartar sauce.

Yield: Four to six servings.

Braised Frogs' Legs with Sherry
TENNESSEE

- 18 pairs frogs' legs
- Salt and freshly ground black pepper
- Flour for dredging
- 8 tablespoons butter
- 2 tablespoons shortening
- 1¼ cups beef broth
- ¼ cup dry sherry
- 1 tablespoon chopped fresh parsley.

1. Preheat the oven to 400 degrees.
2. Place the frogs' legs in a mixing bowl and add cold water. Drain well and sprinkle with salt and pepper.
3. Dredge the frogs' legs, one pair at a time, in flour.
4. Heat the butter and shortening in a heavy iron skillet and, when skillet is very hot, add the frogs' legs. Cook until golden brown on one side. Turn and cook until golden brown on the other. Transfer the frogs' legs to a baking dish and add the broth and sherry to the fat remaining in the skillet. Bring to a boil, stirring with a wooden spoon. Pour this over the frogs' legs and bake twenty minutes. Sprinkle with the parsley and serve.

Yield: Six servings.

Spit-Roasted Saddle of Venison
TENNESSEE

- ½ cup wine vinegar
- 2 carrots, coarsely chopped
- 1 onion, chopped
- 3 sprigs parsley
- 1 clove garlic, crushed
- 10 juniper berries
- 1 sprig fresh rosemary
- 1 teaspoon crushed sage
- 1 five-pound to six-pound saddle of young venison
- 1 bottle dry red wine
- Salt and freshly ground black pepper to taste
- Cranberry and horseradish sauce (page 264).

1. Day before, combine the vinegar, carrots, onion, parsley, garlic, juniper berries, rosemary and sage. Bring just to a boil and pour the mixture over the venison. Add the wine, salt and pepper and let stand overnight.

2. Next day, drain the venison and wipe it dry, reserving marinade. Sprinkle venison with salt and pepper. Place on a spit and roast, basting with the marinade, until dark brown on the surface and rare within. This will require about thirty minutes to one hour, depending on size of venison and proximity to the heat. Serve with cranberry and horseradish sauce.

Yield: Ten to one dozen servings.

Pressed Duck
TENNESSEE

- 6 wild ducks
- ¾ cup olive oil
- 1 large onion, coarsely chopped
- 3 tablespoons dry red wine, preferably a Burgundy or Bordeaux
- 3 tablespoons cognac
- 4 tablespoons sweet butter, melted
- ¼ teaspoon cayenne pepper
- 1½ teaspoons freshly grated horseradish
- 3 tablespoons Cointreau or other orange-flavored liqueur
- 12 slices bacon
- Cooked wild rice.

1. With a sharp knife, carefully trim away the fleshy meat from either side of the breast of each duck. From six ducks this will yield twelve portions. Leave the skin on each portion. Place the meat in a mixing bowl and add the oil and onion. Let stand at least two hours.

2. Chop up the carcasses of the ducks with a cleaver and warm the carcasses in a skillet, stirring frequently. Place the carcasses in a duck press and press to extract as much liquid as possible from the meat and bones. This should yield a scant cup. Bring the extracted liquid to a boil.

3. To the duck juice add the wine, cognac, butter, cayenne, horseradish and Cointreau. Simmer five minutes.

4. Prepare a charcoal fire.

5. Remove the duck breasts from the oil and onion and wrap each portion in a slice of bacon. Skewer with toothpicks. Place the breasts, thus prepared, on the grill six inches away from the heat. For rare duck, cook four minutes on each side; for medium, seven minutes on each side; for well done, ten minutes on each side. Serve with wild rice and the duck sauce.

Yield: Six servings.

Wild Ducks with Madeira
LOUISIANA

4	wild ducks		Piquet's Wild Game Sauce, if available
	Olive oil or melted butter		
	Salt and freshly ground black pepper	4	slices orange
		4	slices lemon
4	apples, peeled, cored and cut into eighths	2	ribs celery with leaves, quartered
4	onions, cut into eighths	½	cup Madeira wine
1	cup chopped celery	2	tablespoons flour
4	slices bacon, cut in half		Cooked wild rice
2	tablespoons A.1. Sauce or		Spiced red apples.

1. Preheat the oven to 275 degrees.

2. Clean the ducks well and rub them with the oil or butter. Sprinkle inside and outside with salt and pepper. Stuff the cavities with equal quantities of the apples, onions and chopped celery. Truss the ducks and place them side by side, breast up, in a roasting pan just large enough to hold them.

3. Arrange two pieces of the bacon on each breast and add water to the pan. There should be only about one-half inch of water around the ducks. Stir in the A.1. or Piquet Sauce and arrange the orange and lemon slices and the celery ribs around the ducks. Bake about three hours, basting occasionally, or until birds are tender.

4. Thirty minutes before ducks are done, remove the bacon strips and add the Madeira. Baste frequently.

5. When done, remove ducks to a serving platter and strain the juices. Blend the flour with about two tablespoons of the juices to make a paste. Stir this into the sauce, using a wire whisk, until sauce boils up and is thickened. Season to taste with salt and pepper and serve wild rice and spiced red apples with the ducks.

Yield: About eight servings.

Wild Duck Country Captain
ALABAMA

- ½ cup flour
- Salt and freshly ground black pepper to taste
- 1 two-and-one-half-pound wild duck or two smaller birds, cut into serving pieces
- 4 tablespoons butter
- ⅓ cup chopped onion
- ⅓ cup finely chopped green pepper
- 1 clove garlic, finely minced
- 1½ teaspoons curry powder
- ½ teaspoon dried thyme
- 2 cups Italian plum tomatoes
- 3 teaspoons dried currants
- ¼ cup toasted almonds
- Buttered rice
- Chopped parsley.

1. Combine the flour, salt and pepper and coat the duck pieces with the mixture.
2. Heat the butter in a large skillet and brown the duck pieces in it. Remove duck pieces and reserve.
3. Add the onion, green pepper, garlic, curry powder and thyme to the skillet and cook, stirring, until onion is golden brown. Add the tomatoes and duck pieces. Cover and cook forty minutes, or until duck is tender. Stir in the currants and almonds and serve with buttered rice tossed with chopped parsley.

Yield: Two to four servings.

Fresh Quail with Grits and Gravy
SOUTH CAROLINA

- 6 quail, skinned and split down the back
- Salted water
- Freshly ground black pepper
- Flour
- Fat or oil for frying
- 2½ cups water
- Salt
- Cooked grits.

1. Wash the quail in water and clean thoroughly. Soak in salted water to cover for three hours.
2. Drain quail and pat dry. Sprinkle with pepper, coat with flour and fry in one-half-inch depth of fat or oil heated in a heavy skillet.
3. Cook about twenty to thirty minutes, turning continuously, until birds have golden crust and are cooked through. Keep warm while making gravy.
4. Pour off all but two tablespoons of the fat from the skillet. Sprinkle fat in skillet with four tablespoons flour. Cook, stirring, one minute. Gradually stir in the two and one-half cups water. Bring to a boil, stirring. Season to taste with salt and pepper and serve over grits.

Yield: Six servings.

Braised Quail
GEORGIA

18	quail	½	green pepper, seeded and chopped
	Flour		
	Salt and freshly ground black pepper	2	cloves garlic, finely minced
		4	cups chicken broth
12	tablespoons butter	¼	cup dry red wine
2	scallions, including green part, chopped		White toast.

1. Preheat the oven to 350 degrees.
2. Coat the quail with a mixture of flour, salt and pepper.
3. Melt the butter in a large Dutch oven and brown four or five quail in it at a time. When all are golden brown, transfer to a roasting pan.
4. Add four tablespoons flour to the Dutch oven. Brown the flour over moderate heat, stirring constantly, but do not let the flour burn or it will have a bitter taste.
5. Add the scallions, green pepper and garlic and cook briefly, stirring. Add the broth, stirring rapidly, and the wine.
6. When the mixture is bubbling and well blended, pour it over the quail. Cover and bake twenty minutes. Reduce the oven heat to 325 degrees and cook until quail are thoroughly tender, one and one-half to two hours. Serve the quail on toast with the sauce separately.

Yield: Nine to eighteen servings.

Halidon Hill Potted Doves
SOUTH CAROLINA

6 doves	1 cup hot chicken broth or water, approximately
4 slices bacon	Flour for dredging
¼ cup finely minced onion	2½ tablespoons peanut oil, lard or butter.
6 slices toasted day-old white bread	
Salt and freshly ground black pepper	

1. Wipe the birds inside and outside with a damp cloth.
2. Cook the bacon in a skillet until crisp. Drain and crumble. Set aside.
3. Pour off all but one tablespoon of fat from the skillet and cook the onion in it, stirring, until onion is wilted. Crumble the toast and add it. Add salt and pepper to taste, the bacon and three-quarters cup of the broth or water. Use the mixture to stuff the birds.
4. Sprinkle the birds with salt and pepper and dredge in flour.
5. Heat the oil, lard or butter and brown the birds in it on all sides. The birds should be quite brown. Add the remaining broth to the skillet, cover closely and cook over low heat until tender, about twenty minutes or longer.

Yield: Three to six servings.

Doves Pontchartrain
LOUISIANA

12 dressed doves	Worcestershire sauce to taste
Salt and freshly ground black pepper	1 lemon, seeded and finely chopped
12 slices bacon	4 slices toast
Boiling chicken broth or water	Chopped parsley.

1. If desired, remove the legs and wings from the doves. Sprinkle the doves with salt and pepper and wrap each dove in a slice of bacon. Secure bacon with toothpicks.
2. Brown the bacon-wrapped doves on all sides in a kettle or casserole. When browned, pour off most of the fat. Add the boiling broth or water to a depth of one-half inch. Add Worcestershire and the lemon. Cover and simmer gently forty-five minutes.

3. Taste the sauce for seasoning. Arrange the ducks, three to a person, on the toast and sprinkle with parsley. Strain the sauce and serve it separately.
Yield: Four servings.

Frogs' Legs Omelet
LOUISIANA

12 pairs frogs' legs	½ cup dry white wine
2 tablespoons olive oil	Salt and freshly ground black pepper to taste
2 tablespoons butter	
½ cup finely chopped onion	¼ cup finely chopped mushrooms
1 small clove garlic, finely minced	
	12 eggs.

1. Rinse the frogs' legs in cold water and pat dry.
2. Heat half the oil and half the butter in an enamel or stainless steel skillet and cook half the onion in it until wilted. Add the garlic and cook briefly. Add the wine and simmer until reduced by half. Add frogs' legs, salt, pepper and the mushrooms. Add water to cover barely. Cover with aluminum foil and simmer until legs are tender. Remove frogs' legs and take the meat from the bones. Set aside. Cook the liquid in the skillet until liquid has a saucelike consistency.
3. Lightly beat the eggs until blended.
4. In a large omelet pan, heat remaining oil and butter. Add remaining onion and cook until wilted. Add the meat from the frogs' legs. Pour in eggs and cook until omelet is cooked on the bottom. Flip the omelet, using a spatula if necessary. Cook until the other side is set. Pour sauce over the omelet and cut it into wedges. Serve hot.
Yield: Six servings.

Baked Christmas Mushroom Omelet
ALABAMA

1 pound mushrooms	¼ cup dry sherry
4 tablespoons butter, melted	Salt and freshly ground black pepper to taste
8 eggs, separated	
3 tablespoons flour	¼ teaspoon cayenne pepper.
2 cups hot milk	

1. Preheat the oven to 350 degrees.
2. Brush the mushrooms with a little of the butter and broil them until done. Let cool. Slice the mushrooms.
3. Beat the egg yolks until light and lemon-colored. Beat the whites until stiff.
4. Place the flour in a mixing bowl and gradually add the hot milk, stirring rapidly with a wire whisk or beater. Add two tablespoons of the melted butter, the egg yolks, sherry, salt, pepper, cayenne and mushrooms. Fold in the whites and pour the mixture into a greased six-cup baking dish. Pour remaining butter on top and bake forty-five minutes.

Yield: Four servings.

Chipped Beef Rarebit
MISSISSIPPI

- 3 tablespoons butter
- 2 small jars (two and one-half ounces each) chipped beef
- 1 teaspoon prepared mustard, preferably Dijon or Düsseldorf
- 2 teaspoons Worcestershire sauce
- 1 teaspoon chili powder
- 4 cups Italian plum tomatoes
- Freshly ground black pepper to taste
- Tabasco sauce to taste (optional)
- 3 cups grated sharp Cheddar cheese
- 3 eggs, well beaten
- 4 slices buttered toast.

1. Heat the butter in a large saucepan. Pull the beef apart with the fingers and add beef to the butter. Cook, stirring, until meat frizzles. Add the mustard, Worcestershire, chili powder, tomatoes, pepper and Tabasco. Do not add salt. Simmer about thirty minutes to make a sauce.
2. Remove the sauce from the heat and stir in the cheese. When the cheese melts, add the eggs. Cook, stirring, just to the boiling point when the rarebit thickens. Do not boil or the eggs may curdle. Serve hot over toast.

Yield: Four servings.

Crackus
MISSISSIPPI

4	tablespoons butter	¾	pound sharp Cheddar cheese, grated
4	tablespoons flour		
½	cup milk	1	small jar (two and one-half ounces) dried chipped beef
2½	cups canned tomatoes, chopped with their liquid		
		2	hard-cooked eggs, chopped
½	teaspoon dry mustard	4	cups cooked rice.

1. Melt the butter and blend in the flour. Gradually stir in the milk and tomatoes. Bring to a boil, stirring.
2. Add the mustard and stir in the cheese until it melts.
3. Fold in the beef and hard-cooked eggs and reheat, but do not boil. Serve over rice.

Yield: Four servings.

Cheese Custard
NORTH CAROLINA

12	saltine crackers, crumbled	2	cups milk
1	cup grated Cheddar cheese	¼	cup butter, melted
3	eggs, lightly beaten	⅛	teaspoon cayenne pepper.

1. Place the crackers in bottom of a greased one-quart casserole. Sprinkle with the cheese. Combine the eggs, milk, butter and cayenne and pour over. Let stand thirty minutes.
2. Preheat the oven to 400 degrees.
3. Bake ten minutes, lower the oven heat to 275 degrees and bake about twenty minutes longer, or until custard is set.

Yield: Four servings.

No-Fail Welsh Rabbit
ARKANSAS

2	tablespoons butter	½	teaspoon dry mustard
2	tablespoons flour	1	tablespoon Worcestershire sauce, or to taste
1	cup stale beer		
2	cups cubed sharp Cheddar cheese		Salt to taste
			Cayenne pepper to taste
2	eggs, well beaten	4	slices toast.

1. Melt the butter and add the flour. Stir in the beer. When the mixture is thickened and smooth, add the cheese, stirring.

2. When the cheese is melted, add the eggs and cook just until the eggs thicken. Do not overcook or the eggs will scramble. Add the mustard, Worcestershire, salt and cayenne. Serve with or on toast.

Yield: Four servings.

Cheese Grits Casserole
KENTUCKY

5 cups water	½ cup butter
1 cup hominy grits	1 egg, separated
½ pound sharp Cheddar cheese, grated	1 teaspoon salt.

1. Bring the water to a boil and gradually stir in the grits. Simmer, covered, twenty-five to thirty minutes, stirring often.

2. Stir in the cheese and butter until melted. Spoon a little of the hot mixture onto the egg yolk, return to the bulk of the mixture, add the salt and mix. Cool to room temperature.

3. Preheat the oven to 350 degrees.

4. Beat the egg white until stiff but not dry and fold into the cooled mixture. Spoon mixture into a greased baking dish and bake, covered, forty minutes. Remove cover, turn oven heat to 375 degrees and bake until top of casserole is slightly browned.

Yield: Six servings.

Quick Big Hominy with Sausage
SOUTH CAROLINA

4 cups corn kernels	2 pounds sausage meat, made into patties.
1 tablespoon baking soda	
½ cup butter	

1. Cover the corn with hot water and let soak overnight.

2. Next morning, drain, cover with more hot water and add the baking

soda. Soak until husks come off and then rinse with several lots of cold water, or until all husks are removed.

3. Place corn in a kettle, cover with hot water, bring to a boil and cook until tender.

4. Drain the corn and toss with the butter. Fry the sausage patties until brown and well cooked and serve around the hot corn on a platter.

Yield: Eight servings.

Vegetables, Main Dish Accompaniments and Salads

Tomatoes and Green Beans au Gratin
ALABAMA

- 2 slices bacon, chopped, or thinly sliced salt pork, chopped
- 1½ cups chopped onions
- 3 medium-size tomatoes, peeled and chopped
- Salt and freshly ground black pepper to taste
- 1 pound green beans
- Salted water
- ½ cup heavy cream
- 1 cup freshly grated Parmesan cheese.

1. Preheat the oven to 350 degrees.
2. Cook the bacon or salt pork and, when the fat is rendered, add the onions. Cook until onions are wilted and add the tomatoes. Bring to a boil and simmer fifteen minutes, stirring occasionally. Add salt and pepper.

3. Remove the tip ends from the beans and break into two-inch lengths. Simmer in salted water to cover about ten minutes until crisp-tender. Drain well. Scatter the beans over a buttered flat baking dish.

4. Bring the cream to a boil and add to the tomato sauce. Pour this over the beans and sprinkle with the cheese. Bake just until thoroughly heated. Glaze lightly under a broiler flame and serve immediately.

Yield: About six servings.

Green Bean Casserole
FLORIDA

1½	pounds green beans, picked over and cut into one-and-one-half-inch lengths (there should be about three cups)	¾	cup chopped onion
		¾	cup chopped green pepper
		¼	cup chopped pimentos
		2	cups homemade or canned well-seasoned tomato sauce
1	tablespoon oil		Tabasco sauce to taste (optional)
3	tablespoons butter		
1	clove garlic, finely minced	1	cup grated Cheddar cheese.

1. Preheat the oven to 350 degrees.

2. Rinse and drain the beans and put them in a four-cup saucepan with cover. Add the oil. Do not add water or salt. Cover the beans and cook them over medium heat, shaking the pan occasionally so the beans do not stick. Cook five to ten minutes, depending on the age of the beans, until they are crisp-tender. Pour beans into a baking dish.

3. Meanwhile, melt the butter and cook the garlic, onion and green pepper in it until the onion is translucent. Stir occasionally.

4. Add the pimentos, tomato sauce and Tabasco if desired to the onion mixture. Simmer briefly and pour the sauce over the beans. Sprinkle with the cheese and bake twenty-five minutes, or until casserole is thoroughly hot and cheese is melted and bubbling.

Yield: About six servings.

Green Beans, Southern Style
GEORGIA

2	pounds green beans	1	small hot pepper (bird's eye peppers are best).
1	ham hock		
2	teaspoons salt		

1. Wash the beans, cut off the ends and snap beans in two.
2. Place the ham hock in a large kettle, cover with water and boil fifteen minutes. Add beans, the salt and hot pepper and more water almost to cover the beans.
3. Bring to a boil, cover and boil forty minutes. Add more water if necessary. Turn off heat and let rest several hours.
4. Simmer thirty-five minutes longer before serving. Serve beans with pieces of ham from hock.
Yield: Six to eight servings.

Green Beans with Brown Butter Sauce
GEORGIA

¼ cup butter	1 pound green beans, cooked and drained
4 tablespoons flour	
2 cups chicken broth	¼ cup chopped pecans.
1 bay leaf	
½ cup grated sharp Cheddar cheese	

1. Brown the butter lightly in a heavy saucepan, but do not allow to burn. Add the flour and gradually stir in the broth.
2. Add the bay leaf and bring to a boil, stirring. Cook one minute. Stir in the cheese until melted. Remove bay leaf.
3. Arrange the beans in a serving dish and pour sauce over. Sprinkle with the pecans.
Yield: Six servings.

Frijoles Negros (Savory Black Beans)
FLORIDA

1 pound dried black beans	½ medium-size onion, coarsely chopped
¼ cup olive oil	
1 clove garlic, unpeeled and mashed	1 cube (two inches) salt pork
	Salt to taste
½ sweet green pepper, coarsely chopped	Fluffy rice.

1. Soak the beans in water to cover for twenty-four hours. Drain; place in a kettle. Add water to come one inch above the top of the beans.

2. Add the oil, garlic, green pepper, onion and salt pork. Bring to a boil and cook for one hour. Add salt and simmer for about thirty minutes longer. If desired, an extra tablespoon of oil may be added before serving. Serve hot in soup plates with fluffy rice.

Yield: About six servings.

Black Beans with Rum
LOUISIANA

2 cups dried black beans	Freshly ground black pepper to taste
2 medium-size onions, coarsely chopped	1 bay leaf
2 cloves garlic, finely minced	1 tablespoon chopped parsley
3 tablespoons bacon drippings	½ teaspoon oregano
3 ribs celery, coarsely chopped	¼ cup dark rum
1 carrot, cut into fine dice	1 cup sour cream.
1 tablespoon salt, or more to taste	

1. Soak the beans overnight in water to cover or add enough water to cover the beans to a depth of one inch, bring to a boil and cook two minutes. Let stand one hour.

2. Cook the onions and garlic in the bacon drippings until onions are wilted. Add to the beans. Add the celery, carrot, salt, pepper, bay leaf, parsley and oregano. Cover and simmer until beans are nearly tender. Add more water if necessary as the beans cook.

3. Meanwhile, preheat the oven to 350 degrees.

4. Turn the beans into a casserole and add half the rum. Cover and bake until beans are thoroughly tender. Just before serving, stir in remaining rum. Serve beans with the sour cream.

Yield: Six servings.

One of the most famous dishes in Louisiana is red beans with rice. The beans are not kidney beans, as many suppose, but kidney beans make an acceptable substitute.

Red Beans with Rice I
LOUISIANA

2 cups dried red beans or kidney beans	½ cup bacon drippings
6 cups water	1 onion
	Hot cooked rice.

1. Wash the beans well until water is clear. Drain. Put the beans in a large bowl and add the six cups water.
2. Heat the bacon drippings in a large kettle or Dutch oven and cook the onion in it gently, stirring occasionally, until onion is amber-colored. Add the beans with their water and bring to a boil. Partially cover and cook three to four hours, or until beans are thoroughly tender and mash easily. If necessary, add more water as the beans cook and stir beans occasionally to prevent them from sticking. When ready to thicken, mash a few beans to thicken the lot. Serve over hot cooked rice.
Yield: Six servings.

Red Beans with Rice II
LOUISIANA

1 cup dried red beans, soaked overnight	1 clove garlic, finely chopped
3 cups water	1 rib celery, chopped
Salt and freshly ground black pepper to taste	¼ cup finely chopped parsley
	1 bay leaf, broken into pieces
3 tablespoons bacon drippings or one small ham hock	1 cup rice, cooked according to package directions.
1 small onion, studded with two whole cloves	

1. Drain the beans and place in a heavy kettle with the water, salt, pepper and bacon drippings or ham hock. Bring to a boil and simmer one and one-half hours. Add the onion, garlic, celery, parsley and bay leaf. Return to a boil and cook one hour longer.
2. Serve on hot rice.
Yield: Four servings.

Fresh black-eyed peas when available are delicious and can be cooked until tender in boiling salted water to cover with bacon, salt pork or bits of ham. The dried black-eyed peas are also excellent.

Black-Eyed Peas
ALABAMA

1 pound dried black-eyed peas	Salt and freshly ground black pepper to taste
¼ pound salt pork	
1 onion, studded with two whole cloves	2 tablespoons grated lemon rind.

1. Day before, place the peas in a bowl and add the salt pork and water to cover to a depth of one inch. Let stand overnight.

2. Next day, drain the peas and salt pork and put both in a large pot with eight cups water. Add the onion, salt and pepper and bring to a boil. Simmer two hours, or until peas are tender. If necessary, add more water as the peas cook to keep them from burning. When ready to serve, stir in the lemon rind.

Yield: About six servings.

Note: A ham bone may be cooked with the peas in place of the salt pork.

Hopping John or Black-Eyed Peas and Rice
SOUTH CAROLINA

3 cups dried black-eyed peas	Salt to taste
½ pound salt pork	Pinch of crushed red pepper
1 onion, chopped	1 cup uncooked rice.
1 bay leaf	

1. Soak the peas overnight in water to cover. Drain.

2. Cook the salt pork in four cups water one-half hour. Add the peas, onion, bay leaf, salt and red pepper and cook one hour.

3. Add the rice and simmer very slowly until rice and peas are soft. Add more water if needed and adjust seasonings to taste.

Yield: Eight servings.

Cabbage Casserole
NORTH CAROLINA

3	cups shredded cabbage	1	cup milk
	Boiling water	⅓	cup heavy cream
1	cup shredded celery	1	egg, lightly beaten
¾	cup soft bread crumbs	2	tablespoons butter
	Salt and freshly ground black pepper to taste	¼	cup freshly grated Parmesan or Cheddar cheese.

1. Preheat the oven to 450 degrees.
2. Place the cabbage in a saucepan and cover with boiling water. Let stand about five minutes. Drain and blend cabbage with the celery.
3. Make a layer of the vegetables in a greased one-and-one-half-quart casserole. Sprinkle with a third of the bread crumbs. Make another layer of vegetables, another of crumbs and another of vegetables. Sprinkle each layer lightly with salt and pepper.
4. Blend the milk, cream and egg; strain over the casserole. Sprinkle with remaining crumbs and dot with butter. Sprinkle with the cheese. Bake fifteen minutes.

Yield: Four servings.

Celery in Cheese Sauce
FLORIDA

4	cups celery, cut into one-inch lengths	½	cup heavy cream
	Salt to taste		freshly ground black pepper to taste
1½	cups chicken broth	¾	cup grated sharp Cheddar cheese
2	celery rib tops with leaves		
3	tablespoons butter		Soft buttered or dry bread crumbs.
3	tablespoons flour		

1. Preheat the oven to 350 degrees.
2. Place the cut-up celery in a saucepan and add water to cover and salt. Bring to a boil, simmer until crisp-tender and drain.
3. Combine the broth with the celery tops and bring to a boil. Strain and reserve the liquid.
4. Melt the butter and stir in the flour with a wire whisk. Add the

strained broth, stirring rapidly with the whisk. When thickened and smooth, add the cream. Simmer five minutes and add salt and pepper. Add the cheese and, when melted, add the celery. Pour into a one-and-one-half-quart casserole, sprinkle with bread crumbs and bake fifteen to twenty minutes.

Yield: Six to eight servings.

Celery with Egg and Lemon Sauce
TENNESSEE

1	cup finely chopped onion		Salt and freshly ground black pepper to taste
4	tablespoons butter		
1	two-pound stalk of celery	2	egg yolks, lightly beaten
2	cups fresh or canned chicken broth		Juice of one lemon.

1. In a large saucepan, cook the onion in the butter until wilted.

2. Trim off the tops of the celery and discard or reserve for soups. Trim off the bottoms of the celery ribs; then cut the ribs of celery into two-inch lengths. Add to the saucepan. Add the broth, salt and pepper and bring to a boil. Simmer until the celery is tender, about half an hour.

3. Combine the egg yolks and lemon juice and stir in a little of the hot broth. Add this to the saucepan, stirring rapidly. Continue stirring and cooking until slightly thickened. Do not overcook or boil or the sauce will curdle. Cover and let stand five minutes.

Yield: Four to six servings.

Corn Oysters
FLORIDA

8	ears corn	¼	cup sifted flour.
3	eggs, separated		
	Salt and freshly ground black pepper to taste		

1. Slit the kernels of the uncooked corn and scrape off the cob with the back of a knife.

2. Beat the egg whites until stiff, adding a pinch of salt.

3. Beat the egg yolks until light and lemon-colored. Add the corn, salt, pepper and flour.

4. Stir the mixture until smooth and fold in the beaten egg whites. Drop the mixture by tablespoonfuls onto a greased skillet or griddle. Cook on both sides until golden brown.

Yield: Six servings.

Francille's Stewed Corn
ARKANSAS

- 12 ears corn, approximately
- ¼ cup bacon drippings
- 2 tablespoons butter
- 3 cups milk, approximately
- 1½ teaspoons salt
- 2 tablespoons light brown sugar
- ¼ teaspoon freshly ground black pepper.

1. Cut off the corn cob tips and scrape the cobs to make one quart of kernels.

2. Heat the bacon drippings and butter in a heavy skillet. Add one cup milk, the salt, brown sugar and pepper.

3. Bring to a boil and add the corn. Turn heat down and simmer gently one and one-quarter hours, stirring frequently with a pancake turner to prevent sticking. Add remaining milk as needed to thin corn.

Yield: Six to eight servings.

Butter-Fried Corn
FLORIDA

- 10 ears corn
- 4 tablespoons butter
- Salt and freshly ground black pepper to taste.

1. Shuck the corn and carefully remove any bits of tassel that remain.

2. Using a sharp knife or a corn scraper, cut off the kernels, not too close to the cob. Gently scrape off kernels remaining on cob.

3. Heat the butter in a saucepan and add the scraped corn. Cook, stirring, five to ten minutes and season with salt and pepper.

Yield: About four servings.

Clara's Eggplant
TENNESSEE

2 medium-size eggplants	2 eggs, lightly beaten
Salt to taste	⅓ cup heavy cream
6 tablespoons butter	¼ teaspoon nutmeg
½ pound chicken livers	Cayenne pepper to taste
Freshly ground black pepper to taste	½ cup soft bread crumbs
½ pound mushrooms, sliced	½ cup freshly grated Parmesan or Cheddar cheese.

1. Preheat the oven to 350 degrees.
2. Select firm eggplants with shiny skins. Peel the eggplants and cut them into one-inch cubes. Place the cubes in a saucepan and add cold water to cover. Add salt and bring to a boil. Simmer just until the eggplant is tender. Do not overcook. Drain the eggplant immediately.
3. Meanwhile, melt two tablespoons of the butter in a skillet and add the chicken livers. Sprinkle with salt and pepper and cook, turning the livers occasionally, until done. Remove and reserve the livers. Add two more tablespoons of the butter to the skillet and cook the mushrooms in it, stirring frequently, until they give up their juices. Cook until most of the liquid evaporates.
4. Chop the eggplant and the livers and combine them. Stir in the mushrooms.
5. Beat together the eggs, cream, nutmeg, cayenne, salt and pepper. Stir this into the eggplant mixture.
6. Pour the mixture into a buttered one-quart casserole. Sprinkle with the bread crumbs and cheese and dot with remaining butter. Bake twenty to thirty minutes.

Yield: Six to eight servings.

Eggplant Soufflé
FLORIDA

- 1 medium-size eggplant
- Boiling salted water
- 2 tablespoons butter
- 3 tablespoons flour
- 1 cup milk
- ½ cup grated sharp Cheddar cheese
- ¾ cup soft bread crumbs
- ¼ cup finely chopped scallions, including green part
- Cayenne pepper to taste
- 2 tablespoons homemade or canned tomato sauce
- Salt and freshly ground black pepper to taste
- 3 eggs, separated.

1. Preheat the oven to 350 degrees.
2. Peel the eggplant and cut it into cubes. Add boiling salted water to cover and simmer just until tender. Drain well and mash the eggplant.
3. Melt butter and, with a wire whisk, stir in the flour. When blended, add the milk all at once, stirring vigorously with the whisk. Remove the mixture from the heat and stir in the cheese and bread crumbs. Add the scallions, cayenne, tomato sauce, salt and pepper. Add the egg yolks and return to the heat. Bring just to a boil.
4. Beat the egg whites until stiff and fold them into the mixture. Pour the mixture into a buttered one-and-one-half-quart soufflé dish and set the dish in a pan of hot water. Place on top of the stove and bring the water in the pan just to a boil. Place in the oven and bake thirty to forty minutes.

Yield: Four servings.

Stuffed Eggplant
MISSISSIPPI

- 2 medium-size eggplants
- Salt to taste
- 8 tablespoons butter
- 1 rib celery, finely chopped
- 1 small onion, finely chopped
- 3 eggs, lightly beaten
- Freshly ground black pepper to taste
- 1 cup soft bread crumbs.

1. Trim off and discard the stem ends of the eggplants. Otherwise, do not peel. Place the eggplants in a large saucepan and add water to cover and salt. Bring to a boil and simmer until eggplants are tender, about thirty minutes, depending on the size of the vegetables. Drain and let cool.

2. Preheat the oven to 400 degrees.

3. Melt six tablespoons of the butter in a skillet and add the celery and onion. Cook briefly, stirring, until vegetables are tender.

4. Split the eggplants lengthwise in half and carefully scoop out the insides, leaving the casings intact. Add the eggplant pulp to the skillet and mash pulp. Cook briefly and add the eggs, salt and pepper. Cook, stirring, until mixture thickens slightly.

5. Stir in all but two tablespoons of the bread crumbs. Spoon the filling into the eggplant casings. Dot with the remaining butter and sprinkle with the remaining crumbs. Bake about fifteen minutes, or until thoroughly heated and golden brown on top.

Yield: Six servings.

Hunt and Polo Eggplant Casserole
TENNESSEE

2	eggplants, peeled and cubed		Nutmeg to taste
	Boiling salted water		Salt and freshly ground black pepper to taste
½	pound chicken livers		
	Melted butter	½	cup soft bread crumbs
2	eggs	½	cup grated mild Cheddar cheese.
½	cup heavy cream		
6	tablespoons butter		
½	pound mushrooms, thinly sliced		

1. Preheat the oven to 350 degrees.

2. Drop the eggplant cubes into boiling salted water to cover. Bring to a boil and simmer just until eggplant is tender. Drain well and mash.

3. Brush the chicken livers with melted butter and place them under the broiler. Cook, turning once, until they are done. Let cool slightly and chop fine. Add them to the eggplant.

4. Beat the eggs with the cream and stir this into the eggplant mixture.

5. Heat two tablespoons of the butter and cook the mushrooms in it, stirring, until they are wilted and most of the liquid evaporates. Add the mushrooms to the eggplant. Add nutmeg, salt and pepper. The mixture will be rather liquid before baking. Turn the mixture into a one-quart casserole.

Sprinkle with the bread crumbs and cheese. Melt the remaining butter and pour it over all. Bake twenty to thirty minutes.
Yield: Six to eight servings.

Homemade Hominy
SOUTH CAROLINA

2 tablespoons lye	1 gallon boiling water
Cold water	2 quarts corn kernels.

1. Put the lye in an iron kettle. Add two cups cold water and stir with a wooden paddle to dissolve.
2. Add boiling water and stir. Add the corn and bring to a boil. Boil twenty-five to forty minutes, stirring all the time, and add more boiling water if corn starts to stick.
3. After twenty-five minutes, spoon some corn into a bowl of cold water and, if the part of the kernel where it was attached to the cob (the eyes) falls off, it is ready to wash.
4. Fill kettle with cold water, stir well and pour off all the water. Repeat the washing and draining five times. The stirring is important because this is what loosens the eyes.
5. Cover corn with cold water and bring to a boil. Drain and repeat four times. Add more cold water, bring to a boil again and boil three to four hours, or until corn swells to maximum. Add water as necessary.
Yield: About two and one-half quarts big hominy.

Fried Hominy Grits
GEORGIA

2½ teaspoons salt		Bacon drippings or lard
5 cups boiling water		Flour
1 cup hominy grits	2	eggs
¼ cup blanched sliced almonds	2	tablespoons water.

1. Day before, add two teaspoons of salt to the boiling water and add the grits gradually, stirring constantly. Cook over low heat, stirring frequently, thirty to forty minutes.
2. Stir in the almonds and let mixture cool to warm.

3. Pack the warm grits into straight-sided iced tea glasses that have been rinsed out with cold water. Chill overnight.

4. Next day, loosen around the grits with a knife and allow to unmold. Cut into one-half-inch-thick circles.

5. Heat the bacon drippings or lard in a heavy iron skillet.

6. Dip the circles in flour and then in the eggs combined with the remaining salt and two tablespoons water.

7. Fry the circles in the hot fat until browned on both sides.

Yield: About twenty circles; five servings.

Sarah's Oando
TENNESSEE

½ cup hominy grits, cooked according to package directions in a double boiler	2 tablespoons butter
	½ teaspoon salt
	1½ cups boiling milk
1 cup yellow corn meal	2 eggs, well beaten.

1. Preheat the oven to 350 degrees.

2. Combine the cooked grits with the corn meal, butter and salt. Pour the milk over and stir to mix.

3. Stir a little of the hot mixture into the eggs. Return all to the bulk of the mixture. Pour into a greased casserole and bake forty to sixty minutes, or until well browned.

Yield: Six servings.

Note: This is similar to the Awendaw bread of South Carolina.

Hominy and Bean Cakes
SOUTH CAROLINA

Bacon drippings	1 cup big hominy, ground
1 tablespoon flour	1 cup cooked red kidney beans, ground
½ cup milk	
1 teaspoon salt	Cayenne pepper to taste.

1. Melt one tablespoon bacon drippings and blend in the flour. Gradually stir in the milk and bring to a boil, stirring. Add the salt.

2. Add the hominy and beans to the sauce and add cayenne to taste (mixture should be hot). Form mixture into cakes.
3. Heat bacon drippings in a heavy skillet and brown the cakes in it on both sides.
Yield: Four servings.

Baked Hominy and Tomatoes
ARKANSAS

3 cups canned or homecooked hominy grits	¼ cup grated sharp Cheddar cheese
1 tablespoon butter	½ teaspoon salt
2 cups canned tomatoes or tomato puree	¼ teaspoon freshly ground black pepper.

1. Preheat the oven to 375 degrees.
2. Combine the hominy, butter, tomatoes and cheese. Add the salt and pepper and pour into an oiled baking dish or casserole.
3. Bake about forty-five minutes.
Yield: Eight servings.

Grits Soufflé
ALABAMA

4 cups cooked grits	Salt to taste
2 cups milk	8 eggs, separated.

1. The grits should be cooked according to package directions. When grits are done, let them cool to room temperature.
2. Preheat the oven to 350 degrees.
3. Bring the milk just to a boil and stir it into the grits. Add salt. Beat the egg yolks and stir them into the grits mixture.
4. Whip the egg whites until stiff and fold them into the mixture. Butter a two-quart baking dish not more than six inches high and pour the mixture into it. Set the dish in a pan of hot water and bake forty-five minutes to one hour. Serve immediately.
Yield: Eight to one dozen servings.

There are three sorts of garden greens that are frequently associated with Southern cooking. These are mustard greens, turnip greens and collard greens. Mustard greens and turnip greens are the more delicate of the three. Collard greens are frequently tough but, for those who enjoy them, they are delicious. In many Southern homes the greens are cooked for several hours before serving.

Mustard Greens, Turnip Greens and Collard Greens
MISSISSIPPI

- 3 pounds mustard greens, turnip greens or collard greens
- 1 onion
- ½ pound salt pork (see note)
- Salt and freshly ground black pepper to taste.

1. Trim the greens and discard hard stems. Wash the greens in several changes of cold water. Put greens in a large pot. If the greens are young and tender, they may be cooked in the water that clings to their leaves. Or add two cups of water to the kettle. Add the remaining ingredients and bring to a boil.

2. Simmer just until greens are tender or cook them one hour or longer. Traditionally, the greens are served with corn bread.

Yield: Six to eight servings.

Note: If desired, cook the salt pork in four cups water until meat is almost tender. This will add flavor to the water. Then add the greens and cook until tender.

Southern-Style Turnip Greens
ARKANSAS

Pick turnip greens carefully. Remove all large, tough stems and brown leaves. Wash thoroughly in several changes of water. Salt may be added to first wash water if greens appear "buggy" to make them turn loose from the leaves, or the individual leaves may be held under running water.

Put the greens into a heavy pan with a tight-fitting cover. Add water to half cover the greens and a ham hock or piece of salt pork. Cover and cook slowly two to three hours. Extra bacon drippings can be added near end of cooking if desired. Check for seasoning before serving.

Mixed Greens with Corn Bread Dumplings
ARKANSAS

2	pounds turnip greens	2	teaspoons sugar
2	pounds mustard greens	1½	cups white corn meal
2½	quarts water	¼	cup flour
1	onion, quartered	1	cup boiling water, approximately.
1	pound salt pork, cubed		
	Salt and freshly ground black pepper		

1. Tear off and discard any tough stems from the greens. If the greens are freshly picked and young, this may not be necessary. In any event, wash the greens in several changes of cold water. Drain.

2. Bring the two and one-half quarts water to a boil in a large kettle and add the onion and salt pork. Simmer thirty minutes and add the greens and salt and pepper to taste. Add one teaspoon of the sugar and simmer about two hours.

3. Meanwhile, combine the corn meal, flour, one teaspoon salt and the remaining sugar in a mixing bowl. Slowly add the boiling water, stirring. Add just enough water to make a stiff, manageable mixture.

4. Wet the palms of the hands, break off bits of corn meal dough the size of walnuts and shape into balls. Drop the balls into the boiling greens. Cover and continue cooking thirty minutes.

Yield: Four or more servings.

Note: Condiments to be served with this dish might include pepper vinegar, malt vinegar, chopped green onions, crumbled crisp bacon and chopped hot green peppers.

Assorted Greens
VIRGINIA

4	pounds collard, turnip or mustard greens, or mixed		Pinch of crushed red pepper
½	pound salt pork		Salt to taste
4	cups cold water	1	onion, minced.

1. Remove large stems from greens and wash greens thoroughly.
2. Put all ingredients in a large pot and boil one to one and one-half hours, or until tender.
3. Drain greens and chop them rather fine. Serve with salt pork, sliced.
Yield: About eight servings.

Mushrooms au Gratin
VIRGINIA

- 3 tablespoons butter
- 2 teaspoons fresh lemon juice
- 1 pound mushrooms, thinly sliced
- 2 tablespoons finely chopped scallions, including green part
- Salt and freshly ground black pepper to taste
- ½ cup milk
- ½ cup heavy cream
- ¼ teaspoon nutmeg
- 2 tablespoons flour
- ⅓ cup soft bread crumbs
- ⅓ cup freshly grated Swiss cheese or Parmesan cheese.

1. Heat one and one-half tablespoons of the butter in a one-quart saucepan and add the lemon juice and mushrooms. Cover closely and cook, shaking the pan, until mushrooms have wilted and given up most of their juices.
2. Add the scallions, salt, pepper, milk and cream and bring to a boil. Add the nutmeg.
3. Blend the flour with the remaining butter, kneading with the fingers. Add mixture, bit by bit, to the mushroom mixture, stirring constantly. When the sauce is thickened, pour the creamed mushrooms into an ovenproof dish and sprinkle with a mixture of the bread crumbs and cheese. Brown under the broiler and serve very hot.
Yield: Four to six servings.

Fried Okra
SOUTH CAROLINA

- 1 pound tender okra
- ½ teaspoon salt
- ⅛ teaspoon freshly ground black pepper
- ⅓ cup yellow corn meal
- ¼ cup bacon drippings.

1. Wash the okra well and cut off the ends. Slice okra into one-quarter-inch rounds. Combine the salt, pepper and corn meal. Toss the okra in the corn meal mixture.
2. Heat the bacon drippings in a large skillet. Add okra slices and sauté until they are tender and golden.

Yield: Four servings.

Limping Susan
SOUTH CAROLINA

4	thick slices bacon, diced	2	cups chicken broth
¾	cup washed, sliced okra		Salt and freshly ground black
1	cup uncooked rice		pepper to taste.

1. Cook the bacon in a skillet until the fat is rendered. Add the okra to the skillet. Sauté until barely tender.
2. Add the rice, broth, salt and pepper. Bring to a boil, cover and simmer until the rice is tender, about twenty-five minutes.

Yield: Six servings.

Heart of Palm (Swamp Cabbage)
FLORIDA

1	three-foot-long heart of palm or swamp cabbage, weighing about two to three pounds	¼	Salt to taste teaspoon thyme.

1. Trim the palm under cold water or palm will discolor. Remove the outer leaves. Cut off the base, which is occasionally bitter. Remove the fibrous upper portion.
2. Soak the trimmed heart of palm in cold water for one hour. Place in a kettle and add water to cover to the depth of one inch. Add salt and the thyme. Bring to a boil and simmer, covered, forty-five minutes, or until tender.

Yield: Four to six servings.

Heart of Palm au Gratin (Swamp Cabbage au Gratin)
FLORIDA

- 2 cups cooked (recipe page 159) or canned heart of palm, cut into one-half-inch rounds
- 1½ tablespoons butter
- 1½ tablespoons flour
- ¾ cup milk
- ¼ cup light cream
- ¾ cup grated sharp Cheddar cheese
- Salt to taste
- Cayenne pepper to taste
- ½ cup toasted soft bread crumbs.

1. Preheat the oven to 400 degrees.
2. Prepare the heart of palm and place it in a buttered baking dish.
3. Melt the butter in a saucepan and stir in the flour with a wire whisk. When blended, add the milk and cream, stirring vigorously with the whisk. Bring to a boil, stirring, and, when the mixture is thickened and smooth, simmer about five minutes. Remove from the heat and add the cheese, salt and cayenne. Pour the sauce over the heart of palm and sprinkle with the bread crumbs.
4. Bake until sauce is bubbling and palm is thoroughly hot.

Yield: Four to six servings.

Fried Plantains
FLORIDA

- 3 firm plantains (see note)
- 1 cup peanut oil
- Salt.

1. Peel the plantains and cut them into one-quarter-inch rounds or smaller.
2. Heat the oil until it is very hot and fry the plantain rounds, a few at a time, like deep-fried potatoes. When crisp and brown, drain on paper towels. While hot, sprinkle with salt.

Yield: Six or seven servings.

Note: Plantains are available in Spanish markets.

French Potato Salad
LOUISIANA

- 8 medium-size potatoes
- Boiling salted water
- 1 teaspoon salt
- ½ teaspoon freshly ground black pepper
- ¼ cup wine vinegar
- 1 tablespoon Pernod, Ricard or other anise-flavored liqueur
- 2 tablespoons beef broth
- ¼ cup dry white wine
- ½ tablespoon chopped tarragon
- 3 tablespoons chopped parsley
- ½ cup oil.

1. Cook the potatoes in boiling salted water until tender but still firm.
2. Peel the potatoes while still warm and cut into slices one-quarter-inch thick. Place in a salad bowl.
3. In another bowl, combine the salt, pepper, vinegar, Pernod, broth and wine. Mix until the salt dissolves.
4. Add the tarragon, parsley and oil and mix well. Pour over the potatoes and toss gently but thoroughly until all the liquid is absorbed.

Yield: Four to six servings.

Hot Potato Salad
KENTUCKY

- 6 medium-size potatoes
- 6 hard-cooked eggs, sliced
- 1 bunch scallions, including green part, finely chopped
- 1½ teaspoons celery seeds
- Salt and freshly ground black pepper to taste
- 1 cup mayonnaise
- 6 slices bacon
- ¼ cup cider vinegar
- ¼ cup hot water
- 3 tablespoons sugar
- 1 dill pickle, diced.

1. Scrub and boil or bake the potatoes until tender. Peel and dice while hot. Add the egg slices, scallions, celery seeds, salt, pepper and mayonnaise.
2. Meanwhile, cook the bacon in a skillet until crisp. Remove and crumble into potato mixture.
3. Add the vinegar, hot water and sugar to bacon drippings in skillet. Bring to a boil and continue boiling, stirring, two minutes. Add the pickle and pour over potatoes. Toss and serve.

Yield: Six servings.

Note: This salad may be chilled and served cold if desired.

Orange-Glazed Sweet Potatoes
KENTUCKY

- 6 medium-size yams or sweet potatoes, scrubbed and boiled or baked until barely tender and peeled
- 1 cup orange juice
- 2 teaspoons grated orange rind
- 1 tablespoon cornstarch
- 3 tablespoons melted butter
- ⅓ cup light brown sugar
- ⅓ cup granulated sugar
- ⅛ teaspoon salt

1. Preheat the oven to 350 degrees.
2. Place the yams or sweet potatoes in a greased shallow baking dish. Combine the remaining ingredients in a small pan and bring to a boil, stirring. Pour over the potatoes and bake thirty minutes, basting occasionally.

Yield: Six servings.

Baked Bourbon Spiced Sweet Potatoes
TENNESSEE

- 4 sweet potatoes
- ⅓ cup sugar
- ½ cup butter
- 2 eggs, lightly beaten
- ½ cup heavy cream
- ¼ teaspoon salt
- ¼ teaspoon nutmeg
- ½ teaspoon cinnamon
- ⅓ cup raisins
- ¼ cup bourbon

1. Preheat the oven to 375 degrees.
2. Scrub the potatoes and bake until tender, about forty minutes. Peel and mash into a bowl.
3. Add the remaining ingredients and mix well. Turn into a greased casserole and bake until heated through, about ten minutes.

Yield: Four servings.

Green Rice Ring
TENNESSEE

1¾ cups uncooked long grain rice	Freshly ground black pepper to taste
4 quarts water	4 tablespoons melted butter
Salt	2 tablespoons butter
1 pound spinach	Buttered small carrots.
3 scallions, including some green part, chopped	

1. Preheat the oven to 300 degrees.
2. Rinse the rice under cold running water. Bring the four quarts water to a boil and add one and one-half teaspoons salt. When water is boiling vigorously, add the rice gradually. Let boil, stirring occasionally, about twenty minutes, or until rice is tender but firm. Drain the rice in a colander and rinse under cold running water.
3. Pick over the spinach to remove any tough stems. Place the spinach and scallions in the container of an electric blender. Blend, stirring down with a rubber spatula, to make a thick puree. Blend the spinach mixture with the rice and add salt and pepper to taste and the melted butter.
4. Butter a ring mold with the two tablespoons of the butter and add the rice. Press the rice firmly in the mold and cover with aluminum foil. Sit the mold in a pan and pour boiling water around mold. Bake twenty to thirty minutes, or until piping hot. Unmold on a round platter and fill the center with buttered carrots.

Yield: Six to eight servings.

Steamboat Rice
LOUISIANA

2 tablespoons oil	¼ teaspoon thyme
2 cups finely chopped onions	1 bay leaf
1 clove garlic, finely minced	Freshly ground black pepper to taste
1 green pepper, cored, seeded and chopped	2 cups homemade or canned tomato sauce
3 cups cubed cooked ham	
¼ cup finely chopped parsley	2 cups fresh or canned chicken broth
¼ cup finely chopped celery	
½ cup chopped scallions, including green part	2 cups uncooked rice.

1. Heat the oil and cook the onions and the garlic in it until onions are wilted. Add the green pepper and ham and cook, stirring, three minutes longer. Add the parsley, celery, scallions, thyme, bay leaf, pepper and tomato sauce. Stir, cover and simmer ten minutes.

2. Remove the cover and add the broth. Bring to a boil; then stir in the rice. Cover and simmer twenty to thirty minutes, or until rice is tender. Remove cover and simmer ten minutes longer. Serve piping hot.

Yield: Six servings.

Dilled Rice for Shrimp

LOUISIANA

- 4 tablespoons butter
- 2 tablespoons chopped onion
- 1½ cups uncooked rice
- 1 cup fish stock or clam juice
- 2½ cups water
- ⅓ cup finely snipped fresh dill weed.

1. Melt the butter in a heavy casserole or skillet and sauté the onion in it until tender but not browned.

2. Add the rice and cook, stirring, three minutes until the rice takes on a transparent appearance and is golden. Stir in the fish stock or clam juice and the water.

3. Bring mixture to a boil, cover and simmer slowly about twenty minutes, or until the liquid has all been absorbed. Add the dill and toss.

Yield: Six servings.

One of the most interesting dishes in Louisiana cuisine bears the abrupt name of Dirty Rice. This is really a jambalaya made with chicken gizzards and livers and, when well made, it is delicious.

Dirty Rice

LOUISIANA

- 2 cups uncooked rice
- 6 cups chicken broth or water
- 1 bay leaf
- 1 cup finely chopped onions
- 2 tablespoons bacon drippings
- ¼ pound chicken livers
- ¼ pound chicken gizzards
- 1 clove garlic, finely minced
- ¾ cup finely chopped scallions, including green part
- ½ cup finely chopped parsley
- Salt and freshly ground black pepper to taste
- Butter.

1. Preheat the oven to 350 degrees.
2. Place the rice in a one-and-one-half-quart saucepan and add four cups broth and the bay leaf. Cover, bring to a boil and simmer exactly fifteen minutes.
3. Cook the onions in the bacon drippings until almost brown. Chop the livers and gizzards fine and add them. Cook, stirring, until brown. Add the garlic, scallions and parsley. Season with salt and pepper and add the remaining broth. Combine the partially cooked rice and the chicken giblet mixture and pour all into a baking pan. Dot with butter and bake fifteen minutes.

Yield: About six servings.

Zucchini Cheese Custard
FLORIDA

4 small zucchini	Pinch of nutmeg
2 medium-size onions	1½ cups grated sharp Cheddar cheese
¼ cup melted butter	
3 eggs, lightly beaten	Salt and freshly ground black pepper to taste.
⅔ cup light cream	

1. Preheat the oven to 350 degrees.
2. Cut the zucchini into two-inch rounds.
3. Peel the onions and cut them into thin rings. Cook the zucchini and onions in the butter until light golden. Do not brown and do not let the zucchini become soft.
4. Spoon the zucchini and onions into a shallow casserole. Combine the eggs, cream and nutmeg and half the cheese. Pour the mixture over the vegetables. Sprinkle with salt, pepper and the remaining cheese. Place the casserole in a baking dish, pour boiling water around casserole and bake thirty-five to forty minutes, or until custard is set.

Yield: Four servings.

Cheese-Stuffed Squash
TENNESSEE

3 medium-size yellow squash	½ teaspoon finely minced garlic
Boiling salted water	¼ cup grated Swiss cheese or Parmesan cheese
2 tablespoons butter	
2 tablespoons finely chopped onion	⅓ cup soft bread crumbs
6 mushrooms, finely chopped	1 tablespoon finely chopped parsley.

1. Preheat the oven to 350 degrees.
2. Split each squash in half lengthwise. With a sharp paring knife, cut away the pulp of each, leaving a rim about one-quarter-inch thick. Reserve the pulp.
3. Drop the shells into boiling salted water and cook three minutes, no longer. Drain.
4. Melt the butter in a skillet, add the onion, mushrooms and garlic and cook until onion is wilted. Add the squash pulp and cook briefly, stirring. Add the cheese, bread crumbs and parsley. Stuff the squash shells with the mixture. Place in a baking dish and bake thirty minutes.

Yield: Six servings.

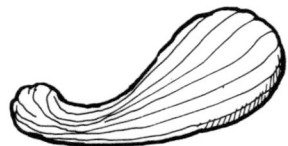

Squash Cakes
MARYLAND

2 medium-size yellow squash or zucchini	½ cup flour, approximately
1 small onion, finely grated	½ teaspoon baking powder
½ teaspoon sugar	Bacon grease, butter or oil for frying.
½ teaspoon salt	
Freshly ground black pepper to taste	

1. Grate the squash or zucchini on a coarse grater to make about two cups.
2. Add the onion, sugar, salt and pepper. Mix well.
3. Combine the flour and baking powder and stir into squash mixture until it holds together and is the consistency of a fritter batter.
4. Heat the bacon grease, butter or oil in a large skillet to a depth of one-half to one-quarter inch. Drop tablespoons of the mixture into the hot fat, flatten with the back of a spoon and cook slowly until golden. Turn the cakes and brown the second side. Drain on paper towels.

Yield: Four servings.

Pecan Squash Casserole
TENNESSEE

3 tablespoons butter	¼ teaspoon nutmeg
½ small onion, finely chopped	2 eggs, lightly beaten
1 cup hot milk	2 cups mashed or sieved cooked squash
1 cup dry bread crumbs	
Salt and freshly ground black pepper to taste	½ cup finely chopped pecans.

1. Preheat the oven to 325 degrees.
2. Heat butter in a small skillet and sauté the onion in it until tender. Add the milk and then pour over the bread crumbs.
3. Mix well. Season with salt, pepper and the nutmeg. Fold in the eggs, squash and pecans. Pour into a greased soufflé dish or baking dish and bake about thirty-five minutes, or until set.

Yield: Four servings.

Spinach and Artichokes, Asphodel Style
LOUISIANA

2 pounds spinach	½ cup heavy cream
1 package frozen artichoke hearts	Salt and freshly ground black pepper to taste
4 slices bacon	Cayenne pepper to taste
½ cup finely chopped onion	1 teaspoon or more Pernod, Ricard or other anise-flavored liqueur
1 tablespoon flour	
1 clove garlic, finely minced	
3 scallions, including green part, trimmed and chopped	¼ cup toasted soft bread crumbs Butter.

1. Trim off any tough stems on the spinach and wash the leaves in several changes of cold water. Shake to remove excess moisture. Put the spinach in a kettle. No additional water is needed. The spinach will cook in the water that clings to the leaves.

2. Cover the kettle and bring to a boil. Stir the spinach leaves around when they wilt and continue cooking briefly until just tender. Set aside.

3. Cook the artichoke hearts according to package directions and set aside.

4. Cook the bacon in a large saucepan until crisp. Remove the bacon, crumble it and reserve.

5. Preheat the oven to 400 degrees.

6. Pour off all but one tablespoon of the fat from the saucepan in which bacon cooked. Add the onion and flour and cook, stirring, but do not brown. Add the garlic and scallions and stir in the cream. Cook until the mixture is thickened and smooth.

7. Drain the spinach well in a colander. Drain the artichokes. Add both vegetables and the reserved bacon to the sauce and season with salt, pepper and cayenne. Add the Pernod and pour mixture into a buttered baking dish.

8. Sprinkle with the bread crumbs, dot with butter and bake until dish is thoroughly hot and nicely browned.

Yield: Six to eight servings.

Broiled Tomatoes
LOUISIANA

6 large firm ripe tomatoes	1 teaspoon chopped fresh or dried rosemary
1 clove garlic	
Salt	Freshly chopped basil
6 teaspoons olive oil	(optional).

1. Core the tomatoes, but do not peel. Cut the tomatoes in half.

2. Slice the garlic into wafer-thin slivers and insert the slivers into the tomato halves. Sprinkle with salt, the oil and rosemary. Rub the bottom of a baking dish with a little oil and arrange the tomatoes in the dish.

3. Place the tomatoes about three inches from a broiler flame and broil until hot and bubbling and edges of tomatoes start to burn. Sprinkle with basil if desired and serve.

Yield: Six servings.

Note: These tomatoes are also good served cold.

Fried Green Tomato Slices
WEST VIRGINIA

4 green tomatoes, thickly sliced	Freshly ground black pepper to taste
½ cup white or yellow corn meal	⅓ cup bacon drippings or pork fat.
¼ teaspoon salt	

1. Dip the tomato slices in the corn meal mixed with the salt and pepper.
2. Heat the bacon drippings or pork fat in a heavy skillet and sauté the slices in it quickly until browned on both sides.

Yield: Six servings.

Tomato Pudding
ARKANSAS

6 tablespoons butter	¼ cup light brown sugar
1 cup chopped onions	2 tablespoons chopped fresh basil
4 cups chopped peeled and cored tomatoes	2 tablespoons chopped fresh parsley
Salt and freshly ground black pepper to taste	1½ cups small white bread cubes or one cup soft bread crumbs.

1. Melt two tablespoons of the butter in a large saucepan and cook the onions in it until wilted. Add the tomatoes and stew them, stirring frequently, until they are reduced by half.
2. Preheat the oven to 375 degrees.
3. Add salt, pepper, brown sugar, basil and parsley to the stewed tomatoes.
4. Pour the bread cubes or crumbs into a one-quart baking dish. Melt the remaining butter and pour over the bread cubes or crumbs. Spoon the tomato mixture over all and cover closely with aluminum foil or a lid. Bake thirty minutes.

Yield: Four to six servings.

Bibb Lettuce Salad

KENTUCKY

- 2 or three heads Bibb lettuce
- 1 teaspoon Dijon or Düsseldorf mustard
- Salt and freshly ground black pepper to taste
- 1 tablespoon wine vinegar or lemon juice
- 3 tablespoons or more peanut oil or olive oil
- ½ clove garlic, finely minced.

1. Pull off the leaves of the lettuce and rinse well under cold running water. Cut or tear the leaves into bite-size pieces. Shake to dry.
2. Put the mustard into a salad bowl and add the salt, pepper, vinegar, oil and garlic, stirring with a wire whick. Add the lettuce and toss.

Yield: Four servings.

Cauliflower Slaw

KENTUCKY

- 1 large head cauliflower, broken into flowerets
- ¼ cup minced scallions, including green part
- ½ cup finely chopped celery leaves
- 1 cup sour cream
- ½ cup homemade French dressing
- 2 teaspoons caraway seeds
- Salt and freshly ground black pepper to taste.

Slice the flowerets thinly and toss with the other ingredients just before serving.

Yield: Six servings.

Cole Slaw

ALABAMA

- 1 small head green cabbage
- ½ to one cup mayonnaise
- 2 tablespoons wine vinegar or lemon juice
- 1 tablespoon grated onion
- ½ teaspoon caraway seeds or celery seeds
- ½ cup finely slivered green or red sweet peppers
- Salt and freshly ground black pepper to taste
- Cayenne pepper to taste (optional).

1. Tear off the tough outer leaves of the cabbage and pare away the core. With a sharp knife on a flat surface, shred the cabbage. There should be about four cups. Place cabbage in a mixing bowl.

2. Add the remaining ingredients and toss well. Serve well chilled.

Yield: About six servings.

Cole Slaw with Capers
SOUTH CAROLINA

1 small head green cabbage	1 teaspoon chopped fresh basil, thyme, tarragon, marjoram or other fresh herb
½ small onion	
Salt and freshly ground black pepper to taste	
2 tablespoons wine vinegar	2 tablespoons capers
3 tablespoons olive oil	1½ cups mayonnaise, approximately.
½ teaspoon Tabasco sauce, or to taste	

1. Peel off the tough outer leaves of the cabbage and pare away the core. Slice the cabbage in half and shred it finely with a sharp knife. There should be about four cups.

2. Place the shredded cabbage in a large mixing bowl. Grate enough onion to make one or two teaspoonfuls and add to cabbage. Add the remaining ingredients, using just enough mayonnaise to bind well. Toss and chill.

Yield: Four to six servings.

Stella's Pensacola Gazpachy Salad
FLORIDA

6 large tomatoes, peeled	2 cups homemade mayonnaise
4 large green peppers, cored and seeded	¼ teaspoon dry mustard
	1 small onion
2 cucumbers, peeled	Salt and freshly ground black pepper to taste
2 ship biscuits (hard tack) or six to eight hard pilot crackers, soaked in cold water	Cayenne pepper to taste.

1. Slice the tomatoes, green peppers and cucumbers as thinly as possible. Place the vegetables and biscuits or crackers in alternate layers in a large salad bowl, spreading each layer with the mayonnaise to which the mustard has been added.

2. Cut the onion in four wedges. Spear each wedge with a toothpick. Push wedges down into salad mixture. Cover and place in refrigerator six hours before serving. Remove onion before serving and stir mixture well with a wooden spoon. Add salt, pepper and cayenne. Do not serve on lettuce.

Yield: Six or more servings.

Shreveport Poppy Seed Dressing
LOUISIANA

½	cup tarragon vinegar		(made by scraping the cut surface of half an onion with a knife)
¼	cup sugar		
1	tablespoon paprika		
1	tablespoon dry mustard	1	egg yolk
½	teaspoon ground ginger	1	tablespoon chopped chutney
1½	teaspoons salt	¾	cup honey
	Cayenne pepper to taste	2	cups peanut or vegetable oil
2	tablespoons onion juice	2	tablespoons poppy seeds.

1. Combine the vinegar and sugar and bring to a boil. Remove from the heat and add the paprika, mustard, ginger, salt, cayenne and onion juice.

2. When cool, beat in the remaining ingredients. Chill and serve with fruit salads. In Shreveport, this dressing is frequently served with sea food cocktails.

Yield: About one quart.

Boiled Salad Dressing
VIRGINIA

1	teaspoon dry mustard	3	egg yolks
3	tablespoons sugar	½	cup cold milk
½	teaspoon salt	¾	cup white vinegar.
2	tablespoons flour		

1. Combine the mustard, sugar, salt and flour in the top of a double boiler.

2. Beat the egg yolks slightly with a wire whisk and beat them into the flour mixture. Stir in the milk and vinegar and cook over boiling water until the mixture is thickened and smooth.

Yield: One and one-half cups.

Cole Slaw Dressing
VIRGINIA

½ cup cider vinegar	Salt to taste
1½ teaspoons dry mustard	¼ to one-half cup sugar
4 eggs	2 tablespoons butter.
2 cups light cream	

1. Combine the vinegar and mustard in the top of a double boiler and let stand ten minutes.

2. Beat the eggs lightly and add them to the vinegar. Add the cream, salt and sugar and cook, stirring with a wooden spoon, until the mixture coats the spoon. Remove the sauce from the heat and swirl in the butter.

Yield: About three cups.

Cooked Bacon Dressing
VIRGINIA

4 slices bacon	
3 eggs	½ cup cider vinegar
1 tablespoon dry mustard	1 cup water
2½ tablespoons flour	¼ teaspoon freshly ground
⅓ cup sugar	black pepper
1 teaspoon salt	1 cup mayonnaise, preferably
½ teaspoon celery seeds, crushed	homemade.

1. Cook the bacon until crisp. Remove and crumble strips. Reserve.

2. Combine bacon drippings with eggs, mustard, flour, sugar, salt, celery seeds, vinegar, water and pepper in a deep saucepan. Beat with a rotary beater.

3. Heat, stirring constantly, until mixture thickens. Remove. Cool slightly and stir in the mayonnaise and reserved bacon bits. Cool and chill.
Yield: About two and one-half cups.
Note: This is excellent on potato salad, chicken salad or spinach salad.

Breads

Hot Water Corn Bread
(Hoe Cake)
MISSISSIPPI

1 cup white corn meal	1¼ cups boiling water, approximately
4 teaspoons sifted flour	
½ teaspoon salt	Shortening for shallow-fat frying.
1 teaspoon sugar	
2 teaspoons baking powder	
6 tablespoons melted shortening	

1. Put the corn meal in a mixing bowl and add the flour, salt, sugar and baking powder. Mix well and stir in the melted shortening.
2. Pour in the boiling water, adding just enough to make a moist but manageable mixture. Wet the hands and shape the dough into patties about one-half-inch thick and four inches in diameter. Heat shortening in a skillet to a depth of about one-quarter inch. Add the patties and cook over moderately high heat on one side. Turn and cook until golden brown on the other.

Yield: Four patties.

Vivian's Corn Bread
FLORIDA

2 cups yellow corn meal	1 teaspoon sugar (optional)
1 cup flour	1 cup milk
1 tablespoon baking powder	3 tablespoons shortening or
2 eggs, lightly beaten	bacon drippings, melted.
1 teaspoon salt	

1. Preheat the oven to 400 degrees.
2. Sift together the corn meal, flour and baking powder into a mixing bowl. Stir in the eggs, salt, sugar if desired, milk and shortening or bacon drippings. Pour into greased nine-inch square pan.
3. Bake twenty to twenty-five minutes, or until bread is firm in the center.

Yield: Six servings.

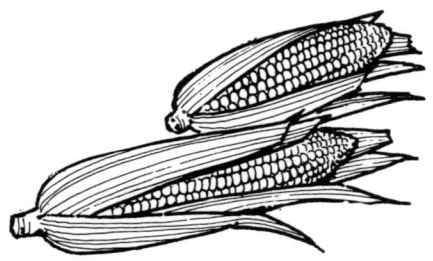

Corn Bread
SOUTH CAROLINA

½ cup lard	1¼ cups flour
½ cup butter	6 teaspoons baking powder
¼ cup sugar	1 teaspoon salt
2 eggs	1¼ cups milk.
1¾ cups white corn meal	

1. Preheat the oven to 450 degrees.
2. Cream the lard, butter and sugar together. Beat in the eggs, one at a time.
3. Sift together the corn meal, flour, baking powder and salt and add alternately with the milk to the butter mixture. Turn into a greased fourteen-by-ten-inch baking pan and bake about twenty-five minutes.

Yield: About thirty-five pieces, each two inches square.

Crackling Corn Bread
MISSISSIPPI

- ¼ pound cracklings, about one cup (see note)
- ⅓ cup sifted flour
- 1½ cups sifted white corn meal
- 1 teaspoon baking soda
- ½ teaspoon salt
- 2 eggs
- 1 cup buttermilk
- 2 cups regular milk
- 3 tablespoons bacon drippings, lard or butter.

1. Preheat the oven to 350 degrees.
2. Place the cracklings in an ovenproof skillet and bake about fifteen minutes. Drain and reserve the cracklings.
3. Sift the flour, corn meal, baking soda and salt into a mixing bowl. Beat the eggs until they are foamy and stir in the buttermilk and half the regular milk. Stir this into the corn meal mixture. Stir in the drained cracklings.
4. Place the bacon drippings, lard or butter in a nine-inch heavy iron skillet and heat it on top of the stove. The bacon drippings should be quite hot but not brown. Pour the corn bread mixture into the skillet. Very carefully pour the remaining cup of regular milk over the top of the corn meal mixture. Do not stir. Bake fifty minutes.

Yield: Eight servings.

Note: Cracklings are rendered pork skins and are much richer than the fried pork skins sold commercially, at least outside the South.

Spoon Bread
MISSISSIPPI

- 3 cups milk
- 1½ cups white corn meal
- ¼ cup butter
- 1 teaspoon salt
- 2 teaspoons baking powder
- 4 eggs, separated.

1. Preheat the oven to 350 degrees.
2. Heat two cups of the milk. Gradually stir into the corn meal set in the top of a double boiler. Add the butter.
3. Bring the mixture to a boil, stirring, and cook ten minutes. Add the salt and cool to lukewarm.

4. Dissolve the baking powder in the remaining milk and beat with the egg yolks into the corn meal mixture. Beat the egg whites until stiff and fold in. Pour into a buttered casserole. Bake about forty minutes, or until well puffed and brown. Serve from the casserole.

Yield: Six servings.

Batter Bread
MARYLAND

2 cups milk	1 teaspoon salt
2 tablespoons butter	1 tablespoon flour
2 eggs, lightly beaten	⅓ cup yellow corn meal
1 tablespoon sugar	1 cup cold cooked rice

1. Preheat the oven to 375 degrees.
2. Heat the milk and butter together. Mix the eggs with the remaining ingredients and then gradually stir the milk mixture into it.
3. Return to the pan and stir and cook over low heat or in the top of a double boiler until mixture thickens. Pour into a buttered baking dish and bake forty minutes, or until well browned.

Yield: Four to six servings.

Deep-Fried Hot Water Corn Bread
ALABAMA

1 cup white corn meal	½ teaspoon salt
1 tablespoon plus one teaspoon flour	1 tablespoon sugar
	1¼ cups boiling water
2 teaspoons baking powder	Fat or oil for deep-frying.

1. Place the corn meal, flour, baking powder, salt and sugar in a bowl. Stir in the water.
2. Heat the fat or oil to 375 degrees. Drop the dough by tablespoons into the hot fat and cook until golden.

Yield: Four servings.

Southern Buttermilk Corn Bread
TENNESSEE

1½ tablespoons butter	½ teaspoon salt
⅓ cup flour	2 eggs, beaten
1½ cups white corn meal	1 cup buttermilk
1 teaspoon baking soda	2 cups regular milk.

1. Preheat the oven to 350 degrees.
2. Heat the butter in an ovenproof nine-inch to ten-inch skillet. A cast iron one is best. Sift together the flour, corn meal, baking soda and salt.
3. Beat in the eggs, buttermilk and one cup of the regular milk. Pour into the hot skillet. Pour remaining cup of regular milk over the top. Do not stir. Bake fifty minutes, or until done.
Yield: Four servings.
Note: Serve, buttered, with creamed chicken.

Fried Corn Meal Mush
SOUTH CAROLINA

½ cup white corn meal	¾ teaspoon salt
2½ cups boiling water	Bacon drippings.

1. Sprinkle the corn meal over the boiling water, stirring briskly. Add the salt and cook thirty minutes over low heat.
2. Pour into a greased loaf pan or bowl and cool until firm. Remove from pan or bowl and cut into slices three-quarters-inch thick.
3. Melt the bacon drippings in a heavy skillet and cook the slices until brown on both sides.
Yield: Four servings.

Corn Meal Sticks
ALABAMA

2 cups water	1 cup grated Edam cheese
1¼ teaspoons salt	Lard for deep-frying.
1½ cups white corn meal	

1. Combine the water and salt in a saucepan. Heat to the boiling point and gradually stir in the corn meal. When thoroughly blended, cook for five minutes, stirring almost constantly. When ready, the mixture should separate from the bottom and sides of the pan.
2. Remove mixture from the heat and stir in the cheese.
3. When cool enough to handle, shape mixture, one heaping teaspoonful at a time, into balls. Using the palms of the hands, roll each ball into a small cigar shape about one-half-inch thick.
4. Drop sticks, a few at a time, into lard heated to 375 degrees. Cook until golden brown and drain on paper towels.

Yield: About fifty; ten servings.

Double Corn Sticks
FLORIDA

4 ears fresh corn	1 teaspoon sugar
1½ cups yellow corn meal	¼ cup butter, melted
½ cup flour	¼ cup finely minced onion
1 tablespoon baking powder	1 cup milk or buttermilk
1¼ teaspoons salt	1 egg, lightly beaten.

1. Preheat the oven to 450 degrees.
2. Remove the husks and silks from the corn; cut the kernels from the cob (about two cups). Set aside.
3. In a large bowl combine the corn meal, flour, baking powder, salt and sugar.
4. Warm the butter in a small skillet. Add the onion and corn and sauté for five minutes. Stir into the flour mixture.
5. Blend in the milk and egg, stirring until mixture is just moistened. Fill eighteen greased corn stick pans about two-thirds full with batter.
6. Bake twenty-five to thirty minutes, or until golden. Let cool in pans for five minutes, carefully remove and serve immediately with sweet butter.

Yield: Eighteen corn sticks.

Crackling Bread Cakes
GEORGIA

1 cup white corn meal	Buttermilk
¼ teaspoon baking soda	½ cup cracklings (crisp pork
1 teaspoon single acting (tartrate) baking powder	rind pieces).

1. Preheat the oven to 400 degrees.
2. Place the corn meal, baking soda and baking powder in a bowl. Add enough buttermilk to make a soft batter. Let rest five minutes. Stir in the cracklings and more buttermilk if needed to make a pancake consistency.
3. Drop by tablespoonfuls onto a hot greased griddle and cook until brown. Turn and brown the other side. Place on a baking pan and bake about ten minutes to complete cooking.

Yield: Four servings.

Lacy Hoe Cakes
GEORGIA

1 tablespoon bacon drippings	1 cup boiling water,
1 teaspoon salt	approximately.
1 cup waterground white corn meal	

1. Add the bacon drippings and salt to the corn meal. Cut in the drippings with a knife. Add boiling water until the batter is fairly runny. Let rest one hour. The corn meal swells.
2. Add more water if necessary to give a batter that flows easily. Spoon by the tablespoonful onto a moderately hot (375 degrees) greased griddle. Cook until brown, turn and cook underside. Hoe cakes must cook thoroughly or they will stick to the griddle. They should be paper-thin and lacy-looking.

Yield: Four servings.

Hush Puppies
KENTUCKY

2	cups white corn meal	1½	cups milk
2¼	teaspoons baking powder	½	cup warm water
1	teaspoon salt		Fat for deep-frying.
½	cup finely minced onion		

1. Sift the corn meal, baking powder and salt into a mixing bowl. Stir in the onion, milk and warm water. Mix well to make a manageable mass. Using the palms, shape the mixture into rounds the size of large walnuts.
2. Heat the fat to about 370 degrees and deep-fry the hush puppies until golden brown and crisp on the outside. These are traditional accompaniments for fried fish.

Yield: About two dozen.

River Road Hush Puppies
LOUISIANA

1	cup white corn meal		Cayenne pepper or chopped hot green peppers to taste
1	cup flour		
1	teaspoon salt	¼	cup chopped scallion tops
½	teaspoon sugar	1	tablespoon finely minced or grated onion
1	teaspoon baking powder		
¾	cup milk		Lard or other fat for deep-frying.
1	egg		

1. Sift the corn meal, flour, salt, sugar and baking powder into a mixing bowl. Make a well in the center and stir in the milk beaten with the egg. When blended, add the cayenne, or hot green peppers, scallion tops and minced onion.
2. Heat the fat for deep-frying (about 375 degrees). Drop the corn meal batter by the spoonful into the fat and cook until golden brown.

Yield: About two dozen.

Lacy Corn Bread
NORTH CAROLINA

1 cup yellow corn meal	½ teaspoon salt
½ cup flour	1½ cups water
½ teaspoon baking soda	Peanut oil.

1. Combine the corn meal, flour, baking soda and salt in a bowl. Add the water and mix to a thin batter.
2. Heat oil to the depth of one-eighth inch in a ten-inch skillet until almost smoking. Pour in a very thin layer of the batter and cook over high heat.
3. Cook until the underside is well browned and the top is lacy over most of its area. Turn and cook a few moments longer. Drain on paper towels and keep warm. Repeat until all the batter is used, being careful to stir batter well before pouring. Thin the batter with water if batter gets too thick and add more oil to the skillet as necessary. The rounds of lacy corn bread can be broken up for serving.
Yield: Eight servings.

Molasses Corn Bread
GEORGIA

¾ cup white corn meal	¾ cup buttermilk
1 cup flour	1 egg, well beaten
1 teaspoon salt	2 tablespoons shortening, melted.
¾ teaspoon baking soda	
½ cup light molasses	

1. Preheat the oven to 425 degrees.
2. Grease an eight-inch cast iron skillet or an eight-inch square pan. Sift the corn meal, flour, salt and baking soda together into a bowl.
3. Add the remaining ingredients and stir until just blended. Pour into the prepared pan and bake twenty minutes, or until done.
Yield: Six servings.

Bacon and Cheese Spoon Bread
GEORGIA

- ½ pound bacon
- 1 clove garlic, finely chopped
- ¾ cup yellow corn meal
- ½ cup white hominy grits
- 2½ cups water
- 2 cups shredded sharp Cheddar cheese
- ¼ pound butter
- ½ teaspoon salt
- 1 cup milk
- 4 eggs, separated
- 1 four-ounce jar or can pimentos, drained and diced.

1. Preheat the oven to 325 degrees.
2. Cook the bacon in a skillet until crisp. Remove, crumble and reserve. Discard all but one tablespoon of the bacon drippings, sauté the garlic in it until tender and reserve.
3. Mix together the corn meal, hominy and water in a saucepan. Bring to a boil, stirring, and cook one minute. Remove from the heat.
4. Stir in the cheese and butter until melted. Add the salt, milk, egg yolks, reserved bacon and garlic and the pimentos.
5. Beat the egg whites until stiff but not dry and fold into the corn meal mixture. Turn into a greased three-quart casserole or soufflé dish and bake about one hour and fifteen minutes, or until set in the middle.

Yield: Six servings.

Grand Hot Cakes
MISSISSIPPI

- ½ cup white corn meal
- 1 tablespoon sugar
- ½ teaspoon salt
- 1 cup boiling water
- 2 eggs, separated
- ¾ cup milk
- 1 cup flour
- 3 teaspoons baking powder
- ¼ cup oil.

1. Place the corn meal, sugar and salt in a saucepan. Stir in the water and cook, stirring, two minutes. Cool.
2. Stir the egg yolks and milk into the cooled corn meal.
3. Sift the flour with the baking powder and stir into the corn meal mixture. Beat the egg whites until stiff and fold with the oil into the mixture.

4. Spoon by tablespoons onto a moderately hot lightly greased griddle and cook until browned. Turn and brown other side.
Yield: Four servings.

Corn Crisps
KENTUCKY

2½ to three cups boiling water	4 tablespoons melted shortening, cooled.
½ cup white corn meal	
1½ teaspoons salt	

1. Preheat the oven to 425 degrees.
2. Pour the boiling water over the corn meal while stirring vigorously.
3. Stir in the salt and shortening. Drop by tablespoons onto a greased baking sheet. The mixture should be thin enough to spread and give three-inch round thin cakes; add more boiling water if necessary.
4. Bake twenty minutes, or until brown and crisp.
Yield: About three dozen.

Cush
NORTH CAROLINA

2 tablespoons bacon drippings	Salt and freshly ground black pepper to taste
2 tablespoons butter	
1 small onion, finely chopped	1 teaspoon ground sage
2 cups crumbled cold corn bread	2 eggs, lightly beaten
1 cup crumbled cold biscuits	Milk.

1. Preheat the oven to 350 degrees.
2. Heat the bacon drippings and butter in a heavy black iron skillet. Add the onion and cook until tender.
3. Add the corn bread, biscuits, salt, pepper and sage and cook, stirring, until lightly browned.
4. Stir in the eggs and enough milk to make a mushlike texture. Bake fifteen to twenty minutes. Serve hot.
Yield: Four servings.

Waffles
TENNESSEE

1½ cups flour	2 eggs, separated
3 teaspoons baking powder	3 tablespoons melted butter,
½ teaspoon salt	syrup, marmalade, jam or
1 tablespoon sugar	honey.
1 cup milk	

1. Sift the flour with the baking powder, salt and sugar into a mixing bowl. Make a well in the center and add the milk, egg yolks and melted butter. Combine rapidly with a fork or wire whisk. The mixture should remain a little lumpy.

2. Beat the egg whites until stiff and fold them into the batter. Cook the batter in waffle irons and serve with melted butter, syrup, marmalade, jelly, jam or honey.

Yield: Six to eight.

Sweet Potato Spoon Bread
GEORGIA

2 medium-size sweet potatoes	½ teaspoon nutmeg
Salt to taste	1 teaspoon allspice
8 tablespoons butter	¼ cup flour
1 tablespoon sugar	2 eggs, separated.

1. Place the potatoes in a large saucepan and add water to cover and salt. Bring to a boil and simmer until potatoes are tender, at least thirty minutes. Drain and peel. Put the potatoes through a ricer into a hot mixing bowl. Beat in the butter, sugar, nutmeg, allspice and flour.

2. Preheat the oven to 400 degrees.

3. Beat the egg yolks lightly and beat them into the potatoes. Beat the egg whites until stiff and fold them into the mixture. Pour the mixture into a buttered one-and-one-half-quart casserole and bake until puffed and brown, about thirty minutes.

Yield: Four to six servings.

Southern-Style Biscuits
SOUTH CAROLINA

- 2 cups flour
- 3 teaspoons baking powder
- ½ teaspoon salt
- 3 tablespoons melted shortening
- ⅔ cup buttermilk, approximately.

1. Preheat the oven to 475 degrees.
2. Sift the flour, baking powder and salt into a bowl.
3. Stir in the shortening and buttermilk to make a soft dough. Work on a floured board lightly until dough can be rolled. Roll out to one-half-inch thickness and cut into rounds.
4. Place rounds on a lightly greased baking sheet and bake ten to twelve minutes.

Yield: About two dozen.

Cheese Biscuits
MISSISSIPPI

- 1½ cups flour
- 2 teaspoons baking powder
- ¼ teaspoon salt
- 6 tablespoons grated sharp Cheddar cheese
- 1 tablespoon melted butter
- Milk.

1. Preheat the oven to 450 degrees.
2. Combine the flour, baking powder and salt. Stir in the cheese. Toss lightly with the butter and approximately two-thirds cup of milk, adding enough milk to make a soft dough that can be dropped from a teaspoon. Toss dough on floured board, pat to one-half-inch thickness and cut with a small biscuit cutter or drop the dough by spoonfuls onto a baking sheet. Brush with milk. Bake ten minutes.

Yield: Three dozen.

Biscuits
MISSISSIPPI

2 cups flour	2 teaspoons baking powder
1 teaspoon sugar	½ cup shortening, melted
½ teaspoon salt	1 cup milk, approximately.

1. Preheat the oven to 425 degrees.
2. Place the flour, sugar, salt and baking powder in a mixing bowl and mix well. Pour in the melted shortening, stirring with a wooden spoon. When blended, add the milk gradually, stirring constantly. Add enough milk to form a soft, manageable dough.
3. Knead the dough about ten strokes. Roll it out on a lightly floured board to approximately one-third-inch thickness. Cut into rounds with a biscuit cutter. Arrange the biscuits about one inch apart on a lightly greased baking sheet and bake twelve to fifteen minutes.

Yield: About one dozen to two dozen.

Beaten Biscuits
VIRGINIA

3 cups flour	3 tablespoons cold lard
½ teaspoon sugar	½ cup cold milk
½ teaspoon salt	½ cup cold water,
3 tablespoons cold butter	approximately.

1. Sift the flour, sugar and salt into a mixing bowl.
2. Add the butter and lard and, with two knives or a pastry blender, cut into the flour until mixture resembles coarse corn meal. Add the milk and enough water to make a stiff dough. Toss mixture with a fork. Knead dough for fifteen minutes; then beat with a mallet for twenty minutes, or until well blistered. Or put dough through the coarse blade of a meat grinder, folding dough over frequently. Or put dough over and over through the rollers of a beaten biscuit machine. When ready, the dough should be smooth and glossy.
3. Preheat the oven to 325 degrees.
4. Roll dough one-half-inch thick and cut into rounds with a small floured biscuit cutter. Prick rounds with a fork and bake thirty minutes on baking sheets.

Yield: Three dozen or more.

Sweet Potato Biscuits
ALABAMA

- 2 cups flour
- 5 teaspoons baking powder
- 1 teaspoon salt
- ¼ cup sugar
- 2 cups mashed cooked sweet potatoes
- ½ cup shortening
- ¾ cup milk, approximately

1. Preheat the oven to 425 degrees.
2. Sift together the flour, baking powder, salt and sugar. Mix in the potatoes and shortening. Add enough milk to make a soft dough for rolling.
3. Knead on a lightly floured board until smooth. Roll out to one-half-inch thickness and cut into rounds with a biscuit cutter. Place rounds on lightly greased baking sheets and bake ten to fifteen minutes. Eat hot.

Yield: About thirty.

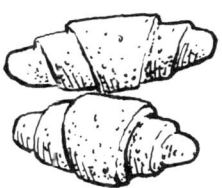

Corn Meal Muffins
ARKANSAS

- 1½ cups sifted self-rising white corn meal
- ½ cup sifted self-rising flour
- 1 cup milk
- 3 tablespoons oil
- 1 egg

1. Preheat the oven to 425 degrees.
2. Mix the corn meal and flour in a bowl. Measure the milk into a two-cup measure and add the oil and unbeaten egg. Mix well.
3. Make a hole in the center of corn meal mixture and pour in milk mixture. Stir until ingredients are just moistened. Fill hot greased muffin pans two-thirds full. Bake eighteen to twenty minutes.

Yield: One dozen medium-size.

Note: In place of self-rising corn meal and flour, use one and one-half cups regular white corn meal, one-half cup flour, three teaspoons baking powder and one-half teaspoon salt.

To avoid heating oven in hot weather, bake the batter as you would pancakes on a hot greased griddle.

Blueberry Muffins
NORTH CAROLINA

3	cups flour	2	eggs, lightly beaten
1	cup sugar	½	cup oil
4	teaspoons baking powder	1	cup milk
1	teaspoon salt	1½	cups blueberries.

1. Preheat the oven to 400 degrees.
2. Mix together the flour, sugar, baking powder and salt in a bowl.
3. Combine the eggs, oil and milk. Stir into the dry ingredients until just moistened.
4. Stir in the berries and spoon into medium-size muffin tins lined with paper liners until they are two-thirds full. Bake twenty minutes. Serve warm.

Yield: Two dozen muffins.

Banana Bread
MISSISSIPPI

½	cup butter	1	teaspoon baking soda
1	cup sugar	¼	teaspoon salt
2	eggs	½	cup chopped pecans
2	cups flour	3	very ripe bananas, mashed.
1	teaspoon baking powder		

1. Preheat the oven to 350 degrees.
2. Cream the butter with the sugar until light and fluffy. Beat in the eggs, one at a time.
3. Sift together the flour, baking powder, baking soda and salt. Toss the pecans with one tablespoon of the flour mixture.
4. Fold the bananas into the butter mixture. Stir in the flour. Fold in the pecans. Turn into a greased 8½-by 4½-by 2½-inch loaf pan and bake forty-five minutes to one hour, or until bread tests done.

Yield: One loaf.

Fried Cream or Custard
ALABAMA

- 1 tablespoon plus one teaspoon flour
- 3 tablespoons cold milk
- ½ cup sugar
- 2 tablespoons cornstarch
- 2 cups hot milk
- 1 stick cinnamon
- 3 eggs, lightly beaten
- ¼ teaspoon salt
- 2 egg whites, lightly beaten
- Cracker crumbs
- Fat or oil for deep-frying.

1. Day before, mix the flour with the cold milk in a saucepan. Mix together the sugar and cornstarch and stir into the flour mixture. Gradually stir in the hot milk. Add the cinnamon stick and heat, stirring, until mixture boils.

2. Cook, stirring, three minutes. Remove cinnamon stick. Add one-half cup of the hot sauce to the eggs. Mix and return to the bulk of the sauce. Cook until eggs cook and mixture thickens a little bit further. Pour into a greased shallow pan so that there is about one-half inch of mixture.

3. Chill overnight. Next day, cut into two-inch squares or strips. Dip in the egg white and then in the crumbs and fry, a few pieces at a time, in a fry basket in fat, or oil heated to 375 degrees. Drain on paper towels and keep warm in the oven while preparing remainder.

Yield: Six servings.
Note: Serve with broiled or roasted chicken.

Light Rolls
SOUTH CAROLINA

- 1 cup shortening
- ½ cup sugar
- 1 tablespoon salt
- 1½ cups boiling water
- 2 eggs, beaten
- 2 packages active dry yeast
- ½ cup lukewarm water
- 5 cups flour, approximately
- Butter.

1. Combine the shortening, sugar, salt and boiling water in a bowl and stir to dissolve the sugar. Let stand until at room temperature.

2. Beat in the eggs.

3. Soften the yeast in the lukewarm water and add to the bowl.

4. Stir in enough flour to make a soft but not sticky dough. Knead until

smooth on a lightly floured board. Place in a clean greased bowl, cover and let rise in a warm place until doubled in bulk.

5. Roll out on a floured board to one-quarter-inch thickness. Cut into two-and-one-half-inch rounds. Place a small piece of butter in the center of each, fold one half over the other and pinch to seal.

6. Place on a greased baking sheet, cover and let rise until doubled in bulk, about forty-five minutes.

7. Preheat the oven to 350 degrees.

8. Bake fifteen to twenty minutes, or until browned and done.

Yield: Three dozen.

Sally Lunn
VIRGINIA

1	package active dry yeast	¼	cup sugar
¼	cup warm water	3	eggs, beaten
1	cup milk, scalded	4	cups flour, approximately
½	cup butter	1	teaspoon salt

1. Soften the yeast in the water and stir to dissolve.

2. Combine the milk, butter and sugar. Stir to melt the butter and dissolve the sugar. Cool to lukewarm.

3. In a large bowl, combine the softened yeast, milk mixture and the eggs. Add three cups of the flour and the salt and beat with a wooden spoon until smooth. Add enough extra flour to make a soft batter. Beat well until smooth and elastic.

4. Place in a clean bowl, cover with a damp cloth and let rise in a warm place until doubled in bulk, about one hour. Knock down and beat well until smooth.

5. Transfer the dough to a greased two-quart Turk's head mold, kugelhof pan or nine-inch angel food pan. Cover with a damp cloth, place in a warm place and let rise until double in bulk, about forty-five minutes.

6. Preheat the oven to 325 degrees.

7. Bake the Sally Lunn about forty-five minutes, or until golden brown and done. Serve hot or warm if possible.

Yield: About ten servings.

Pies, Cakes, Desserts and Cookies

Molasses-Nut Pie
ALABAMA

- 1 cup dark molasses
- 3 tablespoons lemon juice
- ½ teaspoon grated lemon rind
- 2 eggs, separated
- ¼ cup sugar
- 1 tablespoon flour
- ¼ teaspoon nutmeg
- ¼ teaspoon cinnamon
- 1 tablespoon melted butter
- ⅛ teaspoon salt
- ½ cup pecans
- 1 unbaked eight-inch or nine-inch pie shell.

1. Preheat the oven to 350 degrees.
2. Mix the molasses with the lemon juice and rind. Beat the egg yolks with the sugar. Gradually beat in the flour, nutmeg, cinnamon, butter and salt.
3. While beating, add the molasses slowly. Beat the egg whites until stiff but not dry and fold molasses mixture into them. Place the pecans in the bottom of the pie shell and pour the molasses mixture over.
4. Bake ten minutes, reduce oven heat to 325 degrees and bake about twenty-five minutes longer, or until set.

Yield: Six servings.

Guava Pecan Pie
FLORIDA

- 1 cup guava syrup or three-quarters cup guava jelly, heated and diluted with water
- ¾ cup sugar
- 2 tablespoons flour
- 2 egg yolks
- ¼ cup evaporated milk
- Pinch of salt
- 2 tablespoons melted butter
- 1 cup pecan halves
- 1 unbaked nine-inch pie shell

1. Preheat the oven to 425 degrees.
2. Place the guava syrup in a bowl. Combine the sugar and flour and beat with the egg yolks. Stir in the evaporated milk and salt. Stir the mixture into the guava syrup and add the butter. Stir in the pecan halves and pour the filling into the pie shell. Bake ten minutes, reduce oven heat to 325 degrees and bake thirty-five minutes longer, or until set.

Yield: Six servings.

Black Walnut Pie
NORTH CAROLINA

- 3 eggs, lightly beaten
- 1 cup dark corn syrup
- 1 cup firmly packed light brown sugar
- 3 tablespoons butter, melted
- 1 teaspoon vanilla
- ⅛ teaspoon salt
- 1 unbaked nine-inch pie shell, chilled
- ¾ cup black walnuts
- Confectioners' sugar (optional).

1. Preheat the oven to 350 degrees.
2. Combine the eggs, syrup, brown sugar, butter, vanilla and salt.
3. Turn the mixture into the pie shell and sprinkle the black walnuts over the top.
4. Bake until firm, about one hour. If desired, serve sprinkled with confectioners' sugar.

Yield: Eight servings.

Note: One cup peanuts or pecans may be substituted for the black walnuts.

Peanut Pie

GEORGIA

2	eggs	1	cup salted peanuts
1	cup dark corn syrup	1	unbaked nine-inch pie shell
1	cup sugar	2	tablespoons butter.
1	teaspoon vanilla		

1. Preheat the oven to 350 degrees.
2. Combine the eggs, syrup, sugar and vanilla. Stir in the peanuts. Pour the mixture into the pie shell. Dot with the butter.
3. Bake forty-five to fifty minutes, or until the filling is set.

Yield: Six to eight servings.

Walnut Pie

GEORGIA

½	cup butter, at room temperature		Pinch of salt
		1	teaspoon vanilla
1	cup firmly packed dark brown sugar	1	unbaked eight-inch or nine-inch pie shell
1	cup dark corn syrup	1	cup walnut meats.
4	eggs, lightly beaten		

1. Preheat the oven to 375 degrees.
2. Cream together the butter and brown sugar in a mixing bowl. Blend in the syrup. Beat in the eggs.
3. Add the salt and vanilla to the mixture and pour into the pie shell. Arrange the walnuts symmetrically over the top and bake forty minutes, or until set.

Yield: Six to eight servings.

Pecan Pie

LOUISIANA

½	cup sugar	1	teaspoon almond extract
2	tablespoons butter	1	teaspoon vanilla
2	eggs, lightly beaten	1	cup light corn syrup
2	tablespoons flour	1½	cups chopped pecans
¼	teaspoon salt	1	unbaked eight-inch pie shell.

1. Preheat the oven to 350 degrees.

2. Cream together the sugar, butter, eggs, flour, salt, almond extract, vanilla and syrup. Beat well and stir in pecans.

3. Pour mixture into pie shell. Bake thirty to forty-five minutes, or until filling is set.

Yield: Six servings.

Chess Pie I
KENTUCKY

1 cup light brown sugar	2 tablespoons light cream
½ cup granulated sugar	½ cup melted butter
1 teaspoon flour	1 unbaked nine-inch pie shell
2 eggs	Sweetened whipped cream
1 teaspoon vanilla	(optional).

1. Preheat the oven to 325 degrees.

2. Combine the brown sugar, granulated sugar and flour. Add the eggs and mix well. Add the vanilla and cream and blend. Stir in the butter and pour the mixture into the pie shell.

3. Bake thirty to thirty-five minutes, or until the filling is slightly firm. If desired, serve with whipped cream sweetened to taste.

Yield: Six to eight servings.

Chess Pie II
KENTUCKY

½ cup butter, at room temperature	Grated rind of one lemon
	Juice of one lemon
1¼ cups sugar	1 teaspoon vanilla
1 tablespoon yellow corn meal	¼ teaspoon salt
3 eggs	1 unbaked nine-inch pie shell.

1. Preheat the oven to 325 degrees.

2. Cream together the butter and sugar in a mixing bowl, using a wooden spoon. Beat in the corn meal.

3. Add the eggs, one at a time, beating well after each addition. Beat in the lemon rind, lemon juice, vanilla and salt. Pour the mixture into the pie shell. Bake forty-five minutes, or until a knife inserted in the center comes out clean.

Yield: Six to eight servings.

Chess Tarts
NORTH CAROLINA

⅓ cup butter	1 teaspoon grated lemon rind
1 cup sugar	1 teaspoon lemon juice
3 eggs, separated	⅛ teaspoon salt
1 tablespoon yellow corn meal	8 individual two-inch tartlet pans lined with pastry.
¼ cup heavy cream	

1. Preheat the oven to 400 degrees.
2. Cream the butter and sugar together. Beat in the egg yolks. Combine the corn meal and cream and add to the batter. Stir in the lemon rind, lemon juice and salt.
3. Beat the egg whites until stiff but not dry and fold in.
4. Bake the unfilled shells about five minutes until set. Fill with the mixture and bake five minutes. Reduce oven heat to 350 degrees and bake about twenty minutes longer, or until browned and set.

Yield: Eight tarts.

Sweet Potato Pie
ARKANSAS

1½ cups mashed cooked sweet potatoes	¼ teaspoon ground cloves
½ cup sugar	2 eggs, well beaten
½ teaspoon salt	½ teaspoon vanilla
½ teaspoon nutmeg	¼ cup butter
1 teaspoon cinnamon	1 cup hot milk
	1 unbaked nine-inch pie shell.

1. Preheat the oven to 450 degrees.
2. Combine the sweet potatoes, sugar, salt, nutmeg, cinnamon, cloves, eggs and vanilla. Melt the butter in the milk and stir into the potato mixture.
3. Beat with a rotary beater until smooth. Turn into the pie shell. Bake ten minutes, reduce oven heat to 350 degrees and bake forty-five minutes longer, or until a knife inserted in center comes out clean. Cool. Chill.

Yield: Six servings.

Sliced Yam Pie
KENTUCKY

	Pastry for a nine-inch two-crust pie
5	to six cups very thinly sliced raw yams
1	cup light brown sugar
½	teaspoon salt
	Cinnamon to taste
½	cup butter
2	tablespoons water or light cream.

1. Preheat the oven to 350 degrees. Line a nine-inch pie pan with the pastry.
2. Using about one-third of the ingredients at a time, arrange the yams, brown sugar, salt, cinnamon and bits of butter in layers in the pie pan. Pour the water or cream over all.
3. Cover with top crust, seal and cut slits. Bake until potatoes are soft, about one hour. Serve warm or at room temperature.

Yield: Six to eight servings.

Jeff Davis Pie
SOUTH CAROLINA

½	cup butter
1	cup sugar
1	tablespoon flour
3	eggs
1	cup heavy cream
¼	teaspoon salt
½	teaspoon vanilla
1	unbaked nine-inch pie shell.

1. Preheat the oven to 425 degrees.
2. Cream the butter and sugar together until light and fluffy. Beat in the flour, eggs, cream, salt and vanilla.
3. Pour into the pie shell and bake ten minutes. Lower the oven heat to 350 degrees and bake about thirty minutes longer, or until set.

Yield: Six servings.

Sour Cream Pie
NORTH CAROLINA

1	cup sour cream
¾	cup sugar
2	eggs, lightly beaten
¼	teaspoon ground cloves
1	teaspoon cinnamon
½	teaspoon nutmeg
½	cup pecans
1	unbaked eight-inch or nine-inch pie shell, chilled.

1. Preheat the oven to 425 degrees.
2. Combine the sour cream, sugar and eggs. Stir in the cloves, cinnamon, nutmeg and pecans. Pour into the pie shell. Bake fifteen minutes, reduce oven heat to 325 degrees and bake fifteen to twenty minutes longer, or until set and browned.

Yield: Six servings.

Black Bottom Pie
KENTUCKY

14	gingersnaps	4	eggs, separated
5	tablespoons melted butter	6	ounces semisweet chocolate bits
1	tablespoon unflavored gelatin		
¼	cup cold water	1	teaspoon vanilla
1	cup sugar	1	tablespoon dark rum
½	teaspoon salt	¼	teaspoon cream of tartar
¼	cup cornstarch		Whipped cream
2	cups milk		Shaved chocolate.

1. Preheat the oven to 350 degrees.
2. Crush and roll the gingersnaps fine with a rolling pin. Mix with the butter and pat the mixture along the bottom and side of a nine-inch pie pan. Bake seven minutes. Cool thoroughly.
3. Soften the gelatin in the cold water.
4. Combine one-half cup of the sugar with the salt and cornstarch and gradually stir in the milk, using a wire whisk. Bring to a boil and cook, stirring, until thickened.
5. Beat the egg yolks in a mixing bowl and gradually stir in the hot mixture. Return the custard to the heat and cook, stirring, two minutes.
6. Remove the saucepan from the heat and measure out one and one-half cups custard. Add the chocolate bits and vanilla and pour into pie shell. Chill.
7. Add the gelatin to the remaining custard mixture, stirring until gelatin dissolves. Cool to lukewarm and add the rum.
8. Beat the egg whites with the cream of tartar until stiff. Gradually beat in the remaining sugar. Fold the whites into the rum-flavored custard, pour over the chocolate mixture and chill. Serve pie topped with whipped cream and garnished with shaved chocolate.

Yield: Six or more servings.

Chocolate-Butterscotch Pie
KENTUCKY

- 3 cups light brown sugar
- ½ cup butter
- 3 eggs
- 1 teaspoon vanilla
- ½ cup light cream
- 1 ounce (one square) unsweetened chocolate, melted
- 1 unbaked nine-inch pie shell with stand-up edge, chilled
- 1 cup sweetened heavy cream, whipped
- Chocolate shavings.

1. Preheat the oven to 350 degrees.
2. Beat the brown sugar and butter together until creamy. Beat in the eggs, one at a time. Add the vanilla.
3. Beat in the light cream, add the melted chocolate and beat to mix completely. Pour into the pie shell and bake thirty minutes. Reduce the oven heat to 300 degrees and continue to bake about fifty minutes longer, or until set. Cool before decorating with the whipped cream and chocolate shavings. The pie puffs up during cooking, then falls as it cools.
Yield: Eight servings.

Rum Pie
LOUISIANA

- 5 egg yolks
- ¾ cup granulated sugar
- 1 envelope unflavored gelatin
- ¼ cup water
- ¾ cup dark rum
- 2 cups heavy cream
- 1 baked nine-inch graham cracker pie shell, cooled
- 3 tablespoons raw sugar (see note).

1. Beat the egg yolks until they are thick and lemon-colored. Gradually beat in the granulated sugar.
2. Soften the gelatin in the water and add one-quarter cup of the rum. Heat over boiling water until gelatin dissolves. Pour the gelatin mixture into the yolks, stirring briskly. Stir in the remaining rum.

3. Whip the cream and fold it into the custard. Pour the filling into the pie shell and chill.
4. When filling is set, sprinkle the pie with the raw sugar and serve.
Yield: Six servings.
Note: Raw sugar is available in health food stores and some supermarkets.

Chocolate Rum Pie
FLORIDA

3 ounces (three squares) unsweetened chocolate	2 egg yolks
¾ cup sugar	1 teaspoon vanilla
3 tablespoons flour	½ cup butter
½ teaspoon salt	¼ cup rum
1½ cups milk	1 baked nine-inch pie shell
3 tablespoons cornstarch	Whipped cream, flavored to taste with sugar and rum.
1 cup light cream	

1. Melt the chocolate over low heat.
2. Combine the sugar, flour and salt in a mixing bowl. Blend one-half cup of the milk with the cornstarch. Stir the cornstarch mixture into the flour mixture. Add the melted chocolate, the remaining milk and the cream. Add the egg yolks, vanilla and butter, beating constantly.
3. Cook the filling over boiling water until thick. Let cool.
4. Stir in the rum and pour the filling into the pie shell. Top with whipped cream and serve.
Yield: Six or more servings.

Bourbon Pie
KENTUCKY

5 egg yolks	1 baked nine-inch pie shell, cooled
¾ cup sugar	½ ounce (one-half square) unsweetened chocolate, shaved.
1 envelope unflavored gelatin	
¼ cup water	
⅓ cup bourbon	
2 cups heavy cream, whipped	

1. Beat the egg yolks and gradually add the sugar. Beat constantly until the mixture turns a light yellow.

2. Soften the gelatin in the water and heat over boiling water until gelatin dissolves. Add to the egg yolk mixture. Mix well and add the bourbon.

3. Fold in the whipped cream and pour into the pie shell. Sprinkle with the chocolate shavings. Chill for at least six hours before serving.

Yield: Six to eight servings.

Note: One-third cup dark rum may be substituted for the bourbon.

Lime Meringue Pie
FLORIDA

4	tablespoons flour		Grated rind of two limes
5	tablespoons cornstarch	½	cup freshly squeezed lime juice
1½	cups plus five tablespoons sugar	2	drops green food coloring (optional)
½	teaspoon salt	1	baked nine-inch pie shell
2	cups boiling water		Pinch of cream of tartar.
3	eggs, separated		

1. Combine the flour, cornstarch, one and one-half cups of the sugar and the salt in a heavy saucepan and mix thoroughly with a wire whisk. When well blended, add the boiling water gradually, stirring with the whisk. Bring gradually to a boil, stirring constantly. When mixture is thickened, remove from the heat.

2. Beat the egg yolks until they are light and lemon-colored. Spoon a little of the hot mixture into the yolks; then stir the yolk mixture into the sauce. Cook, stirring, two minutes over low heat.

3. Stir in the lime rind, lime juice and food coloring if desired. When all is well blended, pour the filling into the pie shell. Let the filling cool in the shell.

4. Preheat the oven to 425 degrees.

5. Beat the egg whites until they are frothy. Add the cream of tartar. Continue beating until whites stand in peaks, and gradually add the remaining sugar. When whites are thoroughly stiff, spread them roughly on top of the pie filling, leaving peaks. Make certain that the meringue touches the pie shell all around to prevent shrinking of meringue as pie bakes.

6. Bake pie until meringue is browned on top.

Yield: Six to eight servings.

Kentucky Lemon Pie

6 eggs	Grated rind of one lemon
1½ cups light corn syrup	1 tablespoon melted butter
¾ cup sugar	1 unbaked ten-inch pie shell with stand-up edge, chilled
1 teaspoon cornstarch	
½ cup lemon juice	Meringue (recipe below).

1. Preheat the oven to 375 degrees.
2. Beat the eggs with a rotary beater until well mixed. Add the syrup and continue beating.
3. Combine the sugar and cornstarch and add to the egg mixture, beating.
4. Add the lemon juice, lemon rind and butter. Beat until thoroughly mixed.
5. Pour carefully into the pie shell. Bake fifteen minutes. Reduce the oven heat to 300 degrees and cook forty-five minutes longer, or until set. Cool and chill.
6. When ready to top the pie with the meringue, preheat the oven to 350 degrees. Spread the meringue over filling so that the meringue touches the pastry edge all around. Leave the surface rough. Bake ten minutes, or until the meringue is lightly browned. Cool and chill again before serving.

Yield: Eight to ten servings.

Meringue
KENTUCKY

3 egg whites, at room temperature	3 tablespoons confectioners' sugar.
¼ teaspoon cream of tartar	

1. Beat the egg whites until frothy. Add the cream of tartar and continue beating until stiff.
2. Add the sugar, one tablespoon at a time, beating very well after each addition.

Yield: Enough for one nine-inch or ten-inch pie.

Orange Liqueur Chiffon Tart
KENTUCKY

1	envelope unflavored gelatin	1	tablespoon grated orange peel
¼	cup cold water		
4	eggs, separated	1	baked nine-inch pie shell
¾	cup sugar	1	cup heavy cream, whipped
⅓	cup orange juice	2	tablespoons sliced toasted almonds.
¼	teaspoon salt		
2	tablespoons Cointreau or Grand Marnier		

    1. Soften the gelatin in the water. Beat the egg yolks until thick. Beat in one-half cup of the sugar. Beat in the orange juice and salt and heat in the top of a double boiler until mixture thickens. Do not allow to boil.
    2. Stir in softened gelatin until it dissolves. Add the liqueur and orange peel. Cool until mixture starts to thicken. Beat the egg whites until frothy, add the remaining sugar and continue beating until stiff and glossy. Fold into cooked mixture.
    3. Pour filling into the pie shell and chill. Decorate with the whipped cream and sprinkle with the almonds just before serving.
Yield: Six servings.

Lemon Chiffon Pie
SOUTH CAROLINA

¾	cup sugar	3	tablespoons lemon juice
2	tablespoons milk	3	egg whites, stiffly beaten
5	egg yolks	1	baked nine-inch pie shell.
1	tablespoon grated lemon rind		

    1. Preheat the oven to 400 degrees.
    2. Combine one-half cup of the sugar, the milk and egg yolks in the top of a double boiler. Cook over hot water, stirring, until thickened. Stir in the lemon rind and lemon juice and remove from heat. Pour the mixture into a mixing bowl and let cool.
    3. Fold the egg whites and remaining sugar into the mixture and pour into the pie shell. Bake eight to ten minutes.
Yield: Eight servings.

Spiced Carrot Pie
ARKANSAS

1	cup sugar	⅛ teaspoon ground cloves
½	teaspoon salt	1½ cups mashed cooked carrots
1	teaspoon ground ginger	3 eggs, lightly beaten
1	teaspoon cinnamon	1½ cups milk or light cream
½	teaspoon nutmeg	1 unbaked nine-inch pie shell.

1. Preheat the oven to 400 degrees.
2. Combine the sugar, salt and spices. Stir in the carrots and eggs. Add the milk or cream and mix well. Pour the mixture into the pie shell.
3. Bake one hour, or until filling is nearly set. The filling will continue to cook slightly after pie is removed from the oven.

Yield: Six to eight servings.

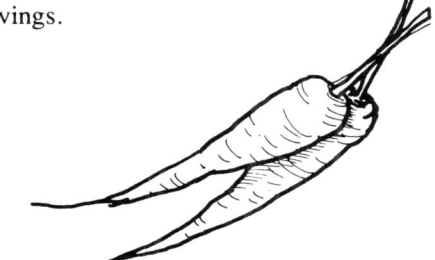

Apple Stack Pie
TENNESSEE

Pastry made according to a standard recipe using three cups flour
4 cups thick applesauce
Sugar to taste
Cinnamon, chopped
Preserved ginger, ground ginger or nutmeg
2 cups heavy cream, whipped.

1. Preheat the oven to 425 degrees.
2. Roll the pastry to one-eighth-inch thickness and cut around a nine-inch pan into circles. There should be about six circles. Bake until golden brown, about twelve minutes.
3. Sweeten the applesauce with sugar and flavor with spice to taste.
4. Just before serving, spread each pastry circle with applesauce and whipped cream, stacking circles like a layer cake.

Yield: Eight servings.

Fried Fresh Peach Turnovers
GEORGIA

2	cups flour	1½	cups peeled and finely chopped peaches
½	teaspoon salt		
4	tablespoons granulated sugar	½	teaspoon cinnamon
1	teaspoon baking powder		Fat or oil for deep-frying
½	cup milk		Confectioners' sugar
1	egg, lightly beaten		Whipped cream.
3	tablespoons melted butter		

1. Sift the flour, salt, one tablespoon of the granulated sugar and the baking powder into a bowl. Combine the milk, egg and butter and stir into the flour mixture to make a soft but not sticky dough.
2. Roll out the dough on a lightly floured board or pastry cloth to one-eighth-inch thickness. Cut into two-and-one-half-inch rounds.
3. Mix together the peaches, cinnamon and remaining sugar and place a tablespoon of this filling in the middle of each round.
4. Moisten around the edge of the round, fold over to make a turnover and press the edge together with the tines of a fork to seal.
5. Deep-fry, two or three at a time, in the fat or oil heated to 375 degrees until golden brown and done, about three minutes. Turn once.
6. Drain on paper towels, sprinkle with confectioners' sugar and serve hot with whipped cream.

Yield: Fourteen to sixteen.

Fried Fruit Turnovers
GEORGIA

1	pound dried peaches, apricots or apples, cooked	1	teaspoon salt
		¾	cup shortening or lard
1	cup sugar, approximately	½	cup ice water, approximately
	Cinnamon or nutmeg to taste		Fat for frying.
4	cups sifted flour		

1. Drain the selected fruit, mash and sweeten with sugar to taste. Add desired spice. Cool.
2. Sift together the flour and salt. Chop in the shortening or lard until the lumps are the size of very small peas. Add the ice water while tossing the

mixture from the bottom of the bowl, using only enough water to form a fairly stiff dough. Press into a ball.

3. Roll out one-third of the dough at a time into a sheet not more than one-eighth-inch thick and about seven inches long. Using a six-inch plate as a guide, cut the dough into circles.

4. Put a one-half-inch layer of prepared fruit on half of each circle, leaving the rim uncovered. Moisten the uncovered rim and fold the other half of the circle over the fruit. Seal and cut away any excess pastry. Crimp the rim.

5. Heat fat to the depth of about one-half inch in a heavy skillet and brown the turnovers on each side. Serve warm or cold.

Yield: Sixteen.

Fresh Peach Pie
GEORGIA

Pastry for a two-crust pie	¼ cup flour
3 cups peeled, sliced fresh peaches tossed with juice of half a lemon to prevent discoloration	⅓ cup light brown sugar
	⅛ teaspoon ground ginger
	1 tablespoon butter.

1. Preheat the oven to 400 degrees.
2. Line an eight-inch pie plate with the pastry.
3. Combine the peaches, flour, brown sugar and ginger and turn the mixture into pie plate. Dot with the butter. Cover with top crust and slash the top. Flute the edges. Bake thirty to forty minutes, or until browned.

Yield: Six servings.

Peach Roll-Ups
GEORGIA

2 cups flour	½ teaspoon cinnamon
4 teaspoons baking powder	2 cups peeled, diced fresh peaches
½ teaspoon salt	
4 tablespoons granulated sugar	½ cup light brown sugar
⅓ cup shortening	1 tablespoon lemon juice
¾ cup milk, approximately	½ cup water
¼ cup soft butter	Whipped cream.

1. Preheat the oven to 400 degrees.
2. Combine the flour, baking powder, salt and one tablespoon of the granulated sugar in a bowl. Cut in the shortening until mixture resembles coarse oatmeal.
3. Gradually add enough milk to make a soft dough. Pat the dough or roll into a rectangle about one-half-inch thick.
4. Brush with the butter and sprinkle with the remaining sugar mixed with the cinnamon.
5. Spread with the peaches and roll like a jellyroll. Cut into one-and-one-half-inch slices and place, cut side up, in a greased nine-by-thirteen-inch baking pan.
6. Combine the brown sugar, lemon juice and water and pour over slices. Bake thirty to forty minutes, or until done. Serve warm with whipped cream.

Yield: Six to eight servings.

Note: The cooked slices can be frozen and stored for up to two months. To serve, bake, uncovered, in a 350-degree oven for about twenty minutes.

Peach Cobbler
ARKANSAS

4 cups sliced fresh peaches, peeled or not as desired	2 tablespoons melted butter
1 cup sugar	¼ cup shortening
3 tablespoons plus three-quarters cup flour	¼ teaspoon salt
	2 tablespoons water.

1. Preheat the oven to 400 degrees.
2. Place the peaches in the bottom of a flame-proof eight-inch square baking dish. Heat until peaches start to simmer.
3. Mix together the sugar and three tablespoons of the flour and sprinkle over the peaches. Add the butter.
4. Place the remaining flour in a bowl, add the shortening and salt and with the fingertips work in the shortening until mixture resembles coarse oatmeal. Mix to a dough with the water.
5. Roll out the pastry on a lightly floured board or pastry cloth to fit the baking dish and place over the peaches. Prick with a fork and bake thirty-five to forty minutes.

Yield: Eight servings.

Rum and Rhubarb Chess Pie
MARYLAND

2	tablespoons butter	2	tablespoons dark rum
1	cup sugar	½	teaspoon salt
¼	cup flour	¼	teaspoon nutmeg
2	eggs, separated	1	partially cooked nine-inch pie shell, prepared according to the next recipe.
1	cup rhubarb, cut into one-half-inch lengths		
¾	cup plus two tablespoons milk		

1. Preheat the oven to 350 degrees.
2. In a mixing bowl and using an electric beater, cream together the butter and sugar. Beat in the flour and then the egg yolks. Stir in the rhubarb, milk, rum, salt and nutmeg.
3. In a separate bowl, beat the egg whites until stiff and fold them into the rhubarb mixture. Pour this into the pie shell and bake forty-five minutes. Let cool before serving.

Yield: Six to eight servings.

Pastry for a Nine-Inch Pie
MARYLAND

1¼	cups sifted flour	¼	cup butter
½	teaspoon salt	3	tablespoons water, approximately.
¼	cup shortening		

1. Preheat the oven to 350 degrees.
2. In a mixing bowl, combine the flour and salt. Using a pastry blender or two knives, cut in the shortening and butter until the mixture resembles coarse corn meal.
3. Sprinkle the water over the mixture a little at a time while tossing lightly with a two-pronged fork. Add just enough water to moisten the flour so that the pastry will hold together. Gather the dough into a ball and roll it out in a circle on a lightly floured board. The pastry should be about one-eighth-inch thick and one and one-half inches larger in diameter than the pie plate. Line the pie plate with pastry. Flute the edge of the pastry and bake five minutes.

Yield: One partially cooked nine-inch pie shell.

Orange Cake
FLORIDA

Cake:
1	cup butter	2	teaspoons baking powder
1½	cups sugar	½	teaspoon salt
4	eggs	1	tablespoon grated orange rind
2¼	cups cake flour	¼	cup orange juice.

Filling:
3	tablespoons flour	1	tablespoon water
2	tablespoons cornstarch	2	egg yolks, lightly beaten
½	cup sugar	¼	cup butter
1	cup orange juice	½	cup heavy cream, whipped
1	teaspoon grated orange rind		(optional).
1	teaspoon unflavored gelatin		

Frosting:
2	egg whites	1	tablespoon light corn syrup
1¾	cups sugar	5	tablespoons orange juice.

1. To prepare cake, grease and flour an eight-inch springform pan or two nine-inch layer pans. Preheat the oven to 325 degrees for the eight-inch pan or to 375 degrees for the layer pans.

2. Beat the butter with the sugar until very light in color and fluffy in texture. Beat in the eggs, one at a time.

3. Combine the flour, baking powder and salt and sift together. Add half the flour mixture, the orange rind and orange juice to the batter and fold in gently. Fold in the remaining flour mixture and pour into the prepared pan or pans.

4. Bake the eight-inch layer about one and one-quarter hours, or until a cake tester inserted in the center comes out clean. Bake the nine-inch layers about thirty minutes, or until they test done.

5. Cool the cake in the pan or pans ten minutes; then remove to a rack and cool before filling and frosting. The deep cake can be sliced into two, three or four layers. Each of the two layers may be halved, if desired, for a four-layer effect.

6. To prepare filling, combine the flour, cornstarch and sugar in a small pan. Add the orange juice and orange rind and mix well.

7. Soak the gelatin in the water.

8. Bring the orange mixture to a boil, stirring constantly. Cook two minutes. Spoon a little of the hot mixture onto the egg yolks and mix. Add the rest of the orange mixture. Cook half a minute longer.

9. Add the soaked gelatin and the butter. Stir to dissolve. Cool and chill, stirring occasionally.

10. Fold in the whipped cream, if desired, just before using to fill the cake layers.

11. To prepare frosting, place all ingredients in the top of a double boiler over rapidly boiling water. Cook seven minutes, beating rapidly all the time. Frosting will be thick and fluffy. Remove from the boiling water and continue to beat until thick enough to hold its shape. Use to frost the cake.

Yield: Ten servings.

Cake à l'Orange
FLORIDA

1 cup butter, at room temperature	½ cup chopped walnuts or pecans
1½ cups sugar	¼ cup orange juice
3 eggs, separated	⅓ Grand Marnier or other orange-flavored liqueur
2 cups flour	
1 teaspoon baking powder	
1 teaspoon baking soda	2 tablespoons slivered blanched almonds.
1 cup sour cream	
Grated rind of one orange	

1. Preheat the oven to 350 degrees.

2. Cream together the butter and one cup sugar until light and fluffy. Beat in the egg yolks.

3. Sift together the flour, baking powder and baking soda and add, alternately with the sour cream, stirring until smooth. Stir in the orange rind and nuts.

4. Beat the egg whites until stiff but not dry and fold them into the batter. Grease a nine-inch tube cake pan and pour in the batter. Bake fifty minutes, or until cake is done when tested with a cake tester.

5. Combine the orange juice, Grand Marnier and remaining sugar and spoon the mixture over the hot cake. Decorate the top with the almonds. Let the cake cool before removing it from the pan.

Yield: Ten servings.

Butter Cake
NORTH CAROLINA

1 cup chopped nuts or nuts mixed with raisins	2 cups flour
4 eggs	1 teaspoon baking powder
2 cups sugar	¼ teaspoon salt
1 teaspoon vanilla	1 cup milk
	½ cup butter.

1. Preheat the oven to 350 degrees.
2. Grease a nine-inch tube pan generously. Line the bottom of the pan with wax paper and grease the paper.
3. Sprinkle the nuts over the bottom of the pan.
4. Beat the eggs until they are lemon-colored and very thick. Gradually beat in the sugar and continue beating until mixture is very thick. Beat in the vanilla.
5. Mix the flour with the baking powder and salt and blend in with the mixer on lowest speed or with a wooden spoon.
6. Heat the milk and butter together in a pan until the butter is melted and the mixture boiling. Pour all at once into the batter and mix just sufficiently to blend all ingredients together. Immediately pour into the prepared pan and bake about fifty minutes, or until done.
7. Cool in the pan ten to fifteen minutes before turning upside down onto a serving plate. The cake will shrink during the cooling.

Yield: Ten to one dozen servings.

Poundcake I
SOUTH CAROLINA

1 cup butter	½ teaspoon almond extract
2 cups sugar	2 cups flour, sifted four times
4 eggs	⅓ cup (one small can) evaporated milk.
1 teaspoon vanilla	

1. Preheat the oven to 350 degrees.
2. Cream the butter and sugar together until very light and fluffy and there is no graininess left from the sugar.
3. Beat in the eggs, one at a time, very well.
4. Beat in the vanilla and almond extract. Fold in the flour alternately with the milk.

5. Pour into an eight-inch tube pan or nine-by-five-by-three-inch loaf pan that has been greased and lined with wax paper.

6. Bake about fifty-five minutes, or until done. Cool slightly in the pan before turning cake out onto a rack. The cake is very tender when hot. The flavor and texture improve on storage.

Yield: Ten to one dozen servings.

Poundcake II
SOUTH CAROLINA

1	cup butter	½	teaspoon baking powder
¼	cup shortening	⅛	teaspoon salt
2½	cups sugar	1	teaspoon vanilla
5	eggs	½	teaspoon lemon extract
3	cups flour	1	cup milk.

1. Cream the butter and shortening together until creamy. Gradually beat in the sugar until mixture is light and fluffy.

2. Beat in the eggs, one at a time.

3. Sift together the flour, baking powder and salt. Add the vanilla and lemon extract to the milk. Fold dry ingredients into batter alternately with the milk.

4. Spoon batter into a lightly greased nine-inch tube pan. Place in the middle of the oven and set the oven for 325 degrees (the oven is not pre-heated). Bake one hour and twenty minutes, or until done.

Yield: One dozen servings.

Pecan-Cherry Cake
GEORGIA

2	cups candied cherries, halved	5	cups flour
2	cups golden raisins	1	teaspoon nutmeg
2	cups bourbon	1	teaspoon cinnamon
1½	cups butter	1	teaspoon baking powder
2	cups granulated sugar	2½	cups (about one pound) shelled pecans, chopped.
1	cup light brown sugar		
6	eggs, separated		

1. Day before, place the cherries and raisins in a bowl and cover with one and one-half cups of the bourbon. Let stand overnight.

2. Next day, preheat the oven to 275 degrees. Line a greased ten-inch tube pan with parchment paper, wax paper or unglazed brown paper and grease again.

3. Cream the butter together with the sugars until very light and fluffy. Beat in the egg yolks, one at a time.

4. Fold in the soaked fruit and the extra bourbon that may be in the bottom of the bowl. Sift together the flour with the nutmeg, cinnamon and baking powder. Take out one-half cup of the mixture and sprinkle over the pecans. Toss to coat.

5. Beat the egg whites until stiff but not dry. Fold the flour mixture and the egg whites into the batter. Fold in the pecans. Spoon the batter into the prepared pan and bake three and one-half to four hours, or until cake tests done.

6. Cool in the pan, then remove from the pan and wrap in cheesecloth soaked in the remaining bourbon. Wrap in wax paper and aluminum foil or place in a tin with a tightly fitting lid. Do not attempt to cut for at least forty-eight hours.

Yield: Two dozen servings.

Jam Cake
SOUTH CAROLINA

¾ cup butter	1 teaspoon nutmeg
1 cup sugar	1 teaspoon allspice
3 eggs	1 teaspoon cinnamon
1 cup black raspberry or blackberry preserves	1 teaspoon baking soda
	¾ cup buttermilk
2½ cups flour	2 tablespoons bourbon.

1. Preheat the oven to 350 degrees.

2. Beat the butter and sugar together until light and fluffy. Beat in the eggs, one at a time.

3. Fold in the preserves. Sift together the flour, nutmeg, allspice, cinnamon and baking soda. Add to batter alternately with the buttermilk, folding in. Fold in the bourbon.

4. Spoon into a greased nine-inch tube pan. Bake fifty minutes.

Yield: Ten to one dozen servings.

Lemon Cake
ALABAMA

- 1 cup butter
- ½ cup shortening
- 2 cups granulated sugar
- 3 eggs
- 3 cups flour
- ½ teaspoon baking soda
- ½ teaspoon salt
- 1 cup buttermilk
- 2 tablespoons grated lemon rind
- ½ cup, approximately, plus one tablespoon lemon juice
- 3 cups confectioners' sugar.

1. Preheat the oven to 325 degrees.
2. Beat one-half cup of the butter, the shortening and granulated sugar together until light and fluffy. Beat in the eggs, one at a time.
3. Sift together the flour, baking soda and salt and stir in alternately with the buttermilk. Stir in one tablespoon of the lemon rind and one tablespoon of the lemon juice.
4. Pour into a greased nine-inch tube pan and bake one and one-quarter hours, or until cake tests done. Cool on a rack.
5. Mix together the remaining butter and the confectioners' sugar until creamy. Add the remaining lemon rind and stir in enough remaining lemon juice to give a pouring consistency. Pour over the cooling cake.

Yield: Ten servings.

Angel Food Cake
TENNESSEE

- 1⅓ cups sugar, sifted twice
- 1 cup sifted cake flour
- ½ teaspoon salt
- 1½ cups egg whites (about twelve whites)
- 1¼ teaspoons cream of tartar
- 1 teaspoon vanilla
- ½ teaspoon almond extract.

1. Preheat the oven to 350 degrees.
2. Add one-third cup of the sifted sugar to the cake flour. Add the salt and sift the mixture together three times.
3. Beat the egg whites, preferably with a wire whisk, until they are foamy and add the cream of tartar. Continue beating until whites are stiff but not dry. Gradually beat in the remaining sugar, one tablespoon at a time. Fold in the vanilla and almond extract. Sift approximately one-quarter cup of the

sugar and flour mixture over the batter. Fold in with a rubber spatula. Continue adding the sugar and flour mixture, folding in after each addition.

4. Pour the batter into an ungreased nine-inch tube pan. Bake about forty-five minutes, or until the top springs back when lightly touched. Immediately turn the pan upside down, suspending tube part over the neck of a funnel or bottle. Let cake stand in the pan until cold, about one and one-half hours.

Yield: One angel food cake; about ten servings.

Sugar Plum Cake
TENNESSEE

Cake:
- ¾ cup shortening
- 1¾ cups granulated sugar
- 4 eggs
- 4 cups flour
- ¾ pound candied orange slices, cut finely with scissors
- 1½ cups coarsely chopped pecans
- 1 eight-ounce package dates, cut small
- 1 three-and-one-half-ounce can flaked coconut
- ⅛ teaspoon salt
- 1 teaspoon baking soda
- ⅔ cup buttermilk
- 1 tablespoon lemon juice
- 1 teaspoon orange extract

Glaze:
- 2 cups confectioners' sugar
- 1 cup orange juice
- 2 teaspoons grated orange rind

1. Preheat the oven to 300 degrees if metal pans are used or to 275 degrees if glass pans are used.
2. Cream the shortening and granulated sugar together very well until light and fluffy. Beat in the eggs, one at a time.
3. Sift half the flour over the orange slice bits, pecans, dates and coconut and mix well.
4. Sift the remaining flour with the salt and baking soda and add alternately with the buttermilk to the creamed shortening mixture. Stir in the lemon juice and orange extract.
5. With the hands, mix in the dredged fruits. Fill two greased and floured nine-by-five-by-three-inch loaf pans with the mixture and bake about

one hour and forty minutes, but start testing for doneness after one hour and fifteen minutes.

6. Let the cakes rest five minutes; then prick all over, while still in the pans, with a skewer or ice pick. Combine the glaze ingredients and spoon over the surface of the cakes while they are still hot.

Yield: Twenty servings.

White Fruitcake

GEORGIA

- 1½ cups butter
- 2 cups sugar
- 6 eggs
- 1 teaspoon nutmeg
- 1 teaspoon vanilla
- ½ cup bourbon
- 2 teaspoons baking powder
- 4 cups sifted flour
- 1 pound candied cherries
- 1 pound candied pineapple, cut into large pieces
- 1 pound shelled pecans.

1. Preheat the oven to 275 degrees.
2. Cream together the butter and sugar. Add the eggs, one at a time, beating well after each addition. Add the nutmeg, vanilla and bourbon. Sift together the baking powder and three cups of the flour and fold into the batter.
3. Dredge the fruit with the remaining flour and place fruit in the oven about five minutes. Add the flour-coated fruit to the batter. Pour into a tube pan and bake three hours.

Yield: Eight or more servings.

Applesauce Fruitcake

TENNESSEE

- ½ cup butter
- 1 cup sugar
- 2 eggs
- 2 cups flour
- 2 teaspoons baking soda
- ½ teaspoon nutmeg
- ½ teaspoon ground cloves
- ½ teaspoon allspice
- ¼ cup port wine or whisky
- 1½ cups applesauce
- 1 pound raisins
- 1 cup diced citron
- 1 cup diced mixed candied peels
- 1 cup drained maraschino cherries
- 2 cups chopped dates.

1. Preheat the oven to 325 degrees.
2. Cream the butter and sugar together well. Beat in the eggs, one at a time. Sift together the flour, baking soda and spices and reserve three tablespoons.
3. Stir in the bulk of the flour mixture alternately with the port or whisky. Stir in the applesauce. Toss the remaining ingredients with the reserved flour mixture and stir in.
4. Spoon the batter into a greased and floured two-and-one-half-quart to three-quart cake tin or springform pan with removable ring. Bake for one and one-half hours, or until the cake tests done.

Yield: One dozen to eighteen servings.

Note: The cake improves on wrapping and storing in a cool place.

Past Perfect Fruitcake
MISSISSIPPI

4	cups shelled pecans	1½	teaspoons baking powder
2	cups unchopped crystallized cherries	¼	teaspoon salt
		4	eggs
5	slices crystallized pineapple, each slice cut into eighths	1	cup sugar
		1	teaspoon vanilla.
1	cup flour		

1. Preheat the oven to 250 degrees.
2. Grease the bottom and sides of a two-quart cake tin and line the bottom of it with brown paper or parchment paper.
3. Combine the pecans, cherries and pineapple in a mixing bowl. Combine the flour, baking powder and salt in a sifter and sift the dry ingredients over the fruits.
4. Combine the eggs, sugar and vanilla in another mixing bowl and beat until blended. Pour this over the fruit and stir with a slotted spoon. Pour the batter into the prepared pan and bake one and one-half hours. At the end of that time, set the cake pan into a pan of boiling water and continue baking fifteen minutes longer.

Yield: One dozen or more servings.

Lane Cake Layers

ALABAMA

1 cup butter	¼ teaspoon salt
2 cups sugar	1 cup milk
1 teaspoon vanilla	8 egg whites, beaten until stiff but not dry.
3¼ cups flour	
3½ teaspoons baking powder	

1. Preheat the oven to 375 degrees.
2. Grease and flour three nine-inch layer pans.
3. Beat the butter and sugar together until very light and creamy. Beat in the vanilla. Sift together the flour, baking powder and salt twice.
4. Stir the flour mixture alternately with the milk into the batter. Stir in one-quarter of the egg whites. Fold in remaining egg whites until just mixed. Spoon into the prepared pans and bake twenty to twenty-five minutes. Cool in the pans for ten minutes; then turn out onto racks for further cooling.

Yield: Three layers; about ten filled and topped servings.

Note: The batter may be baked in a greased and floured ten-inch tube pan or a 13-by-9½-by-2-inch metal pan, in an oven preheated to 350 degrees, for one to one and one-quarter hours.

The cake mellows on storage in a closed container for several days.

Wrapped in plastic wrap or aluminum foil, both layers and large cakes freeze well and are always on hand to be finished with filling and frosting.

For a firmer, closer, slightly more tender texture, three and one-quarter cups cake flour and one and three-quarters cups superfine sugar may be substituted for the flour and sugar in the above recipe. The instructions remain the same.

Lane Cake Filling

ALABAMA

8 egg yolks	¼ teaspoon salt
1¼ cups sugar	1 cup shredded coconut, preferably fresh
Grated rind of one orange	
⅓ cup bourbon	1 cup raisins
½ teaspoon mace	1 cup glacé cherries, quartered.
1¼ cups pecans, chopped	

1. Mix together the egg yolks, sugar and orange rind in a heavy pan or in the top of a double boiler.

2. Stirring constantly, cook the mixture over medium heat until the sugar dissolves and the mixture thickens to coat the back of the spoon. Do not allow the mixture to boil or the egg yolks will be scrambled.

3. Remove from the heat and stir in the remaining ingredients. Cool before using to fill and top a three-layer cake.

Yield: About one quart.

Lady Baltimore Cake
SOUTH CAROLINA

Cake:
- 1 recipe (three layers) lane cake (page 219).

Syrup:
- 1 cup sugar
- ½ cup water
- ½ teaspoon almond extract
- 1 teaspoon vanilla.

White frosting:
- 3 cups sugar
- 1 cup water
- ¼ teaspoon cream of tartar
- 3 egg whites
- ⅛ teaspoon salt
- 1 teaspoon vanilla
- 2 cups pecans, coarsely chopped
- 1½ cups figs, coarsely chopped
- ½ cup raisins
- ⅓ cup cognac (optional).

1. While the cake layers are baking, prepare the syrup by combining the sugar and water in a small pan. Heat, stirring, until the sugar dissolves. Cook six minutes longer without stirring. Stir in the almond extract and vanilla and pour over the cake layers while they are still hot from the oven.

2. To make the frosting, combine the sugar, water and cream of tartar in a saucepan. Heat, stirring, until the sugar dissolves. Continue to heat without stirring until the syrup registers 238 degrees on a candy thermometer or spins a thread.

3. Beat the egg whites and the salt until stiff. Pour the syrup in a steady stream into the beaten egg whites, beating constantly until the frosting stands in peaks. Stir in the vanilla. There will be about two and one-quarter cups frosting. Divide the frosting into two parts.

4. Add the pecans, figs and raisins, soaked overnight in the cognac if desired, to one-half of the frosting and use to fill between the three soaked layers. Use remaining frosting to frost the top and sides of the cake.
Yield: About one dozen servings.

Mrs. D's Moravian Sugar Cake
NORTH CAROLINA

1	cup mashed potatoes
1	cup potato water
1	cup milk, scalded
2	cups granulated sugar
1	package active dry yeast
⅓	cup lukewarm water
9	cups flour, approximately

2	eggs, well beaten
¾	cup melted shortening
1	tablespoon salt
¾	cup butter
1	cup light brown sugar
2	teaspoons cinnamon.

1. Mix together the potatoes, potato water, milk and one cup of the granulated sugar. Cool to lukewarm.

2. Dissolve the yeast in the lukewarm water and add one teaspoon of the remaining sugar.

3. Add yeast mixture and two cups of the flour to cooled potato mixture. Stand in a warm place, covered, for about one hour, or until mixture bubbles.

4. Stir in the eggs, shortening, salt, remaining sugar and enough remaining flour to make a soft dough. Knead lightly on a board. Place in a clean greased bowl and let rise until doubled in bulk, about one and one-half hours.

5. Punch dough down and then spread into a one-half-inch layer in three greased jellyroll pans or other shallow baking pans. Cover and let rise until doubled in bulk, about twenty minutes.

6. Preheat the oven to 375 degrees.

7. Make depressions in the dough and place a knob of butter and a tablespoon or two of the brown sugar mixed with the cinnamon in each hole. Bake about twenty minutes, or until brown and done.

Yield: About four dozen servings.

Note: After kneading, the dough can be left in a clean bowl in a cool place overnight, if desired.

Sweet Potato Pone
GEORGIA

2 cups grated raw sweet potatoes	2 cups milk
1 egg, beaten	½ teaspoon grated fresh or ground ginger
½ cup unsulphured molasses	½ teaspoon cinnamon
3 tablespoons sugar	½ teaspoon nutmeg
3 tablespoons melted butter	½ teaspoon salt
Grated rind of one orange	Heavy cream or ice cream.

1. Preheat the oven to 275 degrees.
2. Combine all the ingredients and pour into a one-and-one-half-quart baking dish. Bake three hours. Serve warm with heavy cream or ice cream.

Yield: Six servings.

Mrs. Mescal Johnston's Rice Custard with Lemon Sauce
ARKANSAS

Custard:

2 cups milk	¼ teaspoon salt
1 cup cooked rice	⅓ cup raisins or nuts
1 tablespoon butter	2 eggs, beaten.
⅓ cup sugar	

Sauce:

½ cup sugar	1 cup boiling water
1 tablespoon cornstarch	2 tablespoons butter
⅛ teaspoon salt	1½ tablespoons lemon juice.
⅛ teaspoon nutmeg	

1. Preheat the oven to 350 degrees.
2. To make custard, heat the milk and add the rice and butter. Stir the sugar, salt and raisins or nuts into the eggs and then slowly stir into hot milk mixture.
3. Pour into a greased baking dish, set in a pan of hot water and bake one hour, or until set. Or pour into four greased custard cups, set in a pan of hot water and bake twelve to fifteen minutes, or until set.

4. For sauce, combine the sugar, cornstarch, salt and nutmeg in a saucepan and gradually stir in the boiling water. Cook, stirring, until thick and clear. Add the butter and lemon juice. Serve with rice custard.
Yield: Four servings.

Banana Pudding
ARKANSAS

4 cups milk	1 teaspoon vanilla
1 cup sugar	Vanilla wafer cookies
⅛ teaspoon salt	3 to four ripe bananas.
4 eggs, separated	

1. Heat the milk, one-half cup of the sugar and the salt in the top of a double boiler. Beat the egg yolks slightly, mix in a little hot milk and return all to the double boiler.
2. Heat, stirring, until custard coats the back of the spoon. Remove from the heat and place in a pan of cold water and stir the custard as it cools. Stir in the vanilla.
3. Preheat the oven to 350 degrees.
4. In the bottom of a greased two-quart baking dish, put a layer of vanilla wafers. Slice over them a layer of bananas and add some of the custard.
5. Repeat until dish is three-quarters full. Beat the egg whites until stiff and gradually beat in the remaining sugar.
6. Spread the meringue on top of the pudding and bake twelve minutes, or until meringue is lightly browned. Cool and chill.
Yield: Six servings.

Bourbon Date Pudding
KENTUCKY

2 eggs	1 cup broken walnuts or pecans
1 cup sugar	1 cup chopped dates
5 tablespoons light cream	1 or two tablespoons bourbon
3 tablespoons flour	(see note)
1½ teaspoons baking powder	Sweetened whipped cream.

1. Combine the eggs and sugar and beat well until light and creamy. Add the cream, flour, baking powder, nuts and dates and spoon into the top of a large double boiler.

2. Cover and cook over boiling water, taking care that all the water does not evaporate from the bottom. Cook about two hours, stirring occasionally. When cooked, add the bourbon. Chill and serve cold with sweetened whipped cream, flavored with bourbon if desired.
Yield: Eight or more servings.
Note: Cognac may be substituted for the bourbon.

Flan
FLORIDA

4 cups heavy cream	Grated rind of half a lime
12 egg yolks	Juice of one lime
1 cup plus five tablespoons sugar	3 tablespoons water.

1. Preheat the oven to 350 degrees.
2. Bring the cream just to a boil.
3. Combine the egg yolks and five tablespoons of the sugar and stir until blended. Gradually add the hot cream to the yolk mixture, stirring constantly. Add the lime rind and lime juice and set aside.
4. Combine the remaining sugar and the water in a saucepan and bring to a boil, stirring. Continue cooking until sugar turns the color of deep amber. Do not burn the sugar, however. Pour caramel around bottom and sides of a warm two-quart baking dish to coat it. Pour in the cream mixture and set the dish in a larger pan. Pour hot water around dish. Bake forty-five minutes to one hour, or until a knife inserted in center comes out clean. Cool, chill and unmold.
Yield: Six to eight servings.

Chocolate Pecan Pudding
VIRGINIA

1 envelope unflavored gelatin	⅛ teaspoon salt
2 tablespoons cold water	½ cup sugar
¼ cup boiling water	1 teaspoon vanilla
2 ounces (two squares) semisweet chocolate	½ cup chopped fresh or toasted pecans
1 tablespoon black coffee	Sweetened whipped cream.
4 egg whites	

1. Soften the gelatin in the cold water. Add the boiling water, stirring until mixture dissolves. Keep warm.
2. Combine the chocolate and coffee and melt over very low heat or in a double boiler, stirring.
3. Whip the egg whites until frothy and add the salt. Beat until stiff but not dry. Gradually beat in the sugar, vanilla and melted chocolate.
4. Stir in the gelatin and pecans and turn into a nine-by-five-inch loaf pan. Chill until firm and serve cut into slices and topped with sweetened whipped cream.

Yield: Six to eight servings.

Lemon Fluff
GEORGIA

7 egg yolks	¼ cup cold water
1¼ cups sugar	7 egg whites
Juice of three lemons	Ladyfingers
Grated rind of two lemons	Sweetened whipped cream.
1 tablespoon unflavored gelatin	

1. Beat the egg yolks with one cup of the sugar until they are light. Add the lemon juice and lemon rind and cook over boiling water, stirring, until thickened.
2. Soak the gelatin in the water; then add to the hot mixture, stirring to dissolve.
3. Beat the egg whites until frothy and begin adding the remaining sugar. Beat until stiff and fold the whites into the yolk mixture. Line a two-quart springform pan with ladyfingers and spoon the lemon fluff into it. Chill until set. Unmold and serve with sweetened whipped cream.

Yield: About eight servings.

Snow on the Mountain
LOUISIANA

Base:

5	egg whites	¼	cup cold water
6	tablespoons sugar	1	cup heavy cream
¼	teaspoon salt	1	teaspoon vanilla
1	envelope unflavored gelatin	1	cup grated coconut.

Sauce:

5	egg yolks	2	tablespoons light rum, or to taste.
1	cup sugar		
2	tablespoons sweet sherry		

    1. To make base, beat the egg whites until stiff. Gradually beat in the sugar and salt.
    2. Soak the gelatin in the water and heat over hot water to dissolve. Fold the gelatin into the beaten egg whites.
    3. Whip the cream until stiff and add the vanilla. Fold the cream into the egg white mixture. Spoon the mixture into lightly oiled custard cups and chill. When ready to serve, unmold onto individual plates or arrange the "balls" in a crystal serving bowl. Sprinkle with the coconut and serve with sauce.
    4. To make sauce, beat the egg yolks until they are slightly thickened and pale yellow. Beat in the sugar. Add the sherry and cook over low heat until thickened and smooth. Do not let the mixture boil. Stir in the rum and reheat without boiling.
    Yield: About six servings.

Bridal Pudding
LOUISIANA

2	envelopes unflavored gelatin	1	teaspoon vanilla
½	cup cold water	1	cup flaked coconut
⅓	cup boiling water		Crushed sweetened strawberries
6	egg whites		
¼	teaspoon salt		Rum sauce (page 267)
¾	cup sugar		Whole strawberries
2	cups heavy cream		(optional).

1. Soften the gelatin in the cold water.
2. Pour the boiling water into the gelatin and stir to dissolve.
3. Beat the egg whites until stiff. Add the salt and gradually beat in the sugar.
4. Fold the gelatin into the egg whites.
5. Beat the cream until stiff and add the vanilla. Fold the cream into the egg whites.
6. Rub the bottom and sides of an eight-inch or nine-inch springform pan with butter. Sprinkle the bottom with half the coconut and pour in the cream mixture. Sprinkle with remaining coconut and chill four hours or overnight.
7. Unmold pudding and serve with crushed sweetened strawberries and rum sauce. If desired, the dessert may be garnished with whole strawberries.

Yield: Six to eight servings.

"Lemmon Syllabub"
MARYLAND

Thinly cut peel (lemon-colored part only) of one lemon	4 cups heavy cream
	⅓ cup lemon juice
	1 cup sugar
1 cup cream sherry	Nutmeg.
1 cup Madeira wine	

1. Soak the lemon peel in the sherry and Madeira for at least one hour.
2. Whip the cream until it just begins to hold its shape. Remove the peel and gradually beat into the cream the wine, lemon juice and sugar until thick. Pour into parfait or wine glasses and sprinkle with nutmeg. Serve immediately.

Yield: Eight servings.

Peppermint Stick Bavarian Cream
LOUISIANA

1 envelope plus one and one-half teaspoons unflavored gelatin	candy canes; crushing can be done easily in an electric blender)
⅓ cup cold water	¼ teaspoon peppermint essence, or to taste
6 egg yolks	Red food coloring
¾ cup sugar	1½ cups heavy cream, whipped
¼ teaspoon salt	Peppermint candies for garnish (optional)
1½ cups milk	Chocolate sauce (recipe below).
¾ cup finely crushed peppermint sticks or candies (about six medium-size	

1. Soak the gelatin in the water.
2. Beat the egg yolks, sugar and salt in a saucepan until well blended. In another saucepan heat the milk and crushed peppermint candies until almost boiling, stirring to dissolve the candy.
3. Gradually beat the hot milk into the egg yolk mixture. Heat over hot water or over low direct heat, stirring continuously until the mixture thickens. Do not allow to boil.
4. Stir in the softened gelatin and stir to dissolve. Set the mixture aside to cool. Stir in the peppermint essence and the red food coloring, remembering that the cream will tone down the shade.
5. Fold in the cream gently but thoroughly and pour into a six-cup mold. Chill four hours or overnight. Unmold and decorate with the candies and serve with chocolate sauce.

Yield: Ten servings.

Chocolate Sauce
LOUISIANA

4 ounces (four squares) unsweetened chocolate	½ cup sugar
2 tablespoons butter	⅛ teaspoon salt
2 tablespoons light corn syrup	½ cup milk
	¼ cup heavy cream.

1. Melt the chocolate with the butter in the top of a double boiler over hot but not boiling water. Add the syrup, sugar and salt and blend.
2. Add the milk and cream and cook, stirring, about ten minutes.

Yield: About one and one-half cups.

Fruited Eggnog Pudding
KENTUCKY

1	cup chopped mixed candied fruits	½	cup dark rum
¼	cup roughly chopped pecans or walnuts	3	envelopes unflavored gelatin
		½	cup cold water
2	tablespoons golden raisins	1	cup bourbon
¼	cup cognac	2	cups heavy cream, whipped
12	egg yolks	2	tablespoons vanilla
¾	cup sugar		Whipped cream for garnish
			Pieces of candied cherries.

1. Soak the mixed fruits, nuts and raisins in the cognac.
2. Beat the egg yolks until very thick, lemon-colored and smooth. Gradually beat in the sugar.
3. Add the rum and beat in well. Chill the mixture until it is at refrigerator temperature, about forty minutes.
4. Soak the gelatin in the water. Heat to dissolve the gelatin. Add the bourbon and stir into the chilled egg mixture quickly and thoroughly.
5. Fold in the whipped cream and vanilla and continue stirring until the mixture begins to thicken. Fold in the soaked fruit and nut mixture and pour into a nine-cup mold which has been rinsed with cold water or lightly oiled.
6. Chill at least five hours or overnight. Unmold and decorate with whipped cream and candied cherries.

Yield: About one dozen servings.

Note: If a nine-cup mold is not available, divide the mixture between a six-cup mold and a three-cup mold. When ready to serve, unmold and place one atop the other.

Trifle
VIRGINIA

- 8 egg yolks, lightly beaten
- ½ cup sugar
- 4 cups milk, scalded
- 1 teaspoon vanilla
- 24 ladyfingers, or a comparable quantity of spongecake, torn into bite-size pieces
- ½ cup medium-dry sherry
- 1 cup strawberry or raspberry preserves
- ⅓ cup slivered blanched almonds or crumbled macaroons (optional)
- ½ cup heavy cream, whipped
- Glacé cherries
- Angelica or one tablespoon slivered blanched almonds.

1. Combine the egg yolks, sugar and milk in a heavy saucepan, beating with a wire whisk to mix well. Heat over medium heat until mixture thickens and coats the back of a spoon. Do not allow custard to boil.
2. Remove from the heat and pour into a cold bowl. Stir in the vanilla and cool to lukewarm.
3. Sprinkle the ladyfingers or spongecake with the sherry and let stand five to ten minutes.
4. Place a layer of the soaked ladyfingers in a two-quart serving bowl, preferably glass.
5. Spread with one-third of the preserves and one-third of the almonds or macaroons. Repeat the layers until all ladyfingers are used.
6. Pour the cooled custard over the ladyfinger arrangement and chill several hours.
7. Decorate with the whipped cream, piped through a rosette tube, and garnish with the cherries and angelica or almond pieces.

Yield: About ten servings.

Trifle Royal
VIRGINIA

- 1 homemade jellyroll, made from four eggs and a standard recipe
- 1 cup strawberry or raspberry preserves
- ½ cup medium-dry sherry
- 8 egg yolks, lightly beaten
- ½ cup sugar
- 4 cups milk, scalded
- 1½ teaspoons vanilla
- 1 teaspoon unflavored gelatin
- 2 tablespoons water
- Whipped cream for garnish.

1. Spread the cooled jellyroll with the preserves. Roll and cut into three-quarter-inch slices. Arrange as many slices as necessary to cover the bottom and sides of a two-quart round glass bowl, dish or casserole. Sprinkle with the sherry.

2. Combine the egg yolks, sugar and milk in a heavy pan. Heat, stirring, over medium heat until the mixture thickens and just coats the back of the spoon. Remove from the heat and pour into a cool bowl to stop the cooking.

3. Stir in the vanilla. Dissolve the gelatin in the water. Add to mixture. Cool to lukewarm or room temperature.

4. Pour one-third of the custard into the lined bowl. Add some of the remaining slices of jellyroll, pushing them down into the custard. Repeat with the remaining custard and jellyroll slices, ending with slices.

5. Chill well, at least several hours. Unmold onto a plate and decorate with whipped cream as desired.

Yield: About ten servings.

Note: If the trifle royal is not to be unmolded, the gelatin may be omitted.

Trifle Pudding

VIRGINIA

½	cup blanched almonds	¼	cup dry sherry
¼	pound candied cherries	1½	teaspoons cornstarch
¼	pound ladyfingers	1½	cups milk
¼	cup tart currant or beach plum jelly	2	large eggs
		4	tablespoons sugar
½	pound almond macaroons	2	cups heavy cream.

1. Preheat the oven to 350 degrees.

2. Place the almonds on a baking sheet and bake until they are toasted, stirring occasionally. Do not let them burn. Turn off oven and let almonds cool.

3. Chop the almonds and chop the candied cherries.

4. Split each ladyfinger in half and smear the split side of each half with jelly. Arrange layers of jelly-smeared ladyfingers and the macaroons over bottom and side of a round glass mixing bowl. Sprinkle with the sherry.

5. Place the cornstarch in a saucepan and gradually add the milk, stirring with a wire whisk. Beat the eggs and add them along with half the sugar. Bring gently to a boil, stirring constantly, to make a custard. Do not cook over

high heat or too long or the custard will curdle. Let cool and fold in chopped cherries.

6. Whip the cream and, before it is stiff, beat in the remaining sugar. Fold the whipped cream into the custard and pour the mixture into the prepared bowl. Chill. When ready to serve, sprinkle with chopped almonds.

Yield: Six servings.

Minetry McCoy's Miracle
TENNESSEE

1	pound sweet butter	1	teaspoon vanilla
2	cups sugar	1	cup chopped pecans
12	eggs, separated	24	double ladyfingers, approximately
48	amaretti (Italian macaroons)		
1	cup bourbon	1½	cups heavy cream, whipped.
4	ounces (four squares) unsweetened chocolate, melted		

1. Day before, cream the butter and sugar together until light and fluffy. Beat the egg yolks until light and beat into creamed mixture.
2. Soak the amaretti in the bourbon.
3. Beat the chocolate into the butter mixture. Add the vanilla and pecans. Beat the egg whites until stiff but not dry and fold into the chocolate mixture.
4. Line a ten-inch springform pan around the side and on the bottom with split ladyfingers. Alternate layers of soaked macaroons and chocolate mixture in the lined pan. Chill overnight.
5. Next day, remove the sides of the pan and decorate the top of the dessert with whipped cream.

Yield: Sixteen to twenty servings.

Stuffed Frozen Oranges
FLORIDA

12	oranges	½	cup sugar, approximately
½	cup water	12	tablespoons heavy cream
1	tablespoon lemon juice	6	tablespoons gin
	Grated rind of one orange	6	sprigs fresh mint for garnish.

1. Cut a one-half-inch slice from the tops of six oranges and carefully scoop out the flesh. This is to provide a hollow shell to be filled later. Place the shells in the freezer.

2. Squeeze the scooped-out flesh to extract the juice. Cut the remaining oranges in half and squeeze to extract the juice. Combine all the juice and add the water, lemon juice and orange rind. Add the sugar according to taste. Stir to dissolve sugar. Pour the mixture into a container for freezing and freeze.

3. Remove the frozen juice for a short time before using. Spoon one tablespoon of the cream into the bottom of each shell; then add a small scoop of the frozen juice. Add another tablespoon cream and another scoop of the frozen juice. Return to the freezer until ready to serve. When ready to serve, add one tablespoon of the gin to each serving and garnish each with a sprig of mint.

Yield: Six servings.

Oranges en Surprise
FLORIDA

6 large navel oranges	Sugar to taste
1 envelope unflavored gelatin	Grand Marnier or other
1½ cups orange juice	orange liqueur to taste.

1. With a sharp paring knife, remove the peel, spiral fashion, from the oranges. Carefully section each orange into a bowl, but leave the pulpy formation or "skeleton" of the orange intact.

2. Soak the gelatin in three-quarters cup orange juice; then heat, stirring to dissolve.

3. Dip the orange sections in gelatin; then replace them neatly in the "skeleton," using a small custard cup as a temporary base. Chill and remove to dessert plates.

4. Sweeten the remaining orange juice with sugar and liqueur. Serve as a sauce with the oranges.

Yield: Six servings.

Ambrosia
FLORIDA

| 4 seedless oranges, peeled and sectioned | 2 tablespoons sugar |
| | ½ cup grated fresh coconut. |

1. Place half the orange segments in a serving bowl. Sprinkle with the sugar and coconut. Add the remaining orange segments.
2. Toss lightly to mix. Cover and refrigerate several hours before serving.

Yield: Six servings.

Bananas à la Turtle Cay
FLORIDA

6 sugar bananas (tiny bananas in islands off Florida)	¼ cup light rum
	¼ cup dark rum
½ cup butter	Lime wedges.
½ cup sugar	

1. Peel the bananas and cut them lengthwise.
2. Melt the butter in a heavy skillet and add the bananas, turning once. As bananas begin to color, sprinkle with the sugar and continue cooking until sugar is caramelized. Stir and turn gently so as not to break the bananas.
3. Combine the rums and heat gently. Pour over the bananas and ignite. Serve with lime wedges.

Yield: Six servings.

Bananas Flambées
FLORIDA

6 ripe bananas, sliced on the bias	½ cup butter
	½ teaspoon cinnamon
Juice of half a lemon	¼ cup cognac
1 cup light brown sugar	Vanilla ice cream.

1. Brush the banana slices with lemon juice. Melt the brown sugar and butter in a flat chafing dish. Add bananas and cook until just tender.
2. Sprinkle bananas with the cinnamon. Warm the cognac and add. Ignite and pour flaming over a ball of ice cream.

Yield: Six servings.

Cooked Custard Ice Cream
ARKANSAS

- 2 cups sugar
- ⅛ teaspoon salt
- ¼ cup cornstarch or one-half cup flour
- 4 cups regular milk, scalded
- 4 eggs, separated
- 1 teaspoon vanilla
- 2 large cans (thirteen ounces) evaporated milk or two and two-thirds cups heavy cream
- 2 cups cold regular milk, approximately.

1. Combine the sugar, salt and cornstarch or flour. Add the scalded milk. Stir until sugar dissolves.
2. Beat the egg yolks in a bowl. Pour a cup of the hot milk mixture into yolks gradually while beating; then return to bulk of milk mixture.
3. Bring to a boil, stirring, and remove from the heat. Add the vanilla and evaporated milk or cream and cool. Beat the egg whites until stiff and fold into custard. Pour into a gallon ice cream freezer can and add the cold milk to fill the can to two-thirds capacity. Freeze in crank-type or electric ice cream maker and serve, or store in home freezer for later use.

Yield: One gallon; about sixteen to twenty servings.

Ginger-Melon Ice
GEORGIA

- 6 cups water
- 3 cups sugar
- 1 tablespoon grated lemon rind
- 1¼ cups lemon juice
- 1½ cups finely chopped preserved ginger
- 3 tablespoons ginger syrup
- 3 cups coarsely grated peeled honeydew melon, apple or shredded pineapple.

1. Heat the water and sugar, stirring until the sugar dissolves. Bring to a boil and boil two minutes. Let cool to room temperature. Chill.
2. Add the remaining ingredients and pour into a large roasting pan. Freeze until mixture is solid around the sides but slushy in the middle. Break up and stir well. Freeze until slushy and serve. If the mixture becomes solid, remove it from the freezer about fifteen to twenty minutes before you wish to serve it.

Yield: Eight to ten servings.

Note: Frozen lemonade concentrate may be substituted for the water, sugar and lemon juice. Reconstitute three six-ounce cans with nine cups water.

Butter Fingers
MISSISSIPPI

½ pound butter	2 teaspoons vanilla
5 tablespoons confectioners' sugar	2 cups chopped pecans
	¼ teaspoon salt.
3 cups flour	

1. Preheat the oven to 350 degrees.
2. Cream the butter and sugar together until creamy.
3. Work in the flour, vanilla, pecans and salt with a wooden spoon or the fingers to make a dough.
4. Divide the mixture into about thirty-six pieces and shape each into a small cigar shape. Place on an ungreased baking sheet and bake fifteen minutes, or until lightly browned.

Yield: About three dozen.

Note: These cookies are best after they have been stored for several days in an airtight tin because the flavor mellows and the texture changes.

Sugar Cookies
ARKANSAS

1 cup shortening	1½ cups sugar
4 cups flour	2 teaspoons baking soda
½ cup milk	½ teaspoon salt
2 eggs	½ teaspoon almond extract.

1. Preheat the oven to 350 degrees.
2. Cut the shortening into the flour with the finger tips or a pastry blender until the mixture is the consistency of corn meal.
3. Combine the remaining ingredients and mix with flour mixture. Gather into a dough and roll to one-eighth-inch thickness.
4. Cut into various shapes and bake on ungreased baking sheets eight to ten minutes, or until lightly browned at the edges.

Yield: Seven dozen two-and-one-half-inch cookies.

Moravian Ginger Cookies
NORTH CAROLINA

⅓	cup dark brown sugar	½	teaspoon ground ginger
¼	cup shortening	½	teaspoon cinnamon
½	cup unsulphured molasses	¼	teaspoon nutmeg
2¼	cups flour	¼	teaspoon ground allspice.
¼	teaspoon baking soda		

1. Heat the brown sugar, shortening and molasses in a small saucepan until shortening melts. Cool.
2. Sift together the remaining ingredients and stir into the cooled mixture. Wrap in wax paper and chill several hours or overnight.
3. Preheat the oven to 375 degrees.
4. Roll out one-quarter of the dough at a time, preferably on a lightly floured pastry cloth, until dough is paper-thin. Use as little extra flour as possible.
5. Cut out with fancy cutters and transfer to a lightly greased baking sheet. Bake four minutes. Cool on a rack.

Yield: Five dozen to six dozen.

Snickerdoodles
TENNESSEE

2¾	cups sifted flour	1½	cups plus one tablespoon sugar
2	teaspoons cream of tartar		
1	teaspoon baking soda	½	teaspoon almond extract
½	teaspoon salt	2	eggs
1	cup shortening, at room temperature	1	tablespoon cinnamon.

1. Preheat the oven to 400 degrees.
2. Sift together the flour, cream of tartar, baking soda and salt.
3. Cream the shortening with one and one-half cups of the sugar and beat in the almond extract and eggs. Combine the two mixtures and chill.
4. Roll the dough into small balls about one-half inch in diameter and roll in a mixture of the remaining sugar and the cinnamon. Place the balls about two inches apart on an ungreased baking sheet and bake eight to ten minutes.

Yield: About five dozen.

Hermits

WEST VIRGINIA

- 4 tablespoons butter, at room temperature
- ½ cup packed light brown sugar
- 1 egg
- 1 cup sifted cake flour
- ½ teaspoon baking powder
- ¼ teaspoon allspice
- ¼ teaspoon ground ginger
- ¼ teaspoon nutmeg
- 1 cup currants or chopped raisins
- ¼ cup chopped walnuts or almonds.

1. Preheat the oven to 350 degrees.
2. Cream the butter in an electric mixer and beat in the brown sugar and egg.
3. Sift together the flour, baking powder, allspice, ginger and nutmeg and add. Fold in the currants and nuts and blend well. Drop by spoonfuls onto a lightly greased baking sheet and bake about ten minutes.

Yield: About two dozen.

Our Aunt Harriet's Favorite Brownies

VIRGINIA

- 2 ounces (two squares) unsweetened chocolate
- ½ cup butter
- 1 teaspoon vanilla
- 3 eggs
- 1¼ cups sugar
- ½ cup flour
- ½ cup chopped walnuts.

1. Preheat the oven to 350 degrees.
2. Melt the chocolate and butter in the top of a double boiler. Stir in the vanilla.
3. Beat the eggs lightly and gradually beat in the sugar. Stir in the chocolate-butter mixture and then the flour and walnuts.
4. Pour into a greased nine-inch square pan and bake twenty-five minutes, or until a crust just forms on the top and the mixture has started to leave the sides of the dish. Let cool in pan and cut into squares.

Yield: About five dozen.

Note: This is a "cakey" style of brownie.

Miscellaneous

Pickles, Relishes and Preserves

Fried Apples
VIRGINIA

6 Red Delicious or Rome apples	⅓ cup butter
	⅓ cup light brown sugar
¼ cup water	2 tablespoons lemon juice

1. Peel, core and slice the apples into thick slices. Place in a skillet with the water and butter. Cook over moderate heat, stirring to prevent sticking, until barely tender.
2. Sprinkle with the brown sugar and lemon juice. Toss, cover and let stand ten minutes before serving.
Yield: Six servings.
Note: Fried apples are served with fried ham slices or homemade sausage for breakfast.

Blackberry and Apple Jelly
ARKANSAS

8 cups unpeeled green apples	4½ cups water
8 cups blackberries	Sugar.

1. Remove stem and blossom ends from the apples, wash the fruit and slice or chop it. Pick over the blackberries and wash and crush them.
2. Place the apples and water in a heavy kettle. Cook very gently for about fifteen minutes, or until almost tender, stirring occasionally.
3. Add the crushed blackberries and cook gently for another ten minutes, stirring frequently.
4. Drain the mixture through a jelly bag, damp cotton flannel or four layers of cheesecloth. Do not squeeze if a clear jelly is desired.
5. Measure the juice and add three-quarters cup sugar for each cup of juice. Stir to dissolve the sugar.
6. Bring mixture to a boil rapidly and cook rapidly, without stirring, for five to ten minutes, or until two drops run together and flake or sheet from the side of a large metal spoon.
7. Pour immediately into hot sterilized jelly glasses. Cover with a thin layer of melted paraffin and cool undisturbed. Cover and store in a cool, dark, dry place.

Yield: About eight six-ounce glasses.

Fig Preserves
ARKANSAS

1 cup baking soda	4 quarts water
6 quarts firm, sound ripe figs	5 pounds (eleven and one-quarter cups) sugar.
6 quarts boiling water	

1. Day before, sprinkle the baking soda over the figs and cover with the boiling water. Let stand fifteen minutes. Drain. Rinse figs in clear cold water and then set to drain while preparing syrup.
2. Mix the four quarts water and the sugar in a saucepan and heat, stirring, until sugar dissolves. Boil without stirring ten minutes and skim.
3. Add the well-drained figs gradually so as not to cool the syrup. Cook rapidly until figs are clear and tender, about two hours. When figs are transparent, lift out carefully and place in shallow pans.
4. Syrup should be as thick as honey. If it isn't, boil some more. Pour over figs, making sure to cover them completely. Leave overnight. Next morning, place cold figs in sterilized jars with stems up.
5. Fill each jar with syrup. Secure caps and process twenty-five minutes in a water bath at simmering temperature. Cool and store in a cool, dark, dry place.

Yield: About one dozen pints.

Quick Apple Preserves
VIRGINIA

4 cups peeled and quartered tart apples that retain their shape	½ teaspoon whole cloves
	½ teaspoon whole allspice
	1 teaspoon nutmeg
4 cups sugar	4 sticks cinnamon.

1. Place the apples in a heavy pan and add water barely to cover. Add the sugar. Tie the spices in a cheesecloth bag and add. Cook slowly, stirring occasionally, until apples are tender but still retain their shape and syrup starts to jell. Remove spice bag.
2. Ladle mixture into hot sterilized jars and adjust caps. Store in the refrigerator.
Yield: About one quart.
Note: Serve with roast pork, ham and poultry.

Cantaloupe and Orange Jam
ARKANSAS

4 cups diced peeled cantaloupe	1 teaspoon grated lemon rind
3 oranges, peeled and diced	4 cups sugar
¼ cup lemon juice	½ teaspoon salt.
1 teaspoon grated orange rind	

1. Combine the cantaloupe, oranges and lemon juice in a heavy kettle. Bring to a boil and simmer fifteen minutes.
2. Add the orange and lemon rinds, the sugar and salt. Boil rapidly about forty-five minutes, or until thick and clear, stirring occasionally. Skim as necessary.
3. Pour into sterilized jelly glasses and cover with a thin layer of melted paraffin. Cool, cover and store in a cool, dark, dry place.
Yield: About six six-ounce glasses.

Peach Conserve
GEORGIA

4 cups ripe peaches	1½ cups sugar.

1. Day before, dip the peaches into boiling water very briefly and peel. Remove the pits and chop the fruit into one-half-inch cubes or slices.

2. Place the peaches in a large bowl and sprinkle with the sugar. Allow to stand overnight.

3. Next day, pour the fruit and juice into a heavy pan and heat very slowly over low heat for about one hour, or until sugar is dissolved and the fruit is tender. Stir gently to prevent sticking.

4. Pour into hot sterilized jars. Seal, cool and store in a cool, dark, dry place.

Yield: About two pints.

Peach Almond Jam
GEORGIA

4 cups finely chopped unpeeled peaches (about three pounds)	7 cups sugar (about three pounds)
½ cup chopped blanched almonds	½ bottle liquid fruit pectin
¼ cup lemon juice	¼ teaspoon almond extract.

1. The unpeeled peaches may be ground, finely chopped or blended quickly in an electric blender. Measure four cups into a heavy kettle.

2. Stir in the almonds, lemon juice and sugar. Put over high heat and stir until the mixture comes to a full rolling boil. Boil hard for one minute, stirring constantly. Remove from the heat.

3. Immediately stir in the pectin and almond extract. Skim off the foam; stir and skim for five minutes to prevent floating fruit. Ladle into hot sterilized jars and cover with a thin layer of melted paraffin wax. Store in a cool, dry, dark place for at least two weeks before using.

Yield: Five to six pints.

Peach Melon Conserve
GEORGIA

6 cups diced peeled peaches	¼ cup chopped preserved ginger
2 cups diced cantaloupe	½ cup chopped pecans.
6 cups sugar	
¼ cup lemon juice	
2 tablespoons syrup from preserved ginger	

1. Place the peaches and cantaloupe in a kettle and simmer gently thirty minutes, stirring to prevent sticking.
2. Add the sugar, lemon juice and syrup and boil rapidly until mixture is thick. Stir to prevent sticking.
3. Stir in the ginger and pecans and pour into hot sterilized jars. Pour two thin layers of paraffin wax over. Cool, cover and store in a cool, dry, dark place.

Yield: About ten jelly jars.

Surinam Preserves
FLORIDA

2 quarts Surinam cherries	Juice of two lemons
2 pounds sugar	½ teaspoon ground cardamom.

1. Rinse the cherries and remove stems. Pit the cherries.
2. Combine the cherries, sugar and lemon juice in a stainless steel or enamel saucepan. Bring to a boil and cook over moderately high heat exactly fifteen minutes, skimming the surface if foam forms. Stir in the cardamom and spoon the mixture into hot sterilized jars. Seal immediately. Cool and store in the refrigerator.

Yield: Three to four cups.

The mayhaw is a hawthorn that is abundant in parts of Louisiana. The fruit is used to make an excellent jelly.

Mayhaw Jelly
LOUISIANA

1 pound ripe mayhaws (part of the fruit should be underripe)	4 cups water, approximately Sugar.

1. Wash the mayhaws and put them in a preserving kettle. Add water to cover, approximately four cups. Bring to a boil and simmer the fruit until tender.
2. Strain the juice through a jelly bag. There should be about five cups. For each five cups of juice, add three cups of sugar and bring to a boil. Boil rapidly to the jelly stage.

3. To test for the jellying point, dip a spoon into the boiling liquid. When the syrup nears the jellying stage, it will drop from the side of the spoon in two drops. When the drops run together and slide off the spoon in a "sheet," the jelly is ready and should be taken off the heat at once. Pour into sterilized glasses and seal at once. Cool and store in refrigerator.

Yield: About two pints.

Damson Jam
VIRGINIA

4 pounds damson plums, pitted, and pits tied in a muslin bag	5 pounds sugar 2 cups water.

1. In a heavy preserving kettle, layer the damsons and the sugar. Add water and heat over high heat until the sugar starts to melt. Reduce heat to low and, when sugar takes on a color, stir the mixture well.

2. Add the bag of pits and continue to cook slowly, stirring occasionally to prevent scorching, until jam is thick and rich. Skim as necessary.

3. Remove bag of pits. Ladle jam into hot sterilized canning jars and adjust caps, or ladle into jelly glasses and cover with two thin (one-eighth-inch) layers of paraffin wax. Cool and store in a dark, dry, cool place.

Yield: About six pints.

A limited crop of Seville oranges is grown in Florida, and some are shipped to gourmet shops in metropolitan areas during late January or early February.

Seville (Bitter) Orange Marmalade
FLORIDA

12 medium-size Seville (bitter) oranges 4 lemons	3 quarts water Sugar.

1. Slice the oranges and lemons very thinly and place in a large bowl. Remove seeds, place in a muslin bag and add to the sliced fruit. Add the water, cover and let stand twenty-four to forty-eight hours.

2. Bring to a boil and simmer gently until the peel is soft, one hour or more. Discard the bag of seeds. Measure fruit and for every cup of fruit add one cup of sugar.

3. Bring to a boil again, stirring until the sugar dissolves. Boil rapidly until two drops form on the edge of the spoon and drop off simultaneously (or for a stiffer marmalade until the drops run together as they fall off). Skim foam from the surface. Pour marmalade into hot sterilized jars and seal. Cool and store in a cool, dark, dry place.

Yield: About nine pints.

Pepper Jelly
TENNESSEE

- 6 medium-size green peppers, cored, seeded and ground
- 5 long yellow sweet peppers if available, ground
- 8 hot green peppers, seeds left in and ground
- 1 onion, ground
- 9 cups sugar
- 1½ cups white vinegar
- ½ cup lemon juice
- 1 bottle liquid fruit pectin
- Green food coloring (optional).

1. Place the peppers, onion, sugar, vinegar and lemon juice in a kettle. Bring to a boil slowly, stirring to dissolve the sugar.

2. Boil five minutes. Stir in the pectin and food coloring if desired. Let stand five minutes, skim, stir and pour into hot sterilized jars. Top with two thin layers of paraffin wax. Cool, cover and store in a cool, dark, dry place.

Yield: About one dozen six-ounce jars.

Note: Serve with meats.

Bourbon Jelly
KENTUCKY

- 1 tablespoon unflavored gelatin
- 1⅓ cups water
- ⅓ cup sugar
- ⅓ cup orange juice
- ⅔ cup bourbon.

1. Soften the gelatin in one-third cup of the water. Heat remaining water to boiling. Add softened gelatin and the sugar. Stir to dissolve.

2. Stir in the orange juice and bourbon and pour into two jelly glasses. Seal. Cool and chill.

Yield: Two jelly glasses.

Note: Serve with poultry, ham or vegetables.

Cucumbers in Butter and Dill
VIRGINIA

3 pounds cucumbers	6 tablespoons butter
6 tablespoons wine vinegar	1½ teaspoons freshly snipped dillweed
2 teaspoons sugar	
2 teaspoons salt	

1. Using a swivel-bladed paring knife, peel the cucumbers. Slice the cucumbers lengthwise and remove seeds with a melon ball cutter or a spoon. Slice each half lengthwise again. Cut each length of cucumber into one-and-one-half-inch pieces.

2. Place the cucumber pieces in a mixing bowl and add the vinegar, sugar and salt. Let stand one hour or so, turning occasionally in the marinade.

3. Meanwhile, preheat the oven to 375 degrees. Butter a baking dish and sprinkle with the dill. Drain the cucumbers and add them to the dish. Bake, uncovered, stirring occasionally, forty-five minutes. Chill and serve cold.

Yield: Four to six servings.

Pickled Garden Carrots
VIRGINIA

1 pound freshly picked small carrots	1 teaspoon sugar
	1 teaspoon mustard seeds
2 cups water	1 teaspoon peppercorns
½ cup wine vinegar	1 bay leaf
1 teaspoon salt	

1. Trim off the carrots at both ends. Wash the carrots well.
2. Combine the carrots with the remaining ingredients and cook until carrots are tender but still crisp. Cooking time will depend on the size of the carrots. Cool the carrots in the liquid; then drain and chill.

Yield: Four to six servings.

Quick Cucumber Pickles
ARKANSAS

4	quarts thinly sliced cucumbers	4	cups sugar
1½	cups thinly sliced onions	1½	teaspoons ground turmeric
⅓	cup salt	1½	teaspoons celery seeds
2	cloves garlic	2	tablespoons mustard seeds
2	quarts crushed ice or ice cubes	3	cups white vinegar.

1. Combine the cucumbers, onions, salt and garlic in a large crock or bowl. Cover the top with the ice and let stand for three hours. The ice removes the bitterness from the cucumbers.
2. Drain the mixture thoroughly in a colander and discard the liquid. If desired, discard the garlic cloves as well.
3. In a large pot, combine the sugar, turmeric, celery seeds, mustard seeds and vinegar. Bring the mixture to a boil and stir until all the sugar is dissolved.
4. Add the drained vegetables and bring to a boil. Cook for five minutes.
5. Pack the hot pickles into hot sterilized jars to within one-half inch of the jar tops. Adjust caps and rings and make sure each cap is firmly sealed.
6. Process the jars in a boiling water bath for five minutes. The boiling water should extend at least one inch above the jars. Remove the jars, adjust seals if necessary, and allow the jars to cool. Store in a cool, dark, dry place.

Yield: Six pints.

Pickled Green Beans
TENNESSEE

- 2 cups cooked whole green beans (drained canned beans or cooked fresh or frozen beans may be used)
- 1 medium-size onion, thinly sliced
- 1 clove garlic, crushed
- 1/3 cup sugar
- 3/4 cup cider vinegar
- 3/4 cup water
- 3 tablespoons oil
- 1/2 teaspoon salt
- 1 teaspoon pickling spice, tied in a muslin bag.

Dressing:
- 1/2 cup sour cream
- 1/4 cup mayonnaise
- 1 teaspoon lemon juice
- 1/4 teaspoon dry mustard
- 1 tablespoon horseradish
- 1/2 teaspoon onion juice
- 2 teaspoons chopped chives.

    1. Alternate the beans and the onion slices in a jar and slip in the garlic clove.
    2. Combine the sugar, vinegar, water, oil, salt and spice bag in a small pan. Bring to a boil and allow to stand until mixture is at room temperature.
    3. Remove the spice bag and pour mixture over beans and onion slices. Refrigerate twelve hours or longer.
    4. To serve, drain the beans and remove garlic clove. Combine the dressing ingredients and toss beans with the dressing.
Yield: Four to six servings.

Whole Artichoke Pickles
KENTUCKY

- 4 quarts small Jerusalem artichokes, washed and scraped
- Salt
- 2 tablespoons alum (see note)
- 8 cups cider vinegar
- 2 tablespoons mustard seeds
- 2 tablespoons whole cloves
- 2 tablespoons celery seeds
- 2 cups sugar
- 1 tablespoon turmeric.

    1. Day before, cover the artichokes with salted water, using one tablespoon salt to every quart water. Let stand overnight.

2. Next day, drain. Cover artichokes with water which has alum in it and let soak twenty-four hours. Drain artichokes and wash well.

3. Combine the vinegar, one cup water, the mustard seeds, cloves, celery seeds, sugar and turmeric in a saucepan. Bring to a boil and simmer twenty minutes. Pack the artichokes in hot sterilized jars and pour syrup over. Seal. Process in a water bath twenty minutes. Adjust caps. Cool and store in a cool, dark, dry place.

Yield: About four quarts.

Note: Alum is available in drugstores.

Crisp Watermelon Pickles
MISSISSIPPI

Rind of one large watermelon	2 tablespoons whole allspice
¼ cup slaked lime (see note)	2 tablespoons whole cloves
10 cups sugar	4 sticks cinnamon.
8 cups cider vinegar	

1. Neatly peel away all green, red and pink portions from the rind. Cut the rind into neat cubes or slices and measure enough rind to make approximately one gallon.

2. Drop the rind into a large kettle of boiling water and simmer five minutes. Drain and cool.

3. Dissolve the slaked lime in two quarts cold water and pour the solution over the rind. Let stand about three and one-half hours. Drain; rinse thoroughly.

4. Cover the rind with clear, cold water, bring to a boil and cook until rind is tender. Drain again.

5. Combine four cups sugar, two cups vinegar and eight cups water. Tie the allspice, cloves and cinnamon in a cheesecloth bag and add it. Bring to a boil and simmer five minutes. Add the rind and return to a boil. Simmer thirty minutes. Remove from the heat and let stand twelve to twenty-four hours.

6. Add the remaining vinegar and sugar and bring to a boil. Simmer until the rind is translucent. If the syrup becomes too thick as it cooks, add a little water occasionally. When rind is cooked, discard the spice bag and pack the rind and syrup into sterilized jars. Seal. Cool and store in a cool, dark, dry place.

Yield: About four quarts.

Note: Slaked lime is available at many drugstores.

Easy Pickled Watermelon Rind
GEORGIA

4 quarts cubed watermelon rind (red flesh and green skin pared away)	1 cup water (optional)
	2 teaspoons whole cloves
	4 tablespoons broken cinnamon pieces.
4 teaspoons salt	
6 cups sugar	
4 cups white vinegar or cider vinegar	

1. Two days before, place the rind in a kettle and add water to cover. Sprinkle with the salt and simmer until rind is tender enough to be pierced with a fork. This should take five to ten minutes, depending on the size of the cubes.

2. Drain the cubes and place in a towel. Squeeze to remove most of the moisture. Place the squeezed rind in a stone crock.

3. Combine the sugar and vinegar in a saucepan. If the vinegar seems particularly acid, dilute with the one cup water. Otherwise, do not use the water. Bring to a boil and cook, stirring, until sugar dissolves. Pour the syrup over the rind. Cover and let stand overnight.

4. Next day, drain the rind and return the syrup to a boil. Pour the syrup over the rind again.

5. Combine the cloves and cinnamon in a cheesecloth bag. Drain the rind once more and bring the syrup to a boil. Pour the syrup over the rind and add the spice bag. Let stand overnight.

6. Next day, discard the spice bag. Bring the rind to a boil in the syrup. Pour into hot sterilized jars and seal. Cool and store in a cool, dark, dry place.

Yield: About four quarts.

Stuffed Oranges and Lemons
GEORGIA

Fruit:
- 10 medium-size lemons
- 10 medium-size oranges

Boiling water.

Syrup:
- 6 cups cider vinegar
- 9 cups sugar
- 1½ cups water
- 3 cups mixed lemon juice and orange juice
- 3 cups grenadine syrup
- 3 sticks cinnamon
- Red food coloring.

Filling:
- 2 cups pitted dates
- 2 cups cranberries
- 2 cups raisins
- 2 cups dried figs
- 1 cup drained watermelon rind pickle, finely chopped
- 2 cups nuts, chopped
- ½ cup drained maraschino cherries, chopped.

1. Test that the fruit fits quart jars. Cut a small slice from end of each piece of fruit and scoop out all pulp. Strain and reserve juice. Discard pulp. Cover fruit shells with boiling water. Simmer twenty minutes. Drain; repeat twice with more water, simmering fifteen and ten minutes.

2. To prepare syrup, combine in a saucepan the vinegar, sugar, water, juices, grenadine, cinnamon sticks and enough food coloring to make the syrup rosy. Heat, stirring to dissolve sugar. Simmer thirty minutes. Add fruit shells. Simmer until shells are tender but not mushy. Remove shells and drain. Reserve syrup.

3. To prepare filling, use the fine blade of a food chopper to grind the dates, cranberries, raisins and figs together. Stir in the watermelon rind pickle, nuts and maraschino cherries.

4. Spoon the fruit and nut mixture into the hot, drained fruit shells. Push down to pack as tightly as possible. Drop three oranges or four lemons, cut ends up, into clean, sterilized quart canning jars.

5. Bring the reserved syrup to a boil and fill jars, leaving one-half-inch head space. Adjust caps. Place on a rack in a water bath so that the jars are

covered by at least one to two inches of boiling water. Bring to a boil again. Boil fifteen minutes.

    6. With tongs or special holder, remove jars and cool. Tighten caps as needed. Next day, test caps for seal. Store in dark, dry, cool place. To use, remove fruit and cut into one-half-inch slices. Spoon a little syrup over slices to moisten and flavor.

    Yield: About eight quart jars, depending on size of fruit.

Pear Relish
GEORGIA

- 10 pounds Keiffer pears, peeled, cored and ground coarsely
- 3 green peppers, seeded and ground
- 3 red sweet peppers, seeded and ground
- 6 onions, ground
- 4 cups cider vinegar
- 4 cups sugar
- 1 teaspoon celery seeds
- 1 tablespoon mixed pickling spices
- 1 tablespoon mustard seeds.

    1. Place the pears, peppers, onions, vinegar and sugar in a large kettle. Tie the celery seeds, pickling spices and mustard seeds in a muslin bag and add to the kettle.

    2. Bring to a boil, stirring occasionally, and simmer about forty minutes. Discard the spice bag. Pour relish into hot sterilized jars and seal immediately. Cool and store in a cool, dark, dry place.

    Yield: About eight pints.

Lime Chutney
FLORIDA

- 2 large or three small limes
- 6 tart apples, peeled, cored and cut into fine dice
- ¼ pound finely chopped suet
- ¼ cup finely chopped candied ginger or equal parts ginger and candied lime peel, if available
- 2 cups currants, chopped
- 2 cups sugar.

1. Squeeze the limes and reserve the juice. Using a spoon, separate the white pulp from the skin. Discard the white pulp. Place the skins in a saucepan and add water barely to cover. Simmer until skins are almost mushy. Drain and mash the skins.
2. Combine the reserved lime juice, mashed lime skins and the remaining ingredients. Stir; then pack in hot sterilized jars. Seal tightly, store in refrigerator but open occasionally to stir. Let stand at least ten days in refrigerator before using.
Yield: About one quart.

Peach Chutney
GEORGIA

4	cups peeled, pitted and finely chopped peaches (about three pounds)	1	tablespoon salt
		1	teaspoon ground allspice
		½	teaspoon cinnamon
¾	cup cider vinegar	½	teaspoon ground cloves
¼	cup lemon juice	½	teaspoon ground ginger
1	cup raisins	7½	cups sugar (about three and one-quarter pounds)
⅓	cup chopped onion		
¼	cup slivered, drained preserved ginger	1	bottle liquid fruit pectin.

1. Put the peaches in a large kettle and add the vinegar, lemon juice, raisins, onion, preserved ginger, salt and spices.
2. Add the sugar and mix thoroughly. Place over high heat and bring to a rolling boil, stirring occasionally. Boil hard one minute, stirring constantly.
3. Remove from the heat and stir in the pectin immediately. Skim off the foam with a metal spoon and stir and skim for five minutes to cool slightly and prevent floating fruit. Ladle into hot sterilized glasses and cover with a one-eighth-inch layer of melted paraffin wax. Store in a cool, dry, dark place.
Yield: About one dozen eight-ounce jars.

Mango Chutney

FLORIDA

- 1½ cups light brown sugar
- 2 cups malt vinegar or cider vinegar
- 1 pound firm, slightly underripe mangoes, peeled and sliced
- ½ pound currants
- ½ pound raisins
- ½ pound blanched almonds
- ⅓ cup sliced green ginger (see note) or one-half cup chopped preserved ginger
- 1 tablespoon salt
- ½ tablespoon white mustard seeds, tied in a cheesecloth bag
- ½ cup chopped onion
- ½ cup chopped green pepper
- 1 teaspoon chopped hot chili pepper or red pepper flakes.

1. Combine the sugar and vinegar and bring to a boil.
2. Stir in the remaining ingredients and simmer thirty minutes, or until syrup is thick and fruit is clear. Discard the spice bag. Ladle the chutney into hot sterilized jars and seal. Cool and store in a cool, dark, dry place.

Yield: Three to four pints.

Note: Green ginger is available in Chinese markets.

Green Tomato Relish

LOUISIANA

- 12 green tomatoes, cored
- ⅓ cup coarse salt
- 24 green peppers
- 6 red sweet peppers (or use this additional amount of green peppers)
- 12 large sweet onions
- 1 gallon boiling water
- 4 cups white vinegar
- 3 cups sugar
- 1 tablespoon whole cloves
- 2 tablespoons stick cinnamon pieces
- 1 teaspoon celery seeds.

1. Chop the tomatoes and sprinkle with the salt. Let stand one hour. Drain.
2. Core and seed green and red peppers and trim away the white veins. Cut peppers into large cubes. Put peppers and the onions through a food chopper. Add half the water and drain immediately in a colander.
3. Add the remaining water and let stand ten minutes. Drain.
4. Add the vinegar and sugar. Tie the cloves, stick cinnamon and cel-

ery seeds in a cheesecloth bag and add it. Bring the mixture to a boil and simmer, uncovered, exactly thirty minutes. Discard the spice bag.

5. Pour the relish into hot sterilized jars and seal. Cool and store in a cool, dark, dry place.

Yield: About six quarts.

Ripe Tomato Pickle
GEORGIA

8 cups ripe tomatoes, cored and chopped	½ teaspoon mace
	½ teaspoon ground cloves
8 cups chopped green cabbage	½ teaspoon ground allspice
4 cups sliced white onions	1 teaspoon ground ginger
6 large green peppers, cored, seeded and chopped	1 tablespoon celery seeds
	1 teaspoon turmeric
4 cups cider vinegar	1 cup salt.
2 pounds light brown sugar	

1. Day before, combine all the ingredients in a large mixing bowl and let stand, stirring occasionally, about one hour.

2. Pour the ingredients into a large cloth bag and let drip overnight. Next day, pour the contents of the bag into a large kettle. Bring to a boil and cook, stirring frequently, one hour. Pour into hot sterilized jars and seal. Cool and store in a cool, dark, dry place.

Yield: About three quarts.

Artichoke Relish
NORTH CAROLINA

4 quarts Jerusalem artichokes, scraped and coarsely ground	1 tablespoon celery seeds
	2 tablespoons mustard seeds
6 onions, coarsely ground	1 tablespoon turmeric
4 green or red sweet peppers, coarsely ground	½ teaspoon cayenne pepper
	6 cups cider vinegar
2 tablespoons coarse salt	3 cups sugar.

Combine all the ingredients in a large kettle. Bring to a boil and simmer thirty minutes, stirring occasionally. Pour into hot sterilized jars and seal. Cool and store in a cool, dark, dry place.

Yield: About fourteen pints.

Green Relish
TENNESSEE

4	cups coarsely ground onions, drained	2	tablespoons coarse salt
4	cups coarsely ground cucumbers, drained	1	tablespoon celery seeds
8	cups coarsely ground seeded green peppers	1	tablespoon mustard seeds
3	hot green peppers, unseeded and ground	2	cups sugar
		2	cups cider vinegar.

Put all the ingredients in a large kettle. Bring to a boil and simmer about thirty minutes. Ladle into hot sterilized jars and seal. Cool and store in cool, dark, dry place.

Yield: About ten pints.

Sauces

Chili Sauce
ARKANSAS

8 pounds ripe tomatoes	1½ cups light brown sugar
3 red sweet peppers, seeded	2 tablespoons salt
3 green peppers, seeded	1 teaspoon freshly ground black pepper
1 small stalk celery	
6 onions, chopped	1 teaspoon dry mustard
3 cloves garlic, minced	2 dried hot red peppers, crushed
1½ teaspoons whole allspice	
1½ teaspoons mustard seeds	2 cups cider vinegar.
1½ teaspoons whole cloves	

    1. Scald, peel, core and chop the tomatoes. Chop the peppers, celery and onions. Add with the garlic to the tomatoes, bring to a boil and simmer for forty-five minutes.

    2. Tie the allspice, mustard seeds and cloves in a muslin bag. Add with the sugar, salt, black pepper, mustard and hot peppers. Boil, uncovered, until thick.

    3. Add the vinegar and boil the sauce to correct the consistency. Discard the spice bag. Pour the sauce into hot sterilized jars and seal. Cool and store in a cool, dark, dry place.

    Yield: Eight pints.

Southern Tomato Sauce
KENTUCKY

10 medium-size tomatoes (about two and one-half pounds)	1 bay leaf
	1 teaspoon basil
¼ pound salt pork, diced	Salt and freshly ground black pepper to taste
¼ cup olive oil	
2 cloves garlic, finely chopped	2 tablespoons butter, cut into small pieces.
1 large onion, finely chopped	
1 six-ounce can tomato paste, preferably the imported Italian kind	

1. Drop the tomatoes two or three at a time into rapidly boiling water and boil for about 10 seconds. Remove and peel with a paring knife. Cut out the stem and discard. Cut the tomatoes in half crosswise and squeeze each half to extract the seeds. Then coarsely chop them in a mixing bowl.

2. In a saucepan gently sauté the salt pork in the oil until brown. Add the garlic and onion and cook until just wilted.

3. Add the prepared tomatoes, tomato paste, bay leaf, basil, and salt and pepper to taste. Bring to a boil and let simmer over very low heat for one hour.

4. When done, swirl in the butter bits and serve.

Yield: About one quart.

Note: This sauce may be frozen.

Hollandaise Sauce
LOUISIANA

½ cup butter, at room temperature	2 tablespoons lemon juice
2 egg yolks	¼ teaspoon salt
	Pinch of cayenne pepper.

1. Divide the butter into three parts. In the top of a double boiler, combine one part of the butter with the egg yolks.

2. Place over hot, nearly boiling water and beat constantly with a wire whisk until the butter is melted.

3. Add the second part of the butter and then the third, stirring constantly.

4. When the sauce thickens, add the lemon juice, salt and cayenne.

Yield: Four servings.

This is one of the most unusual of Florida's specialties. Called Old Sour, it is really a sauce made with lime juice and salt that is aged before using. The sauce is designed for use with fish and sea foods and in salad dressings.

Key West Old Lime Sour
FLORIDA

| 2 cups fresh lime juice, preferably made with thin-skinned key limes | 1½ teaspoons salt. |

1. Strain the lime juice and, using a funnel, pour it into a bottle. Add the salt and shake the bottle.
2. Do not stopper the bottle, but cover the mouth with cheesecloth. Tie with a string and let the lime juice stand at room temperature for about two weeks to age. Seal the bottle and keep it in a cool place. Serve a dash of the sauce on broiled fish, cold fish, in mayonnaise or in French dressings.
   Yield: About two cups.

Tartar Sauce
LOUISIANA

1 cup mayonnaise	1 tablespoon chopped capers
1 clove garlic, finely minced	¼ cup finely chopped parsley
¼ cup finely chopped onion	1 teaspoon Creole mustard or imported mustard such as Dijon or Düsseldorf.
2 tablespoons chopped sour pickle	

Combine all ingredients and serve.
Yield: About one and one-quarter cups.

Lime and Herb Sauce Vinaigrette
FLORIDA

½ cup peanut oil or vegetable oil
¼ cup olive oil
3 to four tablespoons lime juice
Salt and freshly ground black pepper to taste
2 tablespoons finely chopped chives
1 teaspoon finely chopped fresh tarragon or one-half teaspoon dried tarragon
½ teaspoon finely minced garlic
2 tablespoons finely chopped parsley
1 teaspoon Creole mustard or imported mustard such as Dijon or Düsseldorf.

Combine all ingredients in a mixing bowl and beat or shake well. Serve as a salad dressing or with sea food.
Yield: About one and one-quarter cups.

Louisiana Sauce Remoulade

- ¼ cup cold water
- 3 tablespoons dry mustard
- 3 cups corn oil
- 1 cup olive oil
- 2 five-ounce jars horseradish or about one cup fresh horseradish
- 3 tablespoons paprika
- 1 teaspoon celery seeds
- 1½ cups finely minced heart of celery
- 1 one-pound jar Creole mustard
- 1 tablespoon lemon juice Grated rind of one lemon
- 12 whole cloves
- 6 bay leaves.

1. Pour the water into the container of an electric blender. Add the dry mustard. Stir to blend and let stand ten minutes.
2. Add all remaining ingredients except the cloves and bay leaves and blend. Add the cloves and bay leaves and store sauce in glass jars. This sauce may be kept for several weeks in the refrigerator. When the sauce is used, add more horseradish to taste if desired. Serve over chilled shrimp.

Yield: About two quarts.

Mustard Mayonnaise

LOUISIANA

- 2 egg yolks
- 1 tablespoon wine vinegar
  Pinch of cayenne pepper
  Salt and freshly ground white or black pepper to taste
- ¾ cup peanut oil
- ¼ cup olive oil
- 2 to four tablespoons mustard, preferably Creole type, or Dijon or Düsseldorf style
  Lime or lemon juice (optional).

1. Place the egg yolks in a mixing bowl and add the vinegar, cayenne, salt and pepper.
2. Begin beating with a wire whisk and, when well blended, add the oils in a thin stream. Continue beating until mayonnaise is thickened and all the oil has been added.
3. When firm, beat in the mustard. If desired, add a little lime or lemon juice to taste. Serve with cold boiled shrimp.

Yield: About one and one-quarter cups.

Aguacate (Avocado Sauce)
FLORIDA

- 1 ripe avocado
- 1 clove garlic, finely minced
- 1 tablespoon wine vinegar
- Juice of one lime or lemon
- 4 tablespoons olive oil
- Salt and freshly ground black pepper to taste
- 1 green chile, fresh or canned, chopped (optional), or Tabasco sauce to taste
- Fresh coriander leaves, chopped (optional).

1. Peel the avocado and mash the pulp.
2. Immediately blend pulp with remaining ingredients. Serve as a sauce with fish or other sea food.

Yield: One to one and one-half cups.

Sauce for Poached Fish
LOUISIANA

- 2 tablespoons butter
- 2 tablespoons flour
- 1 cup boiling water
- 2 tablespoons catchup
- 1 tablespoon Worcestershire sauce
- Juice of one lemon
- 1 hard-cooked egg, finely chopped
- Salt to taste
- Cayenne pepper to taste.

1. Melt the butter and stir in the flour. Add the water, stirring until blended and smooth.
2. Stir in the remaining ingredients and serve hot with fish.

Yield: About one and one-half cups.

Lobster or Shrimp Cocktail Dressing
MISSISSIPPI

- 1 cup mayonnaise
- 3 tablespoons catchup
- 1 tablespoon tarragon vinegar
- 1 teaspoon Worcestershire sauce
- Lemon juice to taste
- Onion juice scraped from one cut onion.

Combine all ingredients and chill. Serve with cold lobster or shrimp.
Yield: About one and one-quarter cups.

Hot Barbecue Sauce
ALABAMA

- 2 teaspoons Tabasco sauce
- 2½ cups bottled chili sauce
- 1 teaspoon finely minced hot green peppers or canned chile peppers
- ¾ cup oil
- ½ cup lemon juice
- 2 tablespoons tarragon vinegar
- 2 cups chopped onions
- 2 cloves garlic, finely minced
- 1 tablespoon light brown sugar
- 1 bay leaf, crumbled
- 1 teaspoon dry mustard
- 1 teaspoon salt
- ½ cup water.

Combine all ingredients and simmer twenty minutes. Serve with charcoal-grilled hamburgers, spareribs or chicken.
Yield: Six cups.

Barbecue Sauce
MISSISSIPPI

- 1 cup catchup
- Juice of two lemons
- 1 tablespoon Worcestershire sauce
- 2 tablespoons cider vinegar
- 2 tablespoons butter
- Salt and freshly ground black pepper to taste
- 1 teaspoon sugar.

Combine all ingredients, bring to a boil and use to brush poultry, meat or fish as it is barbecued.
Yield: About one and one-half cups.

Pendennis Club Barbecue Sauce
KENTUCKY

- 1 bottle chili sauce
- 1 medium-size bottle catchup
- 1 bottle Worcestershire sauce
- 1 bottle A.1. Sauce
- 1 small bottle Major Grey's chutney
- 1 cup bourbon
- Dry red wine or cider vinegar.

Combine all the ingredients, using enough wine or vinegar to give a pouring consistency. Serve on barbecued spareribs, chicken or hamburgers.

Yield: About seven cups.

Tomato Gravy
ALABAMA

2 tablespoons bacon drippings	½ teaspoon salt
3 tomatoes, peeled and chopped	¼ teaspoon freshly ground black pepper
2 tablespoons flour	⅛ teaspoon baking soda
½ teaspoon sugar	2 cups milk.

1. Heat the bacon drippings in a skillet and cook the tomatoes in it until tender. Sprinkle with the flour, sugar, salt and pepper and stir to mix well. Cook two minutes.

2. Add the baking soda to the milk and stir in the tomato mixture. Bring to a boil, stirring. Spoon over hot biscuits or grits.

Yield: Three cups.

Mississippi Steak Sauce

½ teaspoon dry mustard	¼ teaspoon curry powder
¼ cup wine vinegar	Salt and freshly ground black pepper to taste
¼ cup catchup	
1 teaspoon Worcestershire sauce	1 cup butter, at room temperature.

1. Combine the mustard with the vinegar and let stand ten minutes. Blend with the catchup, Worcestershire, curry powder, salt and pepper.

2. Place the butter in a skillet and place the skillet over very low heat. Stir continuously with a wire whisk and, when the butter is creamy but not melted, gradually stir in the catchup mixture. When all ingredients are blended, remove the sauce from the heat. Serve with charcoal-grilled steak.

Yield: About one and one-half cups.

Cranberry and Horseradish Sauce
TENNESSEE

4 cups cranberries	1½ cups sugar
2 cups water	Horseradish to taste.

1. Place the berries in a saucepan and add the water. Cover and cook until berries pop.
2. Add the sugar and continue cooking fifteen minutes. Let cool and add the horseradish. Mold, if desired, and chill. Serve with game, poultry or meat.

Yield: About three cups.

Port Wine and Horseradish Sauce
MISSISSIPPI

½ cup port wine	1 cup red currant jelly (eight ounces)
⅛ teaspoon nutmeg or mace	
⅛ teaspoon cinnamon	2 tablespoons freshly grated horseradish.
Salt and freshly ground black pepper to taste	

1. Pour the wine into a saucepan and add the nutmeg or mace, cinnamon, salt and pepper. Bring to a boil and reduce by one-third.
2. Heat the jelly over hot water, stirring, until jelly dissolves. Add the wine mixture and horseradish. Serve with game or poultry.

Yield: One and one-half cups.

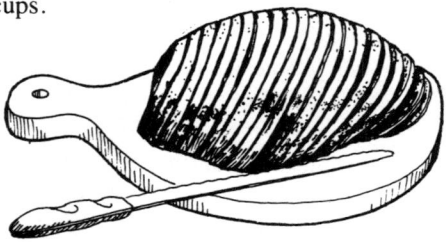

One of the most famous sauces in Louisiana is a honey and curry sauce used on first courses at the Shreveport Club in Shreveport. The sauce is used on fresh fruit and on sea food.

Shreveport Club Honey and Curry Sauce
LOUISIANA

1 cup mayonnaise	Salt to taste
2 tablespoons catchup	Worcestershire sauce to taste
1 tablespoon dry mustard	1 teaspoon onion juice,
2 tablespoons honey	squeezed from grated onion
1 tablespoon curry powder	1 tablespoon preserved ginger
Tabasco sauce to taste	or freshly grated ginger to
1 teaspoon lemon juice	taste.

    1. Spoon the mayonnaise into a mixing bowl. Blend the catchup and mustard together and add to mayonnaise.
    2. Stir in the remaining ingredients and chill.
Yield: About one and one-half cups.

Old-Fashioned Lemon Butter
VIRGINIA

3 lemons	3 eggs
3 cups sugar	4 tablespoons butter.

    1. Grate the rind of the lemons. Squeeze the lemons to extract the juice. Combine the grated rind and the juice.
    2. Place the sugar in a mixing bowl and add the eggs, one at a time, beating well after each addition. Blend with the lemon rind and juice.
    3. Add the butter bit by bit and cook the mixture in the top of a double boiler, stirring constantly, until mixture thickens. Do not boil.
    4. Pour into hot sterilized jars and seal. Cool and store in a cool, dark, dry place. Serve with toast or as a filling for sponge layers.
Yield: About three cups.

Papaya Sauce
FLORIDA

2 large ripe but fairly firm papayas	1 lemon, thinly sliced
	6 whole cloves.
3 cups sugar	
1 teaspoon grated fresh ginger or ground ginger	

1. Peel the papayas and cut them into cubes.
2. Cover the papaya cubes with water and add the remaining ingredients. Bring to a boil and simmer until papaya is thoroughly tender.
Yield: Two to three cups.
Note: Use as you would applesauce.

Rum and Cherry Sauce
LOUISIANA

- 1 cup dark or bing cherry preserves
- ½ cup broken pecans, walnuts or other nuts
- ½ cup dark rum, or more to taste.

Combine all the ingredients and let stand until ready to use. This sauce should be made only with dark rum and not with the light. The sauce will keep indefinitely in the refrigerator and for several weeks in a cool place if tightly sealed.
Yield: About two cups.

Custard Sauce Flavored with Pernod
LOUISIANA

- 4 egg yolks
- 3 tablespoons sugar
- 1 teaspoon cornstarch
- ⅛ teaspoon salt
- 1¾ cups milk, scalded
- 1 tablespoon Pernod.

1. Beat the egg yolks with the sugar until thick and pale. Beat in the cornstarch and salt. Gradually beat in the milk.
2. Pour the mixture into a heavy pan and cook over low heat, stirring constantly, until the mixture thickens and lightly coats the back of the spoon.
3. Remove from the heat and set in a pan of ice water to prevent further cooking. Cool. Stir in the Pernod. Chill.
Yield: About two cups.

Rum Sauce
LOUISIANA

6 egg yolks
1 cup sugar
¾ cup dark rum.

1. Beat the egg yolks until lemon-colored and slightly thickened. Gradually beat in the sugar.
2. Stir in half the rum and cook over boiling water, stirring constantly, until sauce coats a wooden spoon. Do not allow to boil. Stir in the remaining rum.

Yield: About one and one-half cups.
Note: Cognac or kirsch may be substituted for the rum.

Beverages

Eggnog
MISSISSIPPI

6 eggs, separated	1 cup heavy cream
12 tablespoons sugar	Nutmeg.
½ cup bourbon, or more to taste	

1. Place the egg yolks in a mixing bowl and add six tablespoons of the sugar. Beat thoroughly until light and lemon-colored.
2. Beat the egg whites until stiff and gradually add the remaining sugar. Fold the whites into the yolks and add the bourbon gradually, beating thoroughly.
3. Whip the cream and fold it into the egg mixture. Serve immediately in chilled silver mugs or glasses and sprinkle each serving with a little nutmeg.

Yield: Six servings.

John's Eggnog
NORTH CAROLINA

¾ cup sugar	1 pint bourbon
12 eggs, separated	2 cups heavy cream, whipped.

1. Slowly add the sugar to the egg yolks and beat until very stiff and white.
2. Beat the egg whites until stiff. Stir the bourbon into yolk mixture. Mix in whites and the cream with a wire whisk. Chill until served. This is better on the second day.

Yield: One dozen servings.

One of the gentlest and most delicious restoratives for the morning-after is a well-chilled milk punch delicately seasoned with nutmeg. The milk punch served in certain Louisiana homes prior to Sunday brunch also contains cream.

Milk Punch
LOUISIANA

3 cups milk
1 cup light cream
3 tablespoons sugar, or to taste

1 cup bourbon or rye whisky
Nutmeg.

1. Combine the milk, cream and sugar and stir until sugar dissolves.
2. Add the bourbon or whisky and serve with an ice cube in chilled glasses. Sprinkle with nutmeg before serving.

Yield: Four to six servings.

Café Brûlot
LOUISIANA

13 lumps sugar
5 whole cloves
2½ sticks cinnamon
1 lemon

1 orange
1 cup warm cognac
4 to six cups piping-hot strong black coffee.

1. Place the lump sugar in a silver bowl or other suitable container. Add the cloves and cinnamon.
2. Cut the skin from the lemon and the orange, spiral fashion. Add the skins to the bowl and reserve the fruit for another use.
3. Add the cognac and ignite it. Ladle the mixture over and over while flame burns, and pour in coffee. Serve immediately in demitasse cups.

Yield: Ten servings.

Edenton Punch
NORTH CAROLINA

2 fifths cognac
1 bottle Sauterne wine
2 quarts ice cold sparkling water

5 fifths ice cold dry or brut champagne.

1. Place a large block of ice in a punch bowl. Pour the cognac and Sauterne over ice.

2. When mixture is thoroughly cold, add the sparkling water and champagne. Serve immediately.
Yield: Fifty servings.
Note: This is served at hunt breakfasts.

Blackberry Syrup
SOUTH CAROLINA

6 to ten quarts blackberries	Sugar.
3 cups cider vinegar	

1. Place sound ripe fruit in a stone crock and pour the vinegar over the top. Cover top of crock with muslin. Let stand in a cool place for three to four days, stirring twice a day.
2. Strain the mixture through a jelly bag without crushing the fruit. Measure the juice into a pan and add one pound of sugar for every pint of juice.
3. Heat, stirring, until sugar dissolves, bring to a boil and boil gently for five minutes. Bottle and seal and dilute to taste for making a blackberry drink. Store in the refrigerator or in a cool, dark, dry place.
Yield: About three quarts.

Elderberry Blossom Wine
KENTUCKY

3 quarts elderberry blossoms without stems	½ package active dry yeast
	¼ cup lukewarm water
4 gallons boiling water	3 pounds raisins.
9 pounds sugar	

1. Place the blossoms in a five-gallon crock and add the boiling water. Add the sugar and stir until it is dissolved. Let cool.
2. Dissolve the yeast in the lukewarm water and add to the crock. Let stand ten days, stirring several times each day.
3. Strain the mixture into a large glass jug and add the raisins. Let stand three months; then strain into bottles or fruit jars. Seal well.
Yield: About three and one-half gallons.

Scuppernong Nectar
SOUTH CAROLINA

12	pounds scuppernong grapes	1	cup water
1	cup white vinegar		Sugar.

1. Day before, crush the grapes and put in large crock or earthenware bowl. Add the vinegar and water, stir and let stand overnight.
2. Next day, drain juice through a cheesecloth bag. Measure juice into a kettle and for each two cups juice add one cup sugar.
3. Bring to a boil and boil five minutes. Bottle in hot sterilized bottles. Seal and store in a cool, dark, dry place.

Yield: About two quarts.

Mint Julep
KENTUCKY

1	teaspoon sugar		Crushed ice
1	tablespoon water	2	ounces bourbon
4	or five mint leaves		Mint sprig.

1. In a bowl, dissolve the sugar in the water. Add the mint leaves and bruise with muddler or wooden spoon until syrup is green-colored.
2. Fill a julep cup or old-fashioned glass with crushed ice.
3. Pour in the mint syrup and the bourbon. Set the cup in the refrigerator from thirty to sixty minutes to frost. Garnish with mint sprig. Serve with a half-sized straw.

Yield: One serving.

Tarpon Isle Rum Cocktail
FLORIDA

	Juice of one sour orange		Shaved ice
1	jigger dark rum	1	slice sour orange.
2	teaspoons unrefined sugar (sometimes called raw sugar or crude sugar)		

Combine all ingredients except sour orange slice in a cocktail shaker and shake well. Strain and garnish with the sour orange slice.

Yield: One serving.

Salty Dog Cocktail
FLORIDA

3 large grapefruit	9 ounces vodka or gin
3 teaspoons salt, or to taste	Ice cubes.

1. Peel the grapefruit before squeezing because the peel gives a bitter, oily flavor to the juice. Squeeze or press the grapefruit. Divide the juice equally among six all-purpose wine glasses, small tumblers or on-the-rocks glasses. Add one-half teaspoon salt or salt to taste to each glass. Stir until salt is dissolved.

2. Add one and one-half ounces of vodka or gin to each glass. Add two or three ice cubes. Stir and serve.

Yield: Six servings.

Sazerac Cocktail
LOUISIANA

4 dashes absinthe (or use Pernod, Ricard or other anise-flavored liqueur)	4 teaspoons sugar (optional)
	8 ounces bourbon
	Ice cubes
4 dashes Angostura or Peychaud bitters	Lemon peel.

1. Thoroughly chill four old-fashioned glasses.

2. Put a dash of absinthe in each glass and swirl the glass around to coat the inside.

3. Add the bitters to a mixing glass. Add the sugar if desired. Add the bourbon and several large ice cubes. Stir until thoroughly chilled; then strain into the old-fashioned glasses. Twist lemon peel over each glass and serve.

Yield: Four servings.

Candies

Pralines

LOUISIANA

- 2 cups light brown sugar
- 1 cup granulated sugar
- 1 cup water
- 1 cup heavy cream
- 1 teaspoon vanilla
- 2 tablespoons butter
- 3 cups pecans.

1. Combine the sugars, water and cream in a heavy saucepan. Bring to a boil, stirring until sugars dissolve. Cook to the soft ball stage, or until mixture registers 238 degrees on a candy thermometer.
2. Remove from the heat and add the vanilla and butter. Beat until creamy. Add the pecans and spoon mixture onto a buttered marble slab or wax paper.

Yield: Three dozen.

Fudge

MISSISSIPPI

- 2 cups sugar
- ¾ cup heavy cream
- 2 tablespoons light corn syrup
- ⅛ teaspoon cream of tartar
- ⅛ teaspoon salt
- 2 tablespoons butter
- 1 teaspoon vanilla.

1. Place the sugar, cream, syrup, cream of tartar and salt in a heavy pan. Heat, stirring, until the sugar dissolves. Brush down the sides of the pan with hot water to remove splashes and crystals.
2. Heat mixture to boiling and boil without stirring to 234 degrees on a candy thermometer, or until the mixture forms a soft ball when dropped into cold water.
3. Add the butter, but do not stir. Cool to lukewarm, about 110 degrees.
4. Add the vanilla and beat the fudge with a wooden spoon until fudge loses its gloss and is thick and creamy. Pour into a buttered dish (eight-by-eight-by-two inches). Mark into squares and cool.

Yield: One pound, about two dozen pieces.

Chocolate fudge: Add two to four ounces (two to four squares) unsweetened chocolate to the sugar mixture at the beginning of the recipe.

Nut fudge: Add one cup chopped walnuts, pecans, almonds or Brazil nuts just before pouring the fudge into the dish.

Penuche fudge: Substitute light brown sugar for the granulated sugar.

Ginger fudge: Add three-quarters cup finely chopped crystallized gingerroot just before pouring the fudge into the dish.

Divinity
GEORGIA

- 2 cups sugar
- ½ cup light corn syrup
- ½ cup hot water
- ¼ teaspoon salt
- 2 egg whites, stiffly beaten
- 1 teaspoon vanilla
- ½ cup chopped pecans

1. Place the sugar, syrup, water and salt in a heavy two-quart saucepan. Cook, stirring, until the sugar dissolves.

2. Wash the sides of the pan with a brush dipped in water to remove any sugar crystals. Boil, without stirring, until the mixture registers 250 degrees on a candy thermometer, or a little dropped into cold water forms a hard ball.

3. While continuing to beat the egg whites at high speed with an electric mixer, gradually pour in the hot syrup. Add the vanilla and beat until soft peaks are formed and the mixture begins to lose its gloss.

4. Stir in the pecans. Drop by teaspoonfuls onto a baking sheet covered with buttered wax paper, twirling the top of each as you lift spoon.

Yield: About one and one-half pounds.

Chocolate Candy
MISSISSIPPI

- 3 tablespoons butter
- 1 teaspoon vanilla
- ¼ teaspoon salt
- 3 cups sugar
- 3 tablespoons cocoa powder
- 1½ cups milk
- 1 cup pecans or other nuts

1. Rub a large platter with lumps of the butter and sprinkle with the vanilla and salt.

2. Combine the sugar and cocoa powder in a mixing bowl and gradually stir in the milk. Scrape the mixture into an aluminum saucepan and bring to a boil. Cook without stirring to form a medium ball when tested in cold water, or until mixture registers 240 degrees on a candy thermometer.

3. Pour the chocolate mixture onto the platter and, when mixture is cool but not firm, beat well until candy begins to harden. Beat in the nuts and drop the mixture, one teaspoonful at a time, onto a lightly buttered surface.

Yield: About one and one-half pounds.

Caramels
MISSISSIPPI

1¾	cups light corn syrup	2	cups heavy cream
2	cups sugar	1	teaspoon vanilla
1	cup butter	1	cup chopped nuts.

1. Combine the syrup, sugar, butter and one cup of the cream in a saucepan. Bring to a boil and stir in the remaining cream.

2. Cook until mixture forms a firm ball in cold water or registers 242 to 248 degrees on a candy thermometer. Add the vanilla and nuts and turn the mixture into a well-buttered pan. When mixture is nearly cold, cut with scissors into squares.

Yield: About two pounds.

Candied Orange Pecans
GEORGIA

3	cups sugar	1	teaspoon grated orange rind
1	cup orange juice	3	cups pecans.
1½	tablespoons butter		

1. Combine the sugar and orange juice in a saucepan. Use a candy thermometer and cook the mixture to the soft ball stage, 236 degrees. Grease a flat surface with oil or butter.

2. Remove the saucepan from the heat and immediately add the butter and orange rind. Beat with a wooden spoon until the mixture is just ready to set. Quickly add the pecans and continue to beat the mixture until it becomes sugary.

3. Turn the candy onto the greased surface to cool. Quickly separate the nuts with two forks.

Yield: About three cups.

Sugar-Glazed Nuts
GEORGIA

1 cup mixed nuts, such as pecans, walnuts, almonds or filberts	1 cup sugar ⅓ cup light corn syrup ½ cup water.

1. This recipe is a little tricky because there are several variables to be taken into account. It is best prepared on a day with low humidity. In any case, the recipe must be carefully followed where temperatures and sugar crystals are concerned. To begin, fill a skillet with water and bring to a boil. Let the water simmer while proceeding with the recipe.

2. If the nuts are not of freshest quality, place them in a moderately hot oven briefly until they become crisp.

3. Combine the sugar, syrup and one-half cup water in a small saucepan and cook, stirring with a wooden spoon, until the sugar is dissolved. Stop stirring, but continue to cook until 300 degrees is reached on a candy thermometer. As sugar crystals form on the side of the pan, wipe them away with a wet cloth. Cook the syrup until it is a delicate straw color. Do not let syrup become too brown.

4. When the syrup is ready, immediately set the saucepan in the simmering water in the skillet. This is to prevent the syrup from hardening.

5. Drop a few nuts into the syrup and dip them out, one by one. Place them on a greased flat surface to harden. The best way to retrieve the nuts from the syrup is with two forks. Use one to lift one nut at a time, the other to push the glazed nut onto the greased surface. Continue, a few nuts at a time, until all are glazed. One authority on candy-making has written, "A superfluous amount of glaze around the base of the nut indicates the work of an amateur."

Yield: One and one-half cups.

Note: Stir the syrup as little as possible while dipping nuts, to prevent crystallization. If the syrup becomes too thick, it may be reheated, but do not let it brown. If the syrup becomes too solid, add a little water and cook again to original temperature.

Crystallized Grapes
GEORGIA

1 pound Thompson seedless grapes	½ cup water
	Sugar.

1. Cut the grapes into small clusters.
2. Combine the water and one cup sugar and boil five minutes. Remove from the heat. Immediately dip the clusters, one at a time, into the syrup. Sprinkle each cluster generously with sugar and let stand until set.

Yield: One pound.

Index

Aguacate (Avocado Sauce), 261
Almond Soup, 48
Ambrosia, 233
Amandine, Trout, 88
Angel Food Cake, 215
Appetizers, 17-34
  Benne Seed Wafers, 32
  Cheese Balls, 31
  Cheese Straws, 33
  Cherry Tomatoes, Stuffed, 30
  Conch Vinaigrette, 17
  Court Bouillon, 27
  Crab Meat Puffs, 20
  Crab Sauté, 20
  Cucumber and Shad Roe, 21
  Eggs Sardou, 29
  Grits Balls, Deep-Fried, 33
  Ham Biscuits, 29
  Ham and Egg Canapés, 28
  Herb Dip for Raw Vegetables, 32
  Hollandaise Sauce, Easy, 30
  Oyster Appetizer, 20
  Oysters with Cocktail Sauce, 21
  Pecans, Salted, 34
  Pickled Shrimp, 23
  Red Snapper, Chilled, 27
  Red Snapper, Escabeche of, 28
  Seafood and Southern Cocktail Sauce, 26
  Shrimp Cocktail with Celery-Tomato Sauce, 22
  Shrimp Creole, Chilled Gulf Coast, 25
  Shrimp with Hot Sauce, 23
  Shrimp with Lamaze Sauce, 22
  Shrimp Paste, 26
  Shrimp Remoulade, 24
  Shrimps Wilder, 25
  Tomato Freeze with Avocado Topping, 31
  Vegetables, Raw, with Herb Dip, 32
Apples, Fried, 239
Apple Jelly, Blackberry and, 239
Apple Preserves, Quick, 241
Applesauce Fruitcake, 217
Apple Stack Pie, 205

Arkansas Chicken Pie, Mom's, 115
Artichoke (s)
  and Sea Food Casserole, 73
  Spinach and, Asphodel Style, 167
Artichoke Pickles, Whole, 248
Artichoke Relish, 255
Asphodel Style Spinach and Artichokes, 167
Assorted Greens, 157
Au Gratin
  Heart of Palm, 160
  Mushrooms, 158
  Swamp Cabbage, 160
  Tomatoes and Green Beans, 141
Avocado Sauce, 261
Avocado Topping, for Tomato Freeze, 31

Bacon and Cheese Spoon Bread, 184
Bacon Dressing, Cooked, 173
Baked Bourbon Spiced Sweet Potatoes, 162
Baked Catfish, 51
Baked Christmas Mushroom Omelet, 135
Baked Country Ham, Boiled and, 104
Baked Pompano, en Papillote, 70
Baked Red Snapper, 82
Baked Rock Fish, Clam-Stuffed, 49
Baked Stuffed Striped Bass, 50
Banana Bread, 190
Banana Pudding, 223
Bananas
  Flambées, 234
  à la Turtle Cay, 234
Barbecue, 98
Barbecued Chicken, 117
Barbecue Sauce, 262
  Hot, 262
  Pendennis Club, 262
Bass. *See* Striped Bass
Batter Bread, 178
Batter-Fried Chicken, 110
Bavarian Cream, Peppermint Stick, 228
Bean Cakes, Hominy and, 154
Beans. *See* Black Beans, Red beans
Beaten Biscuits, 188

Beef
　Chipped
　　Crackus, 137
　　Rarebit, 136
　Cuban Round Roast, 92
　Grillades, 94
　Hot-ta-Meat Pies, 93
　Piccadillo, 89
　Tamale Pie, 90, 91
　Tripe Creole, 95
Benne Seed Wafers, 32
Beverages, 268-72
　Blackberry Syrup, 270
　Café Brûlot, 269
　Edenton Punch, 269
　Eggnog, 268
　　John's, 268
　Elderberry Blossom Wine, 270
　Milk Punch, 269
　Mint Julep, 271
　Rum Cocktail, Tarpon Isle, 271
　Salty Dog Cocktail, 272
　Sazerac Cocktail, 272
　Scuppernong Nectar, 271
Biscuits, 188
　Beaten, 188
　Cheese, 187
　Ham, 29
　Sausage with Cream Gravy and, 100
　Southern-Style, 187
　Sweet Potato, 189
Bisque
　Crawfish, 35
　Shrimp, 36
Black Beans
　Frijoles Negros, 143
　with Rum, 144
Black Bean Soup, 41
Blackberry and Apple Jelly, 239
Blackberry Syrup, 270
Black Bottom Pie, 199
Black-Eyed Peas, 146
　and Hog Jawl (Jowl), Mrs. Jackson Porter Dick's, 103
　and Rice, 146
Black-Eyed Pea Soup, 39
Black Walnut Pie, 194
Blueberry Muffins, 190
Bog, Chicken, 127
Boiled and Baked Country Ham, 104
Boiled Salad Dressing, 172
Boiled Spareribs, 97
Bouillon, Court, 27, 84

Bourbon Date Pudding, 223
Bourbon Jelly, 245
Bourbon Pie, 201
Bourbon Spiced Sweet Potatoes, Baked, 162
Braised Frogs' Legs with Sherry, 129
Braised Quail, 133
Bread(s), 175-92
　Banana, 190
　Batter, 178
　Biscuits
　　Beaten, 188
　　Cheese, 187
　　Ham, 29
　　Southern Style, 187
　　Sweet Potato, 189
　Cakes, Crackling, 181
　Corn, 176
　　Crackling, 177, 181
　　Hot Water, 175
　　Deep-Fried, 178
　　Lacy, 183
　　Molasses, 183
　　Southern Buttermilk, 179
　　Vivian's, 176
　Corn Crisps, 185
　Corn Meal Muffins, 189
　Corn Meal Mush, Fried, 179
　Corn Meal Sticks, 180
　Corn Sticks, Double, 180
　Cush, 185
　Hot Cakes, Grand, 184
　Lacy Corn, 183
　Lacy Hoe Cakes, 181
　Light Rolls, 191
　Sally Lunn, 192
　Spoon, 177
　　Bacon and Cheese, 184
　　Sweet Potato, 186
　Wafers, Benne Seed, 32
　Waffles, 186
Breakfast Shrimp, Charleston, 78
Breasts, Chicken, Stuffed, 116
Bridal Pudding, 226
Broiled Red Snapper, 79
Broiled Soft-Shelled Crabs, 58
Broiled Tomatoes, 168
Brown Butter Sauce, Green Beans with, 143
Brownies, Our Aunt Harriet's Favorite, 238
Brunswick Stew, 127
Butter
　and Dill, Cucumbers in, 246
　Old-Fashioned Lemon, 265
Butter Cake, 212

Butter Fingers, 236
Butter-Fried Corn, 149
Buttermilk Corn Bread, Southern, 179
Butter Sauce, Brown, Green Beans with, 143
Butterscotch Pie, Chocolate-, 200

Cabbage, Swamp, 159
  au Gratin, 160
Cabbage Casserole, 147
Café Brûlot, 269
Cajun Jambalaya, 126
Cake(s), 210-21
  Angel Food, 215
  Bean, Hominy and, 154
  Bread, Crackling, 181
  Butter, 212
  Fruitcake
    Applesauce, 217
    Past Perfect, 218
    White, 217
  Grand Hot, 184
  Hoe, 175
    Lacy, 181
  Jam, 214
  Lady Baltimore, 220
  Lane
    Filling, 219
    Layers, 219
  Lemon, 215
  Minetry McCoy's Miracle, 232
  à l'Orange, 211
  Orange, 210
  Pecan-Cherry, 213
  Poundcake I, 212
  Poundcake II, 213
  Squash, 166
  Sugar, Mrs. D's Moravian, 221
  Sugar Plum, 216
Canapés, Ham and Egg, 28
Candied Orange Pecans, 275
Candies, 273-77
  Candied Orange Pecans, 275
  Caramels, 275
  Chocolate, 274
  Crystallized Grapes, 277
  Divinity, 274
  Fudge, 273
  Pralines, 273
  Sugar Glazed Nuts, 276
Cantaloupe and Orange Jam, 241
Capers, Cole Slaw with, 171
Caramels, 275

Carrots, Pickled Garden, 246
Carrot Pie, Spiced, 205
Casserole(s)
  Artichoke and Sea Food, 73
  Cabbage, 147
  Cheese Grits, 138
  Eggplant, Hunt and Polo, 152
  Green Bean, 142
  Pecan Squash, 167
Catfish, Baked, 51
Catfish Gumbo, 51
Cauliflower Slaw, 170
Celery
  in Cheese Sauce, 147
  with Egg and Lemon Sauce, 148
Celery Chowder, 43
Celery-Tomato Sauce, for Shrimp Cocktail, 22
Charles Street Trout, 87
Charleston Breakfast Shrimp, 78
Cheese
  Bacon and, Spoon Bread, 184
  Crackus, 137
  Rarebit, 136
  Welsh Rabbit, 137
Cheese Balls, 31
Cheese Biscuits, 187
Cheese Custard, 137
  Zucchini, 165
Cheese Grits Casserole, 138
Cheese Sauce, Celery in, 147
Cheese Straws, 33
Cheese-Stuffed Squash, 165
Cherries
  Surinam Preserves, 243
Cherry Cake, Pecan-, 213
Cherry Sauce, Rum and, 266
Cherry Tomatoes, Stuffed, 30
Chesapeake Bay Fish Stew, 84
Chess Pie
  I, 196
  II, 196
  Rum and Rhubarb, 209
Chess Tarts, 197
Chicken, 108-27
  Barbecued, 117
  Batter-Fried, 110
  Brunswick Stew, 127
  with Corn Bread Stuffing, 111
  'n' Dumplings, 112
  Olivette, 113
  Poulet Floride, 119

Pressed, 119
Seven Hearths, 118
Southern Fried
 I, 108
 II, 108
 III, 109
Chicken Bog, 127
Chicken Breasts, Stuffed, 116
Chicken Crab Bake, 117
Chicken Cream Gravy, 110
Chicken Creole, 123
Chicken Jambalaya, 123
 Cajun, 126
Chicken Loaf, 120
Chicken Pie, Mom's Arkansas, 115
Chicken Pudding, 114
Chicken Spaghetti, 124
Chicken Wings, Gumbo-Style, 122
Chiffon Pie, Lemon, 204
Chiffon Tart, Orange Liqueur, 204
Chili Sauce, 257
Chilled Gulf Coast Shrimp Creole, 25
Chilled Peach Soup, 46
Chilled Red Snapper Appetizer, 27
Chipped Beef
 Crackus, 137
 Rarebit, 136
Chitterlings, 102
Chocolate-Butterscotch Pie, 200
Chocolate Candy, 274
Chocolate Fudge, 274
Chocolate Pecan Pudding, 224
Chocolate Sauce, for Bavarian Cream, 228
Chowder
 Celery, 43
 Clam, Maryland, 39
 Conch, 34
Christmas Mushroom Omelet, Baked, 135
Chutney
 Lime, 252
 Mango, 253
 Peach, 252
Clams, Maryland Fried, 52
Clam Chowder, Maryland, 39
Clam-Stuffed Baked Rock Fish, 49
Clara's Eggplant, 150
Cobbler, Peach, 208
Cocktail Dressing, Lobster or Shrimp, 261
Cocktails
 Mint Julep, 271
 Rum, Tarpon Isle, 271
 Salty Dog, 272

Sazerac, 272
Cocktail Sauce
 Oysters with, 21
 Southern, Sea Food and, 26
Cole Slaw, 170
 with Capers, 171
Cole Slaw Dressing, 173
Collard Greens, 156
Conch Chowder, 34
Conch Salad, Raw, 52
Conch Vinaigrette, 17
Conserve(s)
 Oranges and Lemons, Stuffed, 251
 Peach, 241
 -Melon, 242
Cooked Bacon Dressing, 173
Cooked Custard Ice Cream, 235
Cookies
 Brownies, Our Aunt Harriet's Favorite, 238
 Butter Fingers, 236
 Ginger, Moravian, 237
 Hermits, 238
 Snickerdoodles, 237
 Sugar, 236
Corn
 Butter-Fried, 149
 Francille's Stewed, 149
 Corn Bread, 112
 Crackling, 177
 Hot Water, 175
 Lacy, 183
 Molasses, 183
 Southern Buttermilk, 183
 Vivian's, 176
Corn Bread Dumplings, Mixed Greens with, 157
Corn Bread Stuffing, Chicken with, 111
Corn Crisps, 185
Corn Meal Muffins, 189
Corn Meal Mush, Fried, 179
Corn Meal Sticks, 180
Corn Oysters, 148
Corn Soup, Cream of, 41
Corn Sticks, Double, 180
Country Ham, Boiled and Baked, 104
Court Bouillon, 27, 84
Cow Pea Soup, 44
Crab Bake, Chicken, 117
Crab Cakes I, 53
Crab Cakes II, 54
Crab Gumbo, 55
Crab Meat Imperial, 57

Crab Meat Puffs, Hot, 20
Crabs
    Hard-Shelled, Steamed, 57
    She-
        and Lobster Soup, 37
        Soup, 38
    Soft-Shelled
        Broiled, 58
        Deep-Fried, 55
    Stone, Steamed, 56
Crab Sauté, 20
Crab Soup
    She-, 38
    and Lobster, 37
    South River Club, 38
Crab Stew, 54
Crackling Bread Cakes, 181
Crackus, 137
Cranberry and Horseradish Sauce, 264
Crawfish Bisque, 35
Crawfish Etoufée, 59
Crawfish à la Nage, 58
Cream
    Bavarian, Peppermint Stick, 228
    Fried, 191
    See also Sour Cream
Creamed Oysters, 68
Cream Gravy
    Chicken, 110
    for Sausage and Biscuits, 100
Cream of Corn Soup, 41
Cream of Peanut Soup, 47
Cream of Spinach Soup, 43
Creole
    Chicken, 123
    Gumbo Pontchartrain, 85
    Red Snapper, 81
    Shrimp, 78
        Chilled Gulf Coast, 25
    Tripe, 95
Crisp Watermelon Pickles, 249
Croquettes, Ham, with Egg Sauce, 107
Crystallized Grapes, 277
Cuban Round Roast, 92
Cuban Sausages, 100
Cucumber(s)
    in Butter and Dill, 246
    and Shad Roe, 21
Cucumber Pickles, Quick, 247
Curry Sauce, Honey and, Shreveport Club, 265
Cush, 185

Custard
    Cheese, 137
    Zucchini, 165
    Fried, 191
    Rice, with Lemon Sauce, Mrs. Mescal Johnston's, 222
Custard Ice Cream, Cooked, 235
Custard Sauce, Flavored with Pernod, 266

Damson Jam, 244
Date Pudding, Bourbon, 223
Deep-Fried Frogs' Legs, 129
Deep-Fried Grits Balls, 33
Deep-Fried Hot Water Corn Bread, 178
Deep-Fried Soft-Shelled Crabs, 55
Deep-Fried Spareribs, 98
Deviled Oysters, 62
Desserts, 193-238
Dill, Cucumbers in Butter and, 246
Dilled Rice for Shrimp, 164
Dip(s)
    Herb, for Raw Vegetables, 32
    Pat's Favorite, 32
Dirty Rice, 164
Divinity, 274
Dolphin Fillets Norsaga, 60
Double Corn Sticks, 180
Doves
    Halidon Hill Potted, 134
    Ponchartrain, 134
Dressing(s), 172-73
    Boiled Salad, 172
    Cole Slaw, 173
    Cooked Bacon, 173
    for Lobster or Shrimp Cocktail, 261
    Poppy Seed, Shreveport, 172
Duck(s)
    Pressed, 130
    Wild
        Country Captain, 132
        with Madeira, 131
Dumplings
    Chicken 'n', 112
    Corn Bread, Mixed Greens with, 157

Easy Hollandaise Sauce, 30
Easy Pickled Watermelon Rind, 250
Edenton Punch, 269
Egg(s)
    and Lemon Sauce, Celery with, 148
    Sea Food with, 72
Egg Canapés, Ham and, 28

Eggnog, 268
  John's, 268
Eggnog Pudding, Fruited, 229
Eggplant
  Clara's, 150
  Stuffed, 151
Eggplant Casserole, Hunt and Polo, 152
Eggplant Soufflé, 151
Egg Sauce, for Ham Croquettes, 107
Eggs Sardou, 29
Elderberry Blossom Wine, 270
Escabeche of Red Snapper, 28

Field or Cow Pea Soup, 44
Fig Preserves, 240
Fish, 49–88
  Poached, Sauce for, 261
  See also Red Snapper, Rock Fish
Fish Stew, 82
  Chesapeake Bay, 84
Flambée(s), Bananas, 234
Flan, 224
Florida Chicken (Poulet Floride), 119
Florida Keys Red Snapper, 80
Florida Lobster, Steamed, 61
Francille's Stewed Corn, 149
French Potato Salad, 161
Fresh Peach Pie, 207
Fresh Peach Turnovers, Fried, 206
Fresh Quail with Grits and Gravy, 132
Fried Apples, 239
Fried Chicken
  Batter-, 110
  Southern, 108-9
Fried Clams, Maryland, 52
Fried Corn Meal Mush, 179
Fried Cream, 191
Fried Custard, 191
Fried Fresh Peach Turnovers, 206
Fried Fruit Turnovers, 206
Fried Green Tomato Slices, 169
Fried Hominy Grits, 153
Fried Okra, 158
Fried Oysters, 66
Fried Plantains, 160
Frijoles Negros, 143
Frogs' Legs
  Braised, with Sherry, 129
  Deep-Fried, 129
Frogs' Legs Omelet, 135
Fromage de Tête, 101
Frozen Oranges, Stuffed, 232

Fruitcake
  Applesauce, 217
  Past Perfect, 218
  White, 217
Fruited Eggnog Pudding, 229
Fruit Turnovers, Fried. 206
Fudge, 273
  Chocolate, 274
  Ginger, 274
  Nut, 274
  Penuche, 274
Game, 130–34
  See also Doves, Duck, Quail, Venison
Gazpachy Salad, Stella's Pensacola, 171
Ginger Cookies, Moravian, 237
Ginger Fudge, 274
Ginger-Melon Ice, 235
Grand Hot Cakes, 184
Grapes
  Crystallized, 277
  Scuppernong Nectar, 277
Gravy
  Cream, 100
  Chicken, 110
  Fresh Quail with, 132
  Grits and, 132
  Red-Eye, 106
  Tomato, 263
Green Bean(s)
  with Brown Butter Sauce, 143
  Pickled, 248
  Southern Style, 142
  Tomatoes and, au Gratin, 141
Green Bean Casserole, 142
Green Peppers
  Pepper Jelly, 245
  Green Relish, 256
Green Rice Ring, 163
Greens
  Assorted, 157
  Collard, 156
  Mixed, with Corn Bread Dumplings, 157
  Mustard, 156
  Turnip, 156
    Southern Style, 156
Green Tomato Relish, 254
Green Tomato Slices, Fried, 169
Grenoble Style Pompano, 72
Grenobloise, Red Snapper, 79
Grillades, 94
Grits. *See also* Hominy Grits
Grits and Gravy, Fresh Quail with, 132

Grits Balls, Deep-Fried, 33
Grits Casserole, Cheese, 138
Grouper, Out Island, 60
Guava Pecan Pie, 194
Gumbo
  Catfish, 51
  Chicken, 121
  Crab, 55
  Ponchartrain Creole, 85
  Shrimp, 75
Gumbo-Style Chicken Wings, 122

Halidon Hill Potted Doves, 134
Ham
  Boiled and Baked Country, 104
  Southern Maryland Stuffed, 105
  Virginia, Smithfield or Smithfield-Style, 104
Ham Biscuits, 29
Ham Croquettes with Egg Sauce, 107
Ham and Egg Canapés, 28
Ham Hocks, 106
Ham Soup, Okra, 45
Ham Steak and Red-Eye Gravy, 106
Hard-Shelled Crabs, Steamed, 57
Head Cheese, 101
  Vinaigrette, 102
Heart of Palm, 159
  au Gratin, 160
Herb Dip for Raw Vegetables, 32
Herb Sauce, Vinaigrette, Lime and, 259
Hermits, 238
Hocks, Ham, 106
Hoe Cake, 175
  Lacy, 181
Hog Jawl (Jowl), Black-Eyed Peas and, 103
Hollandaise Sauce, 258
  Easy, 30
Homemade Hominy, 153
Hominy Grits, 153
  Baked, and Tomatoes, 155
  and Bean Cakes, 154
  Fried, 153
  Homemade, 153
  Sarah's Oando, 154
  with Sausage, Quick Big, 138
  Tamale Pie with, 91
Hominy Grits Soufflé, 155
Honey and Curry Sauce, Shreveport Club, 265
Hopping John, 146
Horseradish Sauce
  Cranberry and, 264
  Port Wine and, 264
Hot Barbecue Sauce, 262
Hot Cakes, Grand, 184
Hot Oysters à la Louisiane, 65
Hot Potato Salad, 161
Hot Sauce, for Shrimp, 23
Hot Water Corn Bread, 175
  Deep-Fried, 178
Hunt and Polo Eggplant Casserole, 152
Hush Puppies, 182
  River Road, 182

Ice, Ginger-Melon, 235
Ice Cream, Cooked Custard, 235

Jambalaya, 87
  Cajun, 126
  Chicken, 123
Jam
  Cantaloupe and Orange, 241
  Damson, 244
  Peach Almond, 242
  See also Jellies, Preserves
Jam Cake, 214
Jeff Davis Pie, 198
Jellied Pork (Souse), 103
Jelly
  Blackberry and Apple, 239
  Bourbon, 245
  Mayhaw, 243
  Pepper, 245
John's Eggnog, 268

Kentucky Burgoo, 128
Kentucky Lemon Pie, 203
Key West Old Lime Sour, 258

Lacy Corn Bread, 183
Lacy Hoe Cakes, 181
Lady Baltimore Cake, 220
Lamaze Sauce, Shrimp with, 22
Lane Cake
  Filling, 219
  Layers, 219
"Lemmon Syllabub," 227
Lemon Butter, Old-Fashioned, 265
Lemon Cake, 215
Lemon Chiffon Pie, 204
Lemon Fluff, 225
Lemon Pie, Kentucky, 203
Lemons and Oranges, Stuffed, 251
Lemon Sauce

Egg and, Celery with, 148
for Mrs. Mescal Johnston's Rice Custard, 222
Light Rolls, 191
Lime Chutney, 252
Lime and Herb Sauce Vinaigrette, 259
Lime Meringue Pie, 202
Lime Sour, Key West Old, 258
Limping Susan, 159
Live Shrimp, Steamed, 77
Loaf, Chicken, 120
Lobster, Florida, Steamed, 61
Lobster Cocktail Dressing, 261
Lobster Soup, She-Crab and, 37
Louisiana Red Bean Soup, 40
Louisiana Sauce Remoulade, 260
Louisiane, Hot Oysters à la, 65

Mackerel
  How to Cook, 62
  How to Salt, 61
Madeira, Wild Ducks with, 131
Main Dishes, 89-139
Mango Chutney, 254
Marinated Pork Loin, Roast, 96
Marmalade, Seville (Bitter) Orange, 244
Maryland Clam Chowder, 39
Maryland Fried Clams, 52
Maryland Stuffed Ham, Southern, 105
Mayhaw Jelly, 243
Mayonnaise, Mustard, 260
Meat Pies, Hot-ta-, 93
Melon Conserve, Peach, 242
Melon Ice, Ginger-, 235
Meringue, 203
  Pie, 202-3
    Lemon, 203
    Lime, 202
Meunière
  Pompano, 71
  Trout, 88
Milk Punch, 269
Minetry McCoy's Miracle, 232
Mint Julep, 271
Mississippi Steak Sauce, 263
Mrs. D's Moravian Sugar Cake, 221
Mrs. Jackson Porter Dick's Black-Eyed Peas and Hog Jawl (Jowl), 103
Mrs. Mescal Johnston's Rice Custard with Lemon Sauce, 222
Mixed Greens with Corn Bread Dumplings, 157

Molasses Corn Bread, 183
Molasses-Nut Pie, 193
Mom's Arkansas Chicken Pie, 115
Moravian Ginger Cookies, 237
Moravian Sugar Cake, Mrs. D's, 221
Mousse, Shad Stuffed with Roe and, 74
Muffins
  Blueberry, 190
  Corn Meal, 189
Mush, Fried Corn Meal, 179
Mushroom Omelet, Baked Christmas, 135
Mushrooms au Gratin, 158
Mustard Greens, 156
Mustard Mayonnaise, 260

Nectar, Scuppernong, 271
No-Fail Welsh Rabbit, 137
Nut Fudge, 274
Nut Pie, Molasses-, 193
Nuts, Sugar-Glazed, 276

Oando, Sarah's, 154
Okra
  Fried, 158
  Limping Susan, 159
Okra Ham Soup, 45
Okra Soup, 45
  Ham, 45
Old-Fashioned Lemon Butter, 265
Omelets
  Frogs' Legs, 135
  Mushroom, Baked Christmas, 135
Orange Cake, 210
Orange, Cake à l', 211
Orange-Glazed Sweet Potatoes, 162
Orange Jam, Cantaloupe and, 241
Orange Liqueur Chiffon Tart, 204
Orange Marmalade, Seville (Bitter), 244
Orange Pecans, Candied, 275
Oranges
  and Lemons, Stuffed, 251
  Stuffed Frozen, 232
  en Surprise, 233
Out Island Grouper, 60
Oyster Appetizer, 20
Oyster Pie, 70
Oyster Roast for Twenty-Four, 69
Oysters
  Bienville, 64
  en Brochette, 66
  Casino, 65

with Cocktail Sauce, 21
Creamed, 68
Deviled, 62
Fried, 66
Hot, à la Louisiane, 65
Johnny Reb, 63
Rockefeller, 67
Scalloped, Southern, 69

Papaya Sauce, 265
Paste, Shrimp, 26
Past Perfect Fruitcake, 218
Pastry for a Nine-Inch Pie, 209
Pat's Favorite Dip, 32
Peach Almond Jam, 242
Peach Chutney, 253
Peach Cobbler, 208
Peach Conserve, 241
Peach Melon Conserve, 242
Peach Pie, Fresh, 207
Peach Roll-Ups, 207
Peach Soup, Chilled, 46
Peach Turnovers, Fried Fresh, 206
Peanut Pie, 195
Peanut Soup, Cream of, 47
Pear Relish, 252
Peas. *See* Black-Eyed Peas, Cow Pea Soup, Field or Cow Pea Soup
Pecan-Cherry Cake, 213
Pecan Pie, 195
    Guava, 194
Pecan Pudding, Chocolate, 224
Pecans
    Candied Orange, 275
    Salted, 34
Pecan Squash Casserole, 167
Pendennis Club Barbecue Sauce, 262
Penuche Fudge, 274
Pepper Jelly, 245
Peppermint Stick Bavarian Cream, 228
Peppers, Pork-Stuffed, 99
Pernod, Custard Sauce Flavored with, 266
Piccadillo, 89
Pickled Garden Carrots, 246
Pickled Green Beans, 248
Pickled Shrimp, 23
Pickled Watermelon Rind, Easy, 250
Pickles
    Artichoke, Whole, 248
    Cucumber, Quick, 247
    Tomato, Ripe, 255
    Watermelon, Crisp, 249
    See also Relishes

Pie(s)
    Apple Stack, 205
    Black Bottom, 199
    Bourbon, 201
    Chess
        I, 196
        II, 196
        Rum and Rhubarb, 209
        Chess Tarts, 197
    Chicken, Mom's Arkansas, 115
    Chocolate-Butterscotch, 200
    Chocolate Rum, 200
    Hot-ta-Meat, 93
    Jeff Davis, 198
    Lemon
        Chiffon, 204
        Kentucky, 203
    Lime Meringue, 202
    Molasses-Nut, 193
    Orange Liqueur Chiffon Tart, 204
    Oyster, 70
    Pastry for, 209
    Peach, 207
    Peanut, 195
    Pecan, 195
        Guava, 194
    Sour Cream, 198
    Spiced Carrot, 205
    Sweet Potato, 197
    Tamale, 90
        with Hominy Grits, 91
    Walnut, 195
        Black, 194
    Yam, Sliced, 198
Pine Bark Stew, 83
Plantains, Fried, 160
Plums
    Damson Jam, 244
Poached Fish, Sauce for, 261
Pompano
    Baked en Papillote, 70
    Grenoble Style, 72
    Meunière, 71
Pone, Sweet Potato, 222
Pontchartrain Creole Gumbo, 85
Pontchartrain Doves, 134
Poppy Seed Dressing, Shreveport, 172
Pork
    Barbecue, 98
    Chitterlings, 102
    Head Cheese, 101
        Vinaigrette, 102
    Jellied, 103

Souse, 103
See also Ham, Sausage, Spareribs
Pork Chops
   Bermudiana, 96
   Smothered, 97
Pork Jowl, 103
Pork Loin, Roast Marinated, 96
Pork-Stuffed Peppers, 99
Port Wine and Horseradish Sauce, 264
Potage d'Haricots Rouges, 40
Potatoes. *See* Sweet Potatoes
Potato Salad
   French, 161
   Hot, 161
Potted Doves, Halidon Hill, 134
Poulet Floride, 119
Poundcake I, 212
Poundcake II, 213
Pralines, 273
Preserves
   Apple, Quick, 241
   Fig, 240
   Surinam, 243
   See also Conserve, Jams, Jelly
Pressed Chicken, 119
Pressed Duck, 130
Puddings, Custards and Creams, 222–32
   Banana Pudding, 223
   Bavarian Cream, Peppermint Stick, 228
   Bourbon Date Pudding, 223
   Bridal Pudding, 226
   Chicken Pudding, 114
   Chocolate Pecan Pudding, 224
   Flan, 224
   Fruited Eggnog Pudding, 229
   "Lemmon Syllabub," 227
   Lemon Fluff, 225
   Rice Custard with Lemon Sauce, Mrs. Mescal Johnston's, 222
   Snow on the Mountain, 226
   Sweet Potato Pone, 222
   Tomato Pudding, 169
   Trifle, 230, 231
   Royal, 230
Pumpkin Soup, 42
Punch
   Edenton, 269
   Milk, 269

Quail
   Braised, 133
   Fresh, with Grits and Gravy, 132

Quick Apple Preserves, 241
Quick Big Hominy with Sausage, 138
Quick Cucumber Pickles, 247

Rarebit, Chipped Beef, 136
Raw Conch Salad, 52
Red Bean Soup, Louisiana, 40
Red Beans with Rice
   I, 145
   II, 145
Red-Eye Gravy, Ham Steak and, 106
Red Snapper
   Appetizer, Chilled, 27
   Baked, 82
   Broiled, 79
   Creole, 81
   Escabeche of, 28
   Florida Keys, 80
   Grenobloise, 79
Relishes
   Artichoke, 255
   Cucumbers in Butter and Dill, 246
   Green, 256
   Green Tomato, 254
   Pear, 252
   See also Chutney Pickles
Remoulade, Shrimp, 24
Remoulade Sauce, Louisiana, 260
Rhubarb, Rum and, Chess Pie, 209
Rice
   Black-Eyed Peas and, 146
   Dilled, for Shrimp, 164
   Dirty, 164
   Green, Ring, 163
   Red Beans with, 145
   Steamboat, 163
Rice Custard, with Lemon Sauce, Mrs. Mescal Johnston's, 222
Ripe Tomato Pickle, 255
River Road Hush Puppies, 182
Roast, Oyster, for Twenty-Four, 69
Roast Cuban Round, 92
Roast Marinated Pork Loin, 96
Rock Fish, Clam-Stuffed Baked, 49
Roe, Shad Stuffed with Mousse and, 74
Rolls, Light, 191
Roll-Ups, Peach, 207
Round Steak
   Grillades, 94
Rum, Black Beans with, 144
Rum and Cherry Sauce, 266
Rum and Rhubarb Chess Pie, 209
Rum Cocktail, Tarpon Isle, 271

Rum Pie, 200
  Chocolate, 201
Rum Sauce, 267
  and Cherry, 266

Saddle of Vension, Spit-Roasted, 130
Salad(s)
  Bibb Lettuce, 170
  Cauliflower Slaw, 170
  Cole Slaw, 170
    with Capers, 171
  Potato
    French, 161
    Hot, 161
  Raw Conch, 52
  Stella's Pensacola Gazpachy, 171
Salad Dressing, Boiled, 172
Sally Lunn, 192
Salted Pecans, 34
Salt Mackerel
  How to Cook, 62
Salty Dog Cocktail, 272
Sauce(s), 257-67
  Avocado, 261
  Barbecue, 262
  Hot, 262
  Pendennis Club, 262
  Brown Butter, 143
  Celery-Tomato, 22
  Cheese, 147
  Chili, 257
  Chocolate, 228
  Cocktail
    for Lobster or Shrimp, 261
    for Oysters, 21
    Southern, 26
  Cranberry and Horseradish, 264
  Custard, Flavored with Pernod, 266
  Egg, 107
    and Lemon, 148
  Hollandaise, 258
    Easy, 30
  Honey and Curry, 265
  Hot, 23
  Lamaze, 22
  Lemon, 22
    and Egg, 148
  Lemon Butter, 265
  Lime and Herb, Vinaigrette, 259
  Lime Sour, Key West Old, 258
  Mustard Mayonnaise, 260
  Papaya, 265

  for Poached Fish, 261
  Port Wine and Horseradish, 264
  Remoulade, 267
  Rum, 267
    and cherry, 266
  Steak, Mississippi, 263
  Tartar, 53, 259
  Tomato, 125
    Southern, 257
Sausage(s)
  with Cream Gravy and Biscuits, 100
  Cuban, 100
  Quick Big Hominy with, 138
  Savory Black Beans, 143
Sazerac Cocktail, 272
Scalloped Oysters, Southern, 69
Scuppernong Nectar, 271
Sea Food
  with Eggs, 72
  and Southern Cocktail Sauce, 26
Sea Food Casserole, Artichoke and, 73
Sesame Seeds
  Benne Seed Wafers, 32
Seven Hearths Chicken, 118
Seville (Bitter) Orange Marmalade, 244
Shad Roe, Cucumber and, 21
Shad Stuffed with Mousse and Roe, 74
She-Crab and Lobster Soup, 37
She-Crab Soup, 37
Shellfish, 49-88. *See also* Crawfish, Lobster,
  Oysters, Shrimp
Sherry, Braised Frogs' Legs with, 129
Shreveport Club Honey and Curry Sauce,
  265
Shreveport Poppy Seed Dressing, 172
Shrimp
  Charleston Breakfast, 78
  Dilled Rice for, 164
  with Hot Sauce, 23
  with Lamaze Sauce, 22
  Pickled, 23
  in Sour Cream, 77
  Steamed Live, 77
  à la Turque, 76
Shrimp Bisque, 36
Shrimp Cocktail with Celery-Tomato Sauce,
  22
Shrimp Cocktail Dressing, 261
Shrimp Creole, 78
  Chilled Gulf Coast, 25
Shrimp Gumbo, 75
Shrimp Paste, 26

Shrimp Remoulade, 24
Shrimp Wilder, 25
Sliced Yam Pie, 198
Smithfield or Smithfield-Style Virginia Ham, 104
Smothered Pork Chops, 97
Snickerdoodles, 237
Snow on the Mountain, 226
Soft-Shelled Crabs
    Broiled, 58
    Deep-Fried, 55
Soufflé
    Eggplant, 151
    Grits, 155
Soup(s)
    Almond, 48
    Black Bean, 41
    Black-Eyed Pea, 39
    Celery Chowder, 43
    Clam Chowder, Maryland, 39
    Conch Chowder, 34
    Crab
        She-, 38
        and Lobster, 37
        South River Club, 38
    Crawfish Bisque, 35
    Cream of Corn, 41
    Cream of Peanut, 47
    Cream of Spinach, 42
    Field or Cow Pea, 44
    Okra, 45
        Ham, 45
    Peach, Chilled, 46
    Pumpkin, 42
    Red Bean, Louisiana, 40
    Shrimp Bisque, 36
    Strawberry Cooler, 47
    Tomato, 42
Sour Cream, Shrimp in, 77
Sour Cream Pie, 198
Souse (Jellied Pork), 103
Southern Buttermilk Corn Bread, 179
Southern Cocktail Sauce for Sea Food, 26
Southern Fried Chicken
    I, 108
    II, 108
    III, 109
Southern Maryland Stuffed Ham, 105
Southern Scalloped Oysters, 69
Southern-Style Biscuits, 187
Southern-Style Green Beans, 142
Southern Tomato Sauce, 257

South River Club Crab Soup, 38
Spaghetti, Chicken, 124
Spareribs
    Boiled, 97
    Deep-Fried, 98
Spiced Carrot Pie, 205
Spinach and Artichokes, Asphodel Style, 167
Spinach Soup, Cream of, 43
Spit-Roasted Saddle of Venison, 130
Spoon Bread, 177
    Bacon and Cheese, 184
    Sweet Potato, 186
Squash, Cheese-Stuffed, 165. *See also* Zucchini
Squash Cakes, 166
Squash Casserole, Pecan, 167
Steak, Ham, and Red-Eye Gravy, 106
Steak Sauce, Mississippi, 263
Steamboat Rice, 163
Steamed Florida Lobster, 61
Steamed Hard-Shelled Crabs, 57
Steamed Live Shrimp, 77
Steamed Stone Crab, 56
Stella's Pensacola Gazpachy Salad, 171
Stew(s)
    Brunswick, 127
    Crab, 54
    Fish, 82
        Chesapeake Bay, 84
        Kentucky Burgoo, 128
        Pine Bark, 83
Stewed Corn, Francille's, 149
Stone Crab, Steamed, 56
Strawberry Cooler, 47
Striped Bass, Baked Stuffed. *See* Rock Fish
Stuffed Cherry Tomatoes, 30
Stuffed Chicken Breasts, 116
Stuffed Eggplant, 151
Stuffed Frozen Oranges, 232
Stuffed Ham, Southern Maryland, 105
Stuffed Oranges and Lemons, 251
Stuffed Peppers, Pork-, 99
Stuffed Squash, Cheese-, 165
Stuffed Striped Bass, Baked, 50
Stuffing
    Chicken with Corn Bread, 111
    Mousse and Roe, for Shad, 74
Sugar Cake, Mrs. D's Moravian, 221
Sugar Cookies, 236
Sugar-Glazed Nuts, 276
Sugar Plum Cake, 216
Surinam Preserves, 243

Swamp Cabbage, 159
  au Gratin, 160
Sweet Potato Biscuits, 189
Sweet Potatoes
  Baked Bourbon Spiced, 162
  Orange-Glazed, 162
Sweet Potato Pie, 197
Sweet Potato Pone, 222
Sweet Potato Spoon Bread, 186
Syrup, Blackberry, 270

Tamale Pie, 90
  with Hominy Grits, 91
Tarpon Isle Rum Cocktail, 271
Tartar Sauce, 53, 259
Tart(s)
  Chess, 197
  Orange Liqueur Chiffon, 204
Tomatoes
  Baked Hominy and, 155
  Broiled, 168
  Cherry, Stuffed, 30
  and Green Beans au Gratin, 141
  Slices, Fried Green, 169
Tomato Freeze with Avocado topping, 31
Tomato Gravy, 263
Tomato Pickle, Ripe, 255
Tomato Pudding, 169
Tomato Relish, Green, 254
Tomato Sauce, 125
  Southern, 257
Tomato Soup, 42
Topping, Avocado, 31
Trifle, 230
  Pudding, 231
  Royal, 230
Tripe Creole, 95
Trout
  Amandine, 88
  Charles Street, 87
  Meunière, 88

Turnip Greens, 156
  Southern-Style, 156
Turnovers
  Fried Fresh Peach, 206
  Fried Fruit, 206
  Peach Roll-Ups, 207

Veal
  Grillades, 94
Vegetables, 141–52, 158–69
  Raw, Herb Dip for, 32
Venison, Spit-Roasted Saddle of, 130
Vinaigrette
  Head Cheese, 102
  Lime and Herb Sauce, 259
Virginia Ham, Smithfield or Smithfield-Style, 104
Vivian's Corn Bread, 176

Wafers, Benne Seed, 32
Waffles, 186
Walnut Pie, 195
  Black, 194
Watermelon Pickles, Crisp, 249
Watermelon Rind, Pickled, Easy, 250
Welsh Rabbit, No-Fail, 137
White Fruitcake, 217
Whole Artichoke Pickles, 248
Wild Duck
  Country Captain, 132
  with Madeira, 131
Wine
  Elderberry Blossom, 270
  Port, and Horseradish Sauce, 264
Wings, Chicken, Gumbo-Style, 122

Yam Pie, Sliced, 198

Zucchini Cheese Custard, 165